Gilbert and Sullivan Operettas Adapted for Half-hour Performance

by

ADELE THANE

Publishers   PLAYS, INC.   *Boston*

Library of Congress Cataloging in Publication Data

Sullivan, Arthur Seymour, Sir, 1842-1900.
  [Operas. Selections; arr.]
  Gilbert and Sullivan operettas adapted for half-hour performance.

  Includes melodies, with chord symbols.
  CONTENTS: H.M.S. Pinafore.—The Mikado.—The Pirates of Penzance. [etc.]
  1. Operas, Juvenile. [1. Operas]   I. Gilbert, William Schwenk, Sir, 1836-1911.
II. Thane, Adele.   III. Title.
M1995.S94T5   782.8'1'54   76-29002
ISBN 0-8238-0188-8

Manufactured in the United States of America

CONTENTS

H.M.S. PINAFORE   3
    Or, The Lass That Loved a Sailor
    Music and words to songs   27

THE MIKADO   43
    Or, The Town of Titipu
    Music and words to songs   70

THE PIRATES OF PENZANCE   91
    Or, The Slave of Duty
    Music and words to songs   113

TRIAL BY JURY   123
    A Dramatic Cantata
    Music and words to songs   137

THE GONDOLIERS   149
    Or, The King of Barataria
    Music and words to songs   176

PATIENCE   195
    Or, Bunthorne's Bride
    Music and words to songs   219

THE YEOMEN OF THE GUARD   243
    Or, The Merryman and His Maid
    Music and words to songs   270

IOLANTHE   285
    Or, The Peer and the Peri
    Music and words to songs   312

INDEX OF SONGS   329

NOTE TO THE DIRECTOR

Music for each operetta in this book appears on the pages following the text of the play. The songs included are those indicated by the stage direction "singing," and are shortened and adapted to fit the half-hour format. For non-musical productions of these plays, the lyrics may be recited rather than sung.

Many of the songs which are included here in abridged form may be found in full in Martyn Green's *Treasury of Gilbert and Sullivan* (Simon and Schuster). Complete scores and librettos of Gilbert and Sullivan operettas are published by G. Schirmer.

An excellent book to help the director stage these Gilbert and Sullivan operettas is *The Theatre Student: Gilbert and Sullivan Production* by Peter Kline (Richards Rosen Press). Mr. Kline, a teacher of drama and producer of many works of Gilbert and Sullivan, presents a complete guide to producing Gilbert and Sullivan operettas for students and amateur groups.

H.M.S. PINAFORE

The story of

H.M.S. PINAFORE

On the deck of *H.M.S. Pinafore*, the crew are busy making the ship ready for the visit of Sir Joseph Porter, First Lord of the Admiralty. Little Buttercup, a peddler woman, comes aboard to sell the sailors ribbons and laces for their sweethearts. Ralph Rackstraw, a young sailor, loves the Captain's daughter, Josephine, but he does not aspire to marry her because of their difference in rank. Presently Sir Joseph Porter arrives, accompanied, as usual, by his retinue of admiring sisters and cousins and aunts. Sir Joseph condescends to propose to Josephine, for, as he explains, love levels all ranks. Josephine and Ralph take this as a cue and prepare to elope, but Dick Deadeye, a crusty old sailor, betrays them to Captain Corcoran, and as the couple are about to leave the ship, they are apprehended. Sir Joseph orders Ralph to be put into a dungeon cell. At this point, Little Buttercup reveals that years ago when she was nursemaid to Captain Corcoran and Ralph Rackstraw, she mixed the babies up. Corcoran promptly becomes the seaman and Ralph the captain. Now there is no longer a barrier to the marriage of Ralph and Josephine. Corcoran embraces Little Buttercup and Sir Joseph accepts the proposal of Hebe, one of his cousins.

H.M.S. PINAFORE

Or, The Lass That Loved a Sailor

Characters

RT. HON. SIR JOSEPH PORTER, K.C.B., *First Lord of the Admiralty*
CAPTAIN CORCORAN, *commanding H.M.S. Pinafore*
TOMMY TUCKER, *midshipmite, a very small boy*
RALPH RACKSTRAW ⎫
DICK DEADEYE ⎪
BOATSWAIN ⎬ *sailors*
BOB BECKET ⎭
OTHER SAILORS
JOSEPHINE, *Captain's daughter*
HEBE, *Sir Joseph's cousin*
LITTLE BUTTERCUP, *peddler*
SIR JOSEPH'S SISTERS, COUSINS, AND AUNTS

SCENE 1

TIME: *Nineteenth century.*
SETTING: *Quarterdeck of H.M.S. Pinafore, lying at anchor in Portsmouth Harbor.*
AT RISE: BOATSWAIN, DICK DEADEYE, BOB BECKET, *and* OTHER SAILORS *are busily polishing brasswork, splicing rope, adjusting rigging, etc., under direction of* TOMMY TUCKER, *midshipmite.* TOMMY *carries telescope under arm, and makes tour of inspection about deck.* RALPH RACKSTRAW *is on bridge, at rear, leaning dejectedly against ship's wheel.*

ALL (*Singing*):
> We sail the ocean blue,
> And our saucy ship's a beauty;
> We're sober men and true,

3

And attentive to our duty.
When the balls whistle free
O'er the bright blue sea,
We stand to our guns all day;
When at anchor we ride
On the Portsmouth tide,
We have plenty of time to play.

(LITTLE BUTTERCUP *enters up left with a large basket on her arm and a tray hung from a strap around her neck. Basket and tray hold assorted articles for sale.*)

BUTTERCUP: Ahoy, my hearties! (SAILORS *stop work. She recites.*)

You've got your pay—spare all you can afford
To welcome Little Buttercup on board!

(SAILORS *cheer.* BUTTERCUP *sings.*)

I'm called Little Buttercup, dear Little Buttercup,
Though I could never tell why,
But still I'm called Buttercup, poor Little Buttercup,
Sweet Little Buttercup I!

(*Shows* SAILORS *her wares*)

I've snuff and tobaccy, and excellent jacky,
I've scissors, and watches, and knives;
I've ribbons and laces to set off the faces
Of pretty young sweethearts and wives.
I've treacle and toffee, I've tea and I've coffee,
Soft tommy and succulent chops;
I've chickens and conies, and pretty polonies,
And excellent peppermint drops.
Then buy of your Buttercup, dear Little Buttercup;
Sailors should never be shy;
So, buy of your Buttercup, poor Little Buttercup;
Come, of your Buttercup buy!

(*As* BUTTERCUP *finishes song, all sailors except* RALPH *crowd around her and buy, then step aside. She holds out long peppermint stick to* TOMMY TUCKER.) And this is for you, my little man. (TOMMY *skips offstage sucking candy.*)

BOATSWAIN (*Pinching her cheek*): Little Buttercup, you are the rosiest, the roundest, and the reddest beauty in all of Portsmouth town!

BUTTERCUP: Rosy, am I? And round? (*Laughs*) Have you ever thought of what lurks beneath this gay exterior?

BOATSWAIN: No, my lass, I can't say I ever have.

BUTTERCUP (*Whispering*): Then you do not know that I am haunted by a guilty secret. (*As* SAILORS *gather around her to hear more,* DICK DEADEYE *pushes to front.*)

DICK (*Leering at* BUTTERCUP): What secret, me beauty? (BUTTERCUP *screams and shrinks back.*)

BECKET (*Reassuringly, to* BUTTERCUP): Don't take any heed of *him*—that's only poor Dick Deadeye.

DICK (*Bitterly*): Yes, Deadeye. It's a beast of a name, ain't it?

BUTTERCUP: It's not a nice name.

DICK: I'm ugly, too, ain't I?

BUTTERCUP: Well—you're certainly not handsome.

DICK (*Shaking his fist*): That's it! I'm ugly. (*Turns to crew*) And you all hate me, don't you?

OTHER SAILORS (*Together*): We do!

BOATSWAIN: Well, Dick, you can't expect a chap with such a name as Dick Deadeye to be a popular character—now can you?

DICK: No—it's human nature. I am resigned. (*Walks away.* BUTTERCUP *notices* RALPH RACKSTRAW, *who is slowly making his way down steps from bridge.*)

BUTTERCUP: Who is that unhappy youth?

BOATSWAIN: That is the smartest lad in all the fleet—Ralph Rackstraw. [*"Ralph" is pronounced "Raife."*]

BUTTERCUP (*Aside; dramatically*): That name! Remorse! Remorse!

RALPH (*Coming downstage, sighing heavily*): Ah, pity, pity me! I love—and love, alas, above my station!

BUTTERCUP (*Aside*): He loves—and loves a lass above his station!

OTHER SAILORS (*Together*): Yes, yes, the lass is much above his station! (BUTTERCUP *exits.*)

BOATSWAIN (*Laying sympathetic hand on* RALPH's *shoulder*): Poor lad, you've climbed too high. Our worthy Captain's daughter won't have anything to do with a chap like you. Will she, lads?

OTHER SAILORS (*Together*): No, no!

DICK (*Sneering*): Captains' daughters don't marry sailors. (CAPTAIN CORCORAN *enters on bridge, at rear.*)

BOATSWAIN: My lads, let us greet our Captain as so brave an officer deserves! (*All sailors line up, left and right, facing upstage.*)

CAPTAIN: My gallant crew, good morning!

SAILORS (*Saluting; together*): Sir, good morning! (CAPTAIN and SAILORS *sing as he descends to deck.*)

CAPTAIN (*Singing*):
       I am the Captain of the *Pinafore;*

SAILORS (*Singing*):
>And a right good captain, too!

CAPTAIN (*Singing*):
>You're very, very good,
>And be it understood,
>I command a right good crew;

SAILORS (*Singing*):
>We're very, very good,
>And be it understood,
>He commands a right good crew.

CAPTAIN (*Singing*):
>Though related to a peer,
>I can hand, reef and steer,
>And ship a selvagee;
>I am never known to quail,
>At the fury of a gale,
>And I'm never, never sick at sea!

SAILORS: What, never?

CAPTAIN: No, never.

SAILORS (*Sternly*): What, *never?*

CAPTAIN: Well ... *hardly* ever!

SAILORS (*Singing*):
>He's hardly ever sick at sea!
>Then give three cheers, and one cheer more,
>For the hardy Captain of the *Pinafore!*

CAPTAIN (*Singing*):
>I do my best to satisfy you all—

SAILORS (*Singing*):
>And with you we're quite content.

CAPTAIN (*Singing*):
> You're exceedingly polite,
> And I think it only right
> To return the compliment.

SAILORS (*Singing*):
> We're exceedingly polite,
> And he thinks it only right
> To return the compliment.

CAPTAIN (*Singing*):
> Bad language or abuse,
> I never, never use,
> Whatever the emergency;
> Though "Bother it" I may
> Occasionally say,
> I never use a big, big D!

SAILORS: What, never?

CAPTAIN: No, never!

SAILORS (*Closing in on* CAPTAIN, *pointing fingers accusingly at him*): What, *never?*

CAPTAIN (*Embarrassed*): Well—uh—*hardly* ever!

SAILORS (*Singing*):
> Hardly ever swears a big, big D!
> Then give three cheers, and one cheer more,
> For the well-bred Captain of the *Pinafore!*
> (SAILORS *give three hearty cheers and exit up left on fourth cheer.* CAPTAIN's *smile changes to an expression of sorrow, and he sits on capstan with bowed head.* BUTTERCUP *re-enters up right without basket and tray.*)

BUTTERCUP: Sir, you are sad.

CAPTAIN: Yes, Buttercup, I'm sad and sorry.

BUTTERCUP: Then confide in me. (*Dramatically*) Fear not!—I am a mother.

CAPTAIN: My daughter, Josephine, is sought in marriage by the great Sir Joseph Porter, the First Lord of the Admiralty—a most eligible suitor—but, for some reason, she refuses to marry him.

BUTTERCUP: Ah, poor Sir Joseph! I know too well the anguish of a heart that loves in vain. (*Gazes ardently at* CAPTAIN *and sighs.* JOSEPHINE *enters up left. She carries basket of flowers.*) There is your daughter now. I will leave you to reason with her. (BUTTERCUP *hurries out up right.*)

CAPTAIN (*Looking after her*): A plump and pleasing person! (*Crosses to* JOSEPHINE) Come, come, my child, you must look your best. Sir Joseph Porter will soon be here to claim your promised hand.

JOSEPHINE: Oh, Father, Sir Joseph is a great and good man, but I cannot love him. My heart is already given.

CAPTAIN (*Surprised*): Given? And to whom?

JOSEPHINE: He is a humble sailor on board your own ship.

CAPTAIN (*Shocked*): Impossible! A common sailor?

JOSEPHINE: Yet I love him just the same.

CAPTAIN: My dear Josephine, I attach little value to rank and wealth, but the line must be drawn somewhere. (*Sound of cannon in distance is heard.* CAPTAIN *goes right and looks offstage.*) Here comes Sir Joseph in his barge, attended by his sisters, and his cousins, and his aunts, who go wherever he goes. Retire to your cabin, my child. (*Handing her a photograph*) Take this picture of Sir Joseph with you. It may help to bring you to a more sensible frame of mind. (CAPTAIN *ascends bridge,* JOSEPHINE *looks at photograph and makes a face, then exits up left. All sailors enter and crowd along rail, ad libbing excitedly as they watch barge approach.* BOATSWAIN *lifts* TOMMY TUCKER *to his shoulder.* TOMMY *adjusts telescope, takes a look through it and waves wildly.* SIR JOSEPH'S SISTERS, COUSINS AND AUNTS *are heard laughing offstage. They enter singing.*)

SISTERS, COUSINS AND AUNTS (*Dancing around deck; singing*):
        Gaily tripping, lightly skipping,
        Flock the maidens to the shipping!
        Sailors sprightly always rightly
        Welcome ladies so politely!
(*Sailors bow to* SISTERS, COUSINS AND AUNTS *with exaggerated flourish, then line up to welcome* SIR JOSEPH.)

CAPTAIN (*On bridge*): Now give three cheers for the Right Honorable Sir Joseph Porter, First Lord of the Admiralty!

SAILORS: Hurrah! Hurrah! Hurrah!

TOMMY TUCKER (*Cheering alone*): Hooray! (TOMMY *gives command.*) 'Ten-*shun!* (SAILORS *snap to attention.* SIR JOSEPH *enters with his cousin* HEBE *on his arm.*)

SIR JOSEPH (*Singing*):
        I am the monarch of the sea,
        The ruler of the Queen's Na-vy,
        Whose praise Great Britain loudly chants.

SISTERS, COUSINS AND AUNTS (*Singing*):
        And we are his sisters and his cousins and his aunts!
        His sisters and his cousins and his aunts!

SIR JOSEPH (*Singing*):
        When at anchor here I ride,
        My bosom swells with pride,
        And I snap my fingers at a foeman's taunts;

ALL (*Singing*):
>And so do his sisters and his cousins and his aunts!
>His sisters and his cousins and his aunts!

SIR JOSEPH (*Singing*):
>But when the breezes blow,
>I generally go below,
>And seek the seclusion that a cabin grants!

ALL (*Singing*):
>And so do his sisters and his cousins and his aunts!
>His sisters and his cousins,
>Whom he reckons up by dozens,
>And his aunts!

SIR JOSEPH (*To crew*): My good men, I am going to tell you the story of my life. It may inspire you to follow my own excellent example. (*Stands center and clears throat*) From the very beginning of my career, I courted success. I began as an office boy in a law firm. (*Singing*)
>I cleaned the windows and I swept the floor,
>And I polished up the handle of the big front door.
>Then I was promoted to the post of junior clerk.
>I served the writs with a smile so bland,
>And I copied all the letters in a big round hand.

Finally I became a lawyer and was given a partnership (*Tittering self-consciously*)—which was the only *ship* I'd ever seen!

DICK DEADEYE (*Aside*): He doesn't know a gunnel from a funnel!

SIR JOSEPH (*Continuing*):
>I grew so rich I was sent to Parliament.
>I always voted at my party's call,
>And I never thought of thinking for myself at all.
>As a matter of fact (*Chants or sings*)—
>I thought so little, they rewarded me
>By making me the Ruler of the Queen's Na-vy!

Now landsmen all, whoever you may be,
If you want to rise to the top of the tree,
Stick close to your desks and never go to sea,
And you *all* may be Rulers of the Queen's Navy!
(SIR JOSEPH *inspects crew through his monocle.*) You have
a remarkably fine crew, Captain Corcoran.

CAPTAIN (*Proudly*): It *is* a fine crew, Sir Joseph.

SIR JOSEPH (*Waving vaguely at line of sailors*): Desire that
splendid seaman to step forward. (DICK DEADEYE *steps forward.*) No, no, the other splendid seaman. (*Points to* RALPH.
DICK *steps back, scowling.*)

CAPTAIN: Ralph Rackstraw, three paces to the front!

SIR JOSEPH (*Sternly to* CAPTAIN): If what?

CAPTAIN: I beg your pardon—I don't think I understand you.

SIR JOSEPH: If you *please.*

CAPTAIN: Oh, yes, of course. (*To* RALPH) If you please. (RALPH
*steps forward, salutes and, at the same time, stamps his
right foot.* SIR JOSEPH *steps back surprised. Then he taps*
RALPH *on shoulder and signals him to turn around.* RALPH
revolves in place, salutes smartly and stamps again. SIR JOSEPH *watches closely, then returns his salute.*)

SIR JOSEPH: Well done! You're a remarkably fine fellow.

RALPH: Yes, your honor. (*Salutes once more, stamping foot.* SIR
JOSEPH *again returns salute, and tries to stamp foot. He
brings one boot down on his other boot, grimaces in pain, and
hops about, then recovers.*)

SIR JOSEPH: Rackstraw, can you dance a hornpipe?

RALPH: No, your honor.

SIR JOSEPH: That's a pity—all sailors should dance a hornpipe. (SAILORS *do hornpipe step.* SIR JOSEPH *stops them with an imperious wave of his hand.*) Rackstraw, can you sing?

RALPH: I can 'um a little, your honor.

SIR JOSEPH: Then 'um this—er—*hum* this at your leisure. (*Gives him sheet of music.*) It is a song that I have composed to teach the principle that a British sailor is any man's equal—excepting mine. Now, Captain Corcoran, a word with you in your cabin, on a tender and sentimental subject.

CAPTAIN: Aye, aye, Sir Joseph. Boatswain, see that extra grog is served out to the ship's company.

BOATSWAIN: Beg pardon, sir. If what, sir?

CAPTAIN: If what?

BOATSWAIN: If you *please*, sir.

SIR JOSEPH: The gentleman is quite right. If you *please*.

CAPTAIN (*Impatiently*): If you *please!*

SIR JOSEPH (*Singing*):
> For I hold that on the seas,
> The expression, "if you please,"
> A particularly gentlemanly tone implants.

SISTERS, COUSINS, AND AUNTS (*Singing*):
> And so do his sisters and his cousins and his aunts!
> His sisters and his cousins and his aunts!

(SIR JOSEPH *exits, followed by* HEBE, SISTERS, COUSINS AND AUNTS, CAPTAIN, *and* TOMMY TUCKER.)

BOATSWAIN: Sir Joseph is a true gentleman, courteous and considerate to the very humblest.

RALPH (*With sudden inspiration*): We are not the very humblest! Sir Joseph has explained our true position to us. He says a British seaman is any man's equal—excepting his. Messmates, my mind's made up! Although I lack birth—

BECKET: You have a berth here on board ship.

RALPH (*Continuing*): I shall speak to the Captain's daughter at once and tell her of the honest love I have for her.

OTHER SAILORS (*Together*): Aye, aye!

BOATSWAIN (*Taking sheet of music from* RALPH): Heave ho, my lads, we'll sing this song Sir Joseph has composed for us, and we'll wet our whistles with a tot of grog to sing it all the better! (SAILORS *exit, dancing hornpipe.* RALPH *remains behind, leaning pensively on rail at right.* JOSEPHINE *enters up left.*)

JOSEPHINE (*Unhappily*): It's no use—I can't endure Sir Joseph's attentions. (*Sees* RALPH) Ralph Rackstraw!

RALPH: Aye, lady—no other than poor Ralph Rackstraw.

JOSEPHINE (*Aside; overcome by emotion*): Be still, my heart! (*Aloud; in formal tones*) Why poor Ralph Rackstraw?

RALPH: I am poor in happiness, lady. For six weary months I have been torn by anxiety and doubt. (*Looks about, then dramatically*) Josephine, I am a British sailor—and I love you!

JOSEPHINE: Sir, what audacity! (*Aside*) Oh, my heart, my beating heart! (*Aloud*) Sir, you forget the difference in our ranks. (*Proudly*) I am a captain's daughter.

RALPH: I forget nothing, lady. I love you desperately, but I am proud and I cannot stoop to implore. I have spoken and I await your answer.

JOSEPHINE: You shall not wait long. (*Aside*) If only he were more highly born, or I more lowly! (*Aloud*) Ralph Rackstraw, I reject your love! Go and cast your eyes on some village maiden—not your Captain's daughter. (*With a haughty toss of her head*, JOSEPHINE *exits.*)

RALPH (*Despairingly*): She scorns my love—yet I adore her! Can I go on living—despised, rejected? No, no, it's not to be expected! (*Calling off*) Shipmates, ahoy! Come here! (*All sailors enter.*)

SAILORS (*Ad lib*): Aye, aye, my boy! What cheer? (*Etc.*)

BECKET: What did she say?

RALPH: She rejected me.

DICK DEADEYE: Oho, I told you so!

RALPH: My heart is breaking! I can live no longer! (*To* BOATSWAIN) Bill, give me your pistol.

BOATSWAIN (*Handing him pistol; with kindly sincerity*): Always ready to help a fellow sailor! (JOSEPHINE *enters on bridge, followed by* BUTTERCUP.)

RALPH: When I am gone, tell the maid I loved her well. (*Puts pistol to his head. Sailors cover their ears.*)

JOSEPHINE (*Screaming from bridge*): Stop! I love you!

OTHER SAILORS (*Uncovering ears*): Stop! She loves you!

RALPH (*Incredulously, lowering pistol*): Loves me?

JOSEPHINE: Loves you! (*She rushes down steps to his side. He tosses pistol overboard and takes her in his arms.*)

OTHER SAILORS *and* BUTTERCUP: She loves him! (BOATSWAIN *and* BUTTERCUP *join* RALPH *and* JOSEPHINE *at center to recite.*)

JOSEPHINE:

>This very night,

BUTTERCUP:

>With bated breath

RALPH:

>And muffled oar—

JOSEPHINE:

>Without a light,

BUTTERCUP:

>As still as death,

RALPH:

>We'll steal ashore.

JOSEPHINE:

>A clergyman

RALPH:

>Shall make us one

BOATSWAIN:

>At half-past ten,

JOSEPHINE:

>And then we can

RALPH:

>Return, for none

BOATSWAIN:

>Can part them then!

DICK DEADEYE (*Down right, aside to audience*): Ralph thinks he's won his Josephine—but he has reckoned without Dick Deadeye! The Captain shall hear of this. (*He slinks off.*)

OTHER SAILORS (*Singing*):

> Let's give three cheers for the sailor's bride
> Who casts all thought of rank aside—
> Who gives up home and fortune, too,
> For the honest love of a sailor true!

(*All sailors cheer. Curtain*)

* * * * *

SCENE 2

TIME: *That night.*

SETTING: *Same as Scene 1.*

AT RISE: *Moonlight floods deck. Lighted lanterns are hung in rigging and on rail of bridge.* CAPTAIN CORCORAN *is on bridge, sadly strumming a guitar and reciting.* BUTTERCUP *is seated in shadow on deck, gazing sentimentally at* CAPTAIN.

CAPTAIN (*Reciting*):

> Fair moon, to thee I sing,
> Bright regent of the heavens,
> Say, why is everything
> Either at sixes or at sevens?

BUTTERCUP: How sweetly he sings to the unconscious moon! (CAPTAIN *sighs and rests guitar against bridge rail. He descends to deck and sees* BUTTERCUP.)

CAPTAIN: Buttercup! Still on board? You should have gone ashore at dusk.

BUTTERCUP: I waited, hoping to see you smile before I left.

CAPTAIN: Ah, Little Buttercup, I fear it will be a long time before I smile again. Misfortunes crowd upon me! My kindly crew is rebellious—my daughter loves a common sailor—and Sir Joseph is angry because she refuses him. He even threatens a court-martial!

BUTTERCUP (*Clasping his hand*): Dear Captain, you have one friend who remains true.

CAPTAIN (*Genuinely moved*): Oh, sweet Buttercup, your loyalty touches my heart. I long to return your love, but our stations are so far apart, we can only remain friends.

BUTTERCUP (*Releasing his hand*): I understand. You are rich and lofty, and I am poor and lowly. (*Warningly*) But take care! There is a change in store for you!

CAPTAIN: A change?

BUTTERCUP: Aye! (*Sings*)
> Things are seldom what they seem,
> Skim milk masquerades as cream;
> Highlows pass as patent leathers;
> Jackdaws strut in peacock feathers.

CAPTAIN: Very true, so they do.

BUTTERCUP (*Singing*):
> Black sheep dwell in every fold;
> All that glitters is not gold;
> Storks turn out to be but logs;
> Bulls are but inflated frogs.

CAPTAIN: Yes, I know, that is so.

BUTTERCUP (*Singing*):
> You will learn the truth with sorrow,
> Here today and gone tomorrow.

(*Speaks*) Farewell! (BUTTERCUP *exits up left melodramatically.*)

CAPTAIN (*Bewildered*): What does she mean? Is there a new misery in store for me? (SIR JOSEPH *enters up right in a huff.*)

SIR JOSEPH: Captain Corcoran, I'm afraid your daughter won't do! She refuses to hear my suit.

CAPTAIN (*Tactfully*): Perhaps she is dazzled by your exalted rank.

SIR JOSEPH (*Pompously*): Naturally she would be.

CAPTAIN: If your lordship would only tell her that love levels all ranks, she might yield at once.

SIR JOSEPH: A capital suggestion! (JOSEPHINE *enters*.) I'll try it now—here she comes. (*Goes to* JOSEPHINE) Madam, I believe you are appalled by my exalted rank. If this is so, your hesitation is uncalled for.

JOSEPHINE: Then, sir, you agree that the high and the lowly may be happy together, if they love one another?

SIR JOSEPH: Madam, love is a platform on which all ranks meet. That is my official opinion.

JOSEPHINE: Your official opinion! (*Brightly*) I thank you, Sir Joseph. I *did* hesitate, but I will hesitate no longer. (*Aside*) He little thinks how eloquently he has pleaded his rival's cause! (*Exits laughing.* CAPTAIN *and* SIR JOSEPH *shake hands.* SIR JOSEPH *joyously cavorts about deck, as* CAPTAIN *sings, then runs up steps to bridge and slides down bannister.*)

CAPTAIN (*Singing*):
      Never mind the why and wherefore,
      Love can level ranks, and therefore,
      Though his lordship's station's mighty,
      Though stupendous be his brain,
      Though your tastes are mean and flighty
      And your fortune poor and plain,

CAPTAIN *and* SIR JOSEPH (*Singing*):
      Ring the merry bells on board-ship,
    (SIR JOSEPH *rings ship's bell.*)

Rend the air with warbling wild,
For the union of his lordship
With a humble captain's child!
(SIR JOSEPH *exits, dancing hornpipe and waving to* CAP-
TAIN.)

CAPTAIN: At last my fondest hopes are crowned! My only daughter is to be the wife of a Cabinet Minister. (DICK DEADEYE
sneaks on deck.)

DICK (*In a hoarse whisper*): Captain!

CAPTAIN (*Startled*): Deadeye! What are you doing here?

DICK: I've come to give ye warning. This very night Miss Josephine is planning to elope with Ralph Rackstraw!

CAPTAIN: Good heavens! Thank you for warning me, Dick. I will
stop their flight. (CAPTAIN *gets cat-o'-nine-tails hanging in
corner, strikes deck with it and goes up on bridge.*) I'll conceal myself behind this wheel. (*Crouches behind wheel.*)

DICK (*Aside; gloating*): Ha, ha! They are foiled! (OTHER SAIL-
ORS *enter left on tiptoe, followed by* RALPH *and* BOATSWAIN.
JOSEPHINE *enters right on tiptoe, accompanied by* BUTTER-
CUP.)

ALL (*Singing*):
Carefully on tiptoe stealing,
Breathing gently as we may,
Every step with caution feeling,
We will softly steal away.
(CAPTAIN *stamps and cracks cat-o'-nine-tails, while remain-
ing hidden.*)

ALL: What was that?

DICK: It was the cat!

ALL (*Reassured*): Oh—it was the cat.

CAPTAIN (*Coming forward on bridge*): You're right—it *was* the cat! (*Flourishes cat-o'-nine-tails. All recoil. Politely*) Josephine, I insist upon knowing where you are going, for my crew, though excellent fellows, are scarcely fit company for a lady like you.

RALPH: Proud Captain, I know I am only a humble sailor, but I am a true-born Englishman.

BOATSWAIN (*Singing*):
> He is an Englishman!
> For he himself has said it,
> And it's greatly to his credit,
> That he is an Englishman!

(SIR JOSEPH, HEBE, *and* SISTERS, COUSINS, AND AUNTS *enter gradually on bridge.*)
> For he might have been a Roosian,
> A French, or Turk, or Proosian,
> Or perhaps, I-tal-i-an!

SAILORS (*Singing*):
> But in spite of all temptations
> To belong to other nations,
> He remains an Englishman!

CAPTAIN (*Trying to restrain his anger*): Far be it from me to disparage any British sailor, but (*Points to* RALPH) to seek to marry your Captain's daughter, why (*Exploding*) *damme!*—it's too bad! (SIR JOSEPH *recoils at* CAPTAIN's *language. An elderly* COUSIN *faints on wheel and sends it spinning around.*)

HEBE (*Clinging to* SIR JOSEPH *for protection*): Oh, the monster! He—he *swore!*

SIR JOSEPH (*To* CAPTAIN, *highly indignant*): My pain, sir, and my distress are not easy to express. My amazement—my surprise—

CAPTAIN: My lord, one word—the facts—hear me!

SIR JOSEPH: I will hear nothing! Go stand in the corner! You are in disgrace. (CAPTAIN *stands in corner at back and hangs his head.* SIR JOSEPH *speaks to sailors as he descends to deck.*) I'll teach you all to refrain from strong language! For I haven't any sympathy with ill-bred taunts.

SISTERS, COUSINS, AND AUNTS (*Together*): No more have his sisters, nor his cousins, nor his aunts.

SIR JOSEPH (*Turning to* RALPH): Now, tell me, my fine fellow, how did your Captain come to forget himself? I am sure you have given him no cause for annoyance.

RALPH: Please, your honor, I'm only a deck-hand—

SIR JOSEPH: Don't be ashamed of that.

RALPH: Your honor, love comes to every one of us. Josephine—

JOSEPHINE (*Running to* RALPH *and throwing herself into his arms*): Darling! (SIR JOSEPH *collapses and is caught by* BUTTERCUP *who fans him with a red bandanna handkerchief.*)

RALPH (*Smiling at* SIR JOSEPH *over* JOSEPHINE's *shoulder*): She is the bright beacon that guides my ship into the port of happiness.

SIR JOSEPH (*Struggling to his feet, seething with rage*): Insolent sailor, you shall repent of this! Seize him! (DICK DEADEYE *seizes* RALPH.)

JOSEPHINE: Oh, Sir Joseph, spare him, for I love him dearly!

SIR JOSEPH (*Coldly*): I will teach this presumptuous mariner to discipline his affections. Have you a dungeon on board?

DICK (*Chuckling*): We have!

SIR JOSEPH: Then load this man with chains and take him there at once! (DICK *starts to lead* RALPH *away*.)

BUTTERCUP (*Loudly*): Wait! (*All turn to her*.) The time has come for me to confess a crime that has been concealed too long. (*Stands center and sings*)
>Many years ago,
>When I was young and charming,
>As some of you may know,
>I practiced baby-farming.
>Two tender babes I nursed:
>One was of low condition;
>The other, upper crust,
>A regular patrician.
>Oh, bitter is my cup!
>However could I do it?
>I mixed those children up,
>And not a creature knew it!
>In time each little waif
>Forsook his foster-mother;
>The well-born babe was Ralph—
>Your Captain was the other!

(CAPTAIN *has slowly come downstage as he listens to* BUTTERCUP'S *revelation*.)

SIR JOSEPH: Am I to understand that Ralph is really the Captain, and the Captain is Ralph?

BUTTERCUP: Aye, aye, your honor.

SIR JOSEPH: Dear me! (*Commanding*) Corcoran—Rackstraw, to the front, march!

CAPTAIN *and* RALPH (*Together*): If what, your lordship?

SIR JOSEPH: Ah, yes—if you *please!* (CAPTAIN *and* RALPH *step forward*. SIR JOSEPH *switches their hats;* CAPTAIN *now wears* RALPH'S *straw sailor hat and* RALPH *wears* CAPTAIN'S *cocked hat*.) I congratulate you both. (*Shakes their hands*)

CAPTAIN *and* RALPH (*Together*): Thank you, your lordship.

SIR JOSEPH (*To* CAPTAIN): I need not tell you, Seaman Corcoran, that after this change in your condition, my marriage with your daughter is out of the question.

CAPTAIN (*Imploring*): Don't say that, your honor! Love levels all ranks.

SIR JOSEPH: Hmm-m—not as much as that! (*Handing* JOSEPHINE *to* RALPH) Here, take her, sir—she's yours.

RALPH *and* JOSEPHINE (*Embracing; together*): Oh, bliss! Oh, rapture!

CAPTAIN *and* BUTTERCUP (*Embracing; together*): Oh, rapture! Oh, bliss!

SIR JOSEPH (*Plaintively*): What shall *I* do? I cannot live alone.

HEBE (*Calling from bridge*): Cheer up, Cousin Joseph! I'll not desert you! (*Descending to deck*) I'll stay with you as long as I live!

SIR JOSEPH (*Groaning*): Oh, don't do that!

HEBE: But I'd rather! (*Gives him peck on cheek*)

SIR JOSEPH (*Resigned; reciting*):
Then tomorrow morn our vows shall all be plighted,
Three loving pairs on the same day united.
(*All sing finale—a medley of "Pinafore" songs.*)

CAPTAIN (*Pointing to* RALPH; *singing*):
For he's the Captain of the *Pinafore*;

ALL (*Singing*):
And a right good captain, too!

CAPTAIN (*Singing*):
>And though before my fall
>I was captain of you all,
>I'm a member of the crew.

ALL (*Singing*):
>Then give three cheers, and one cheer more,
>For the former Captain of the *Pinafore!*

BUTTERCUP (*Singing*):
>For he loves Little Buttercup, dear Little Buttercup,
>Though I could never tell why;
>But still he loves Buttercup, poor Little Buttercup,
>Sweet Little Buttercup, aye!

SIR JOSEPH (*Singing*):
>I am the monarch of the sea,
>And when I've married thee
>(*To* HEBE)
>I'll be true to the devotion that my love implants;

HEBE (*Singing*):
>Then goodbye to your sisters, and your cousins, and
>>your aunts—
>(SIR JOSEPH *throws kisses to* SISTERS, COUSINS AND AUNTS)
>Especially your cousins,
>Whom you reckon up by dozens,
>And your aunts!

ALL (*Singing*):
>For he is an Englishman,
>And he himself has said it,
>And it's greatly to his credit
>That he is an Englishman!
>(*Curtain*)

THE END

Characters: 13 male (including 6 Other Sailors, extras) ; 9 female (including 6 Sisters, Cousins, and Aunts, extras). Additional Sailors and Sisters, Cousins and Aunts may be added if desired.

Playing Time: 30 minutes.

Costumes: Nineteenth-century period dress. Sir Joseph and Captain Corcoran wear ceremonial uniforms, cocked hats, white gloves, swords. Tommy Tucker wears navy blue uniform, white gloves. Sailors wear white uniforms, navy blue jackets, straw sailor hats. Dick Deadeye wears black patch over one eye. Josephine, Sisters, Cousins, and Aunts and Hebe wear long dresses and hats, and they carry parasols, reticules, etc. Hebe carries lorgnette. Buttercup wears cotton dress with full skirt, white apron, cape and bonnet trimmed with buttercups.

Properties: Telescope; small basket of flowers; photograph; cat-o'-nine-tails; monocle; sheet of music; red bandanna handkerchief; basket and tray on strap for Buttercup—tray contains various small articles including peppermint stick; guitar.

Setting: Ship's quarterdeck. There is a raised platform (the bridge) at rear, reached by flight of steps at left. Ship's wheel is on bridge. Mast is up center, behind bridge. Rigging hangs at sides of deck. Capstan and coils of rope are at right. Up center, in front of bridge, is ship's bell. Exits left and right lead to cabins, lower decks. Painted backdrop shows sky, water, and ships at anchor in distance.

Lighting: Lanterns, moonlight effect, as indicated in text.

Sound: Cannon shots.

Music for songs on following pages.

WE SAIL THE OCEAN BLUE

Sailors

We sail the o-cean blue, And our sau-cy ship's a beau-ty; We're so-ber men and true, And at - tentive to our du-ty. When the balls whis-tle free O'er the bright blue sea, We stand to our guns all day; When at an - chor we ride On the Ports-mouth tide, We've plen-ty of time for play.

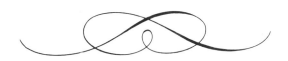

27

I'M CALLED LITTLE BUTTERCUP

Buttercup

I'm called Little Buttercup, dear Little Buttercup,

Though I could never tell why, But still I'm called

Buttercup, poor Little Buttercup, Sweet Little Buttercup

I! I've snuff and to-bac-cy, and ex-cel-lent jack-y, I've

scissors and watches and knives; I've ribbons and laces to

set off the faces Of pretty young sweethearts and wives. I've

treacle and toffee, I've tea and I've coffee, Soft tom-my and

suc-cu-lent chops; I've chickens and conies and

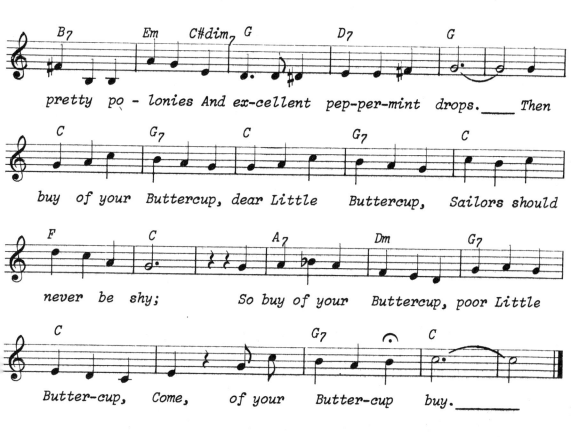

pretty po - lonies And ex-cellent pep-per-mint drops.____ Then

buy of your Buttercup, dear Little Buttercup, Sailors should

never be shy; So buy of your Buttercup, poor Little

Butter-cup, Come, of your Butter-cup buy._____

I AM THE CAPTAIN OF THE PINAFORE

1. I am the captain of the Pin-a-fore! And a right good captain too! You're ver-y, ver-y good, And be it understood I command a right good crew. We're very, very good And be it understood He commands a right good crew. Tho' re-la-ted to a peer, I can hand reef and steer And ship a sel-va-gee; I am never known to quail At the

2. I do my best to sat-is-fy you all-- And with you we're quite content. You're ex-ceeding-ly po-lite And I think it only right To return the compli-ment. We're exceedingly polite He thinks it only right To return the compli-ment. Bad language or a-buse, I never, never use, What-ever the e-mer-gen-cy; Tho' "bother it" I may_____ Oc-

fury of a gale, And I'm never, never sick at sea! What,
casionally say, I never use a big, big D! What,

never? No, never! What, never? Hardly
never? No, never! What, never? Hardly

ever! He's hardly ever sick at sea! Then
ever! Hardly ever swears a big, big D! Then

give three cheers and one cheer more for the hardy captain of the
give three cheers and one cheer more for the hardy captain of the

Pin-a-fore!
Pin-a-fore!

GAILY TRIPPING

Gai-ly trip-ping, Light-ly skip-ping, Flock the

maidens to the shipping; Gai-ly trip-ping, Lightly skip-ping,

Flock the maidens to the shipping. Sailors sprightly Al-ways

right-ly Wel-come la - dies so po - lite - ly.

I AM THE MONARCH OF THE SEA

Sir Joseph

I am the monarch of the sea, The ruler of the Queen's Na-vee Whose praise Great Britain loudly chants And we are his sisters and his cousins and his aunts His sisters and his cousins and his aunts.

Sir Joseph

When at anchor here I ride, My bosom swells with pride And I snap my fingers at a foeman's taunts. And so do his sisters and his cousins and his aunts. And so do his sisters and his cousins and his aunts.

Sir J.

But when the breezes blow I generally go be-low And

33

seek the seclusion that a cabin grants! And so do his sisters and his

cousins and his aunts His sisters and his cousins Whom he reckons up
by

dozens and his aunts! ____

WHEN I WAS A LAD

Sir Joseph

1. When I was a lad I served a term   As   office boy
2. As office   boy I made such a mark That they gave me
   the

to   an attorney's firm. I cleaned the windows and I swept the floor
post of a junior clerk I served the writs with a smile so bland And

And I

polished up the handle of the big front door.   *That now I am the*
copied all the letters in a hand so free

ruler of the Queen's Navee.

THINGS ARE SELDOM WHAT THEY SEEM

Buttercup *Dm*

Things are seldom   what they seem,   Skim milk masque-

rades as cream; Highlows pass as patent leathers; Jackdaws strut in

peacocks feathers. Black sheep dwell in every fold, All that glitters

is not gold Storks turn out to be but logs Bulls are but inflated frogs.

He will learn the truth with sorrow Here today and gone tomorrow!

NEVER MIND THE WHY AND WHEREFORE

Captain

Never mind the why and wherefore, Love can

level ranks and therefore Tho' his Lordship's station's mighty Tho'
stu-

pendous be his brain, Tho' your tastes are mean and flighty And your

Captain, Sir Joseph

fortune poor___ and plain,   Ring the merry

bells on boardship, Rend the air with warbling wild,   For the

union of his Lordship With a humble captain's child.

CAREFULLY ON TIPTOE STEALING

Sailors

G / Am

Careful-ly on tip-toe steal-ing, Breathing

F#dim / G / D₇

gen-tly as we may, Ev-'ry step with cau-tion

G / G#dim₇ / D₇ / G

feel-ing, We will soft - ly steal a - way.

HE IS AN ENGLISHMAN

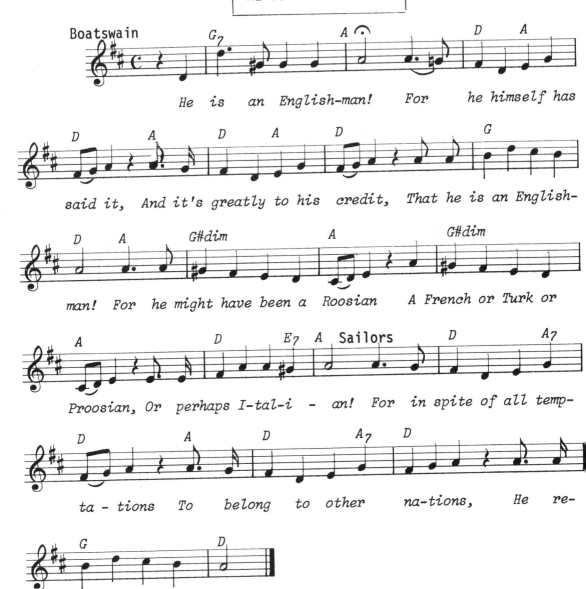

Boatswain

He is an English-man! For he himself has said it, And it's greatly to his credit, That he is an English-man! For he might have been a Roosian A French or Turk or Proosian, Or perhaps I-tal-i - an! For in spite of all temp-ta - tions To belong to other na-tions, He re-mains an English - man!

A MANY YEARS AGO

A many years a-go, When I was young and charming, As some of you may know, I practised baby farming. Two tender babes I nurs'd: One was of low con-dition, The other, up-per crust, A re-gu-lar pa-trician. Oh, bitter is my cup! How-e-ver could I do it? I mixed those children up, And not a creature knew it! In time each little waif Forsook his foster mother: The wellborn babe was Ralph, Your captain was the other!

39

THE MIKADO

The story of

THE MIKADO

Nanki-Poo, the only son of the Mikado, the Emperor of Japan, has run away from home to escape marrying Katisha, an ugly old harridan. He arrives in the town of Titipu disguised as a wandering minstrel. Ko-Ko, the town tailor, has been condemned to death for flirting, under a recent decree of the Mikado. However, instead of being executed, Ko-Ko has been promoted to the rank of Lord High Executioner by his fellow townspeople, who reason that Ko-Ko is the ideal man for the job because, as next to die, he cannot cut off another's head until he cuts his own off. Consequently there have been no more executions in Titipu. A group of schoolgirls enter. Among them is Ko-Ko's lovely ward, Yum-Yum, whom Nanki-Poo has met while singing at a seaside resort. It is to see her again that he has come to Titipu, but she is engaged to marry Ko-Ko.

Preparations are being made for the wedding when word comes that the Mikado is about to arrive. He is angry because Ko-Ko has not yet executed anyone, and a victim must be found quickly. Nanki-Poo offers himself as the victim, provided he can first marry Yum-Yum and live with her for a month. Ko-Ko reluctantly consents. The Mikado and Katisha arrive, and the Mikado asks whether his orders have been carried out. Ko-Ko gives the Mikado a false certificate of Nanki-Poo's execution. Katisha, who has discovered Nanki-Poo's disguise, reads the certificate and reveals with horror that Ko-Ko has executed the Mikado's son. As Ko-Ko is being led off to execution, Nanki-Poo and Yum-Yum enter and announce that they have just been married. There is general rejoicing as all sing "For he's gone and married Yum-Yum."

THE MIKADO

Or, The Town of Titipu

Characters

THE MIKADO OF JAPAN
NANKI-POO, *his son, disguised as a wandering minstrel*
KO-KO, *Lord High Executioner of Titipu*
POOH-BAH, *Lord High Everything Else*
PISH-TUSH, *a noble lord*
YUM-YUM ⎫
PITTI-SING ⎬ *sisters, wards of Ko-Ko*
PEEP-BO ⎭
KATISHA, *an elderly lady*
GO-TO, *a boy, Ko-Ko's attendant*
SCHOOLGIRLS
NOBLES
GUARDS

SCENE 1

SETTING: *Courtyard of Ko-Ko's palace in Titipu. Main entrance is up center through pagoda arch, beyond which part of garden is seen. Screens right and left are painted to suggest sliding panels. There are low platforms on each side of stage where taborets and cushions are placed for sitting. Down left are a low table and cushion. Porcelain pottery and vases of flowers are set about stage.*

AT RISE: PISH-TUSH *and* NOBLES *are posed about stage, standing and sitting.* POOH-BAH *is seated at table down left, writing Japanese characters on scroll with brush and ink.*

PISH-TUSH *and* NOBLES (*Singing*):
      If you want to know who we are,
      We are gentlemen of Japan:

On many a vase and jar—
On many a screen and fan,
(*They open fans and fan themselves.*)
We figure in lively paint;
Our attitude's queer and quaint—
You're wrong if you think it ain't, oh!
(*Imitating jerky movements of puppets*)
If you think we are worked by strings,
Like a Japanese marionette,
You don't understand these things:
It is simply Court etiquette.
(*All bow*)
Perhaps you suppose this throng
Can't keep it up all day long?
If that's your idea, you're wrong, oh!

(NANKI-POO *enters up center in great excitement. He is a charming young man, dressed as a minstrel, who loves the maiden* YUM-YUM. *Guitar is slung on his back and he carries a sheaf of papers in his hand.*)

NANKI-POO: Oh, tell me, gentlemen, where will I find the fair maiden named Yum-Yum? (PISH-TUSH, *a serious individual, answers him.*)

PISH-TUSH (*Haughtily*): Who are you to ask this question?

NANKI-POO: I am Nanki-Poo, a wandering minstrel who sings songs for every occasion. (*Plays guitar and sings*)
A wandering minstrel I—
A thing of shreds and patches,
Of ballads, songs and snatches,
And dreamy lullaby!
My catalogue is long,
Through every passion ranging,
And to your humors changing
I tune my supple song!

PISH-TUSH: And what might be your business with Yum-Yum?

NANKI-POO: It is this: A year ago I was a member of the Titipu
Town Band—I played the second trombone. One day I met
Yum-Yum, and we fell in love. But she was betrothed to her
guardian, Ko-Ko, a cheap tailor, and there was no hope for
us. In despair I left town and traveled far away. Then, a
month ago, I heard that Ko-Ko had been condemned to death
for flirting! Imagine my delight! I hurried back here, hoping
to find Yum-Yum free.

PISH-TUSH: It is true that Ko-Ko was condemned to death for
flirting, but he was reprieved at the last moment, and raised
to the exalted rank of Lord High Executioner. You see, our
great Mikado decided that Japanese men should be more
serious-minded, and so he decreed (*Recites*)—
> That all who flirted, leered or winked
> (Unless connubially linked)
> Should forthwith be beheaded.

NANKI-POO: Merciful heavens!

PISH-TUSH: You can well understand that this was a most un-
popular law. The people of Titipu sought to circumvent it
by freeing Ko-Ko. (*Recites*)
> And so we straight let out on bail
> A convict from the county jail,
> Whose head was next
> On some pretext
> Condemned to be mown off,
> And made *him* Headsman, for we said,
> "Who's next to be decapited
> Cannot cut off another's head
> Until he's cut his own off."

Of course this ruling put an end to all executions and made
the public happy. (*Recites*)
> And we are right, I think you'll say,
> To argue in this kind of way;
> And I am right
> (*Points closed fan at himself*)

And you are right
(*Points fan at* NANKI-POO)
And all is right
(*Opens fan with a snap*)—
Too-loo-ra-lay!
(*Fans himself rapidly*)

NOBLES (*Reciting*):
And you are right,
And we are right,
And all is right—
Too-loo-ra-lay!
(NOBLES *exit right and left, repeating business with fans.*)

NANKI-POO (*Shaking his head in wonder*): To think that Ko-Ko, the cheap tailor, is now Lord High Executioner of Titipu! Why, that's the highest rank a citizen can attain! (POOH-BAH *rises, with scroll in hand. He is a pompous, smug, self-satisfied character who speaks with a superior manner.*)

POOH-BAH: It is. But Ko-Ko holds only *one* public office, whereas *I* (*Indicating column of characters on scroll*)—hold *thirteen!*

PISH-TUSH (*Aside to* NANKI-POO): That is Pooh-Bah, the most important person in Titipu—at least, *he* thinks he is!

POOH-BAH (*Strutting about, his nose in air*): I can trace my ancestry back to a protoplasmal primordial atomic globule. I was born sneering. (*Stopping beside* NANKI-POO) But I always do my best to overcome my family pride. When all the great officers of state refused to serve under an ex-tailor, I unhesitatingly accepted all their posts. I am consequently (*Pointing to characters on scroll one at a time*) First Lord of the Treasury, Lord Chief Justice, Commander-in-Chief, Lord High Admiral, Master of the Buckhounds, Groom of the Back Stairs, Archbishop of Titipu, Lord Mayor, both acting and elect (*Indicating remaining characters on scroll*), et cetera, et cetera—all rolled into one. And at a salary! Yes, I have humiliated myself by taking pay for my services. (*Rolls up scroll and tucks it into his sash*)

NANKI-POO (*Smiling*): It does you credit.

POOH-BAH: Ah, but I don't stop at that. I also retail state secrets at a very low figure. For instance, any further information about Yum-Yum would come under the head of a state secret. (NANKI-POO *gives him two coins.* POOH-BAH *sneers at them.*) Another humiliation—and, I think, a cheap one! (*Pockets coins and regards* NANKI-POO *with disdain*) My advice to you, young man, is to leave this town and forget Yum-Yum. She is returning from school today to marry Ko-Ko.

NANKI-POO (*With bowed head*): And I have journeyed for a month only to find that my case is hopeless! Yum-Yum is to marry Ko-Ko.

POOH-BAH: And if I am not mistaken, Ko-Ko is even now approaching.

NANKI-POO (*Sadly*): Oh, sorrow! Sorrow! (*He exits.* POOH-BAH *and* PISH-TUSH *stand downstage as* NOBLES *enter, and line up on platforms left and right.*)

NOBLES (*Singing with great dignity*):
>Behold the Lord High Executioner!
>A personage of noble rank and title—
>A dignified and potent officer,
>Whose functions are particularly vital!
>Bow down, bow down,
>(*All bow low*)
>To the Lord High Executioner!
>Bow down, bow down,
>To the Lord High Executioner!

(Ko-Ko *enters. He is an insignificant-looking man, irritable and constantly perplexed by the demands of his office. He is attended by* GO-TO, *a small boy who carries* KO-KO's *badge of office, a huge ceremonial sword in sheath.*)

Ko-Ko (*Singing as he comes down center*) :
>Taken from the county jail
>By a set of curious chances;
>Liberated then on bail,
>On my own recognizances;
>Wafted by a favoring gale
>As one sometimes is in trances,
>To a height that few can scale,
>Save by long and weary dances;
>Surely, never had a male
>Under such like circumstances
>So adventurous a tale,
>Which may rank with most romances.

Nobles (*Singing*) :
>Bow down, bow down,
>To the Lord High Executioner!

Ko-Ko (*To* Nobles) : Gentlemen, I am much touched by this reception.

Nobles (*Bowing and bleating like sheep*) : Ba-a-a-a-a!

Ko-Ko (*Bowing and bleating*) : Ba-a-a-a! Thank you, my noble sheep. (*Continues his speech*) I can only hope that I shall always deserve your favors.

Nobles: Ba-a-a-a!

Ko-Ko: Ba-a-a-a! If I should ever be called upon to perform my duty as executioner, I assure you that there will be no difficulty in finding plenty of people whose execution would be a benefit to society. I've got a little list of those who never will be missed! (Ko-Ko *produces long scroll that reaches down to floor. He hands upper end of scroll to* Go-To, *lifts boy onto table, then gets down on hands and knees and reads list, beginning at bottom of scroll and rolling it up as he crawls along floor. Singing or reciting*)

There's the pestilential nuisances who write for autographs—

All people who have flabby hands and irritating laughs—

All children who are up on dates, and floor you with 'em flat—

All persons who in shaking hands, shake hands with you like *that*—

(*Pantomimes shaking hands with arm held high*)

And that singular anomaly, the girl who's not been kissed—

I don't think *she'd* be missed—I'm *sure* she'd not be missed!

NOBLES (*Reciting or singing*):

He's got her on the list, and I'm *sure* she'll not be missed!

KO-KO (*Reciting or singing*):

And the fellow in a card game, who politely trumps your ace,

And says, "Rotten luck, old chap!"—I've got him on the list!

And the people who eat peppermint and puff it in your face,

They never would be missed—they never would be missed!

And apologetic statesmen of a compromising kind,

Such as—What d'ye call him—Thing'em-bob, and likewise—Never mind,

And Tut-tut-tut—and What's-his-name, and also You-know-who—

The task of filling up the blanks I'd rather leave to *you*.

But it really doesn't matter whom you put upon the list,

For they'd none of 'em be missed—they'd none of 'em be missed!

NOBLES (*Reciting or singing*):
>You may put 'em on the list and they'll none of 'em
>be missed!

(KO-KO *gives rolled-up scroll to* GO-TO, *who sits down on table with sigh of relief.* NOBLES *form groups and converse in pantomime.* KO-KO *crosses to* POOH-BAH.)

KO-KO: Pooh-Bah, I want to consult you as to the amount I ought to spend on my approaching marriage.

POOH-BAH: Certainly. In which of my capacities? As First Lord of the Treasury, Lord Chamberlain, Attorney-General, Chancellor of the Exchequer, Privy Purse, or Private Secretary?

KO-KO: Suppose we say as Private Secretary.

POOH-BAH: As your Private Secretary, I shall discuss this matter with you (*Staring pointedly at* PISH-TUSH, *who is eavesdropping on conversation*)—in private! (POOH-BAH *and* KO-KO *exit down right.* PISH-TUSH *hurries off after them, and* GO-TO *follows carrying sword and scroll. Procession of* SCHOOLGIRLS, *including* YUM-YUM, PEEP-BO *and* PITTI-SING, *enters up center with short running steps, fluttering their fans.* NOBLES *look on.*)

GIRLS (*Singing as they enter*):
>Schoolgirls we, eighteen and under,
>From scholastic trammels free,
>And we wonder—how we wonder!—
>What on earth the world can be!

(YUM-YUM, PEEP-BO, *and* PITTI-SING *come downstage.*)

YUM-YUM, PEEP-BO *and* PITTI-SING (*Singing*):
>Three little maids from school are we,
>Pert as a schoolgirl well can be,
>Filled to the brim with girlish glee,
>Three little maids from school!

YUM-YUM (*Singing*):
> Everything is a source of fun!
> (*Giggles behind fan*)

PEEP-BO (*Singing*):
> Nobody's safe, for we care for none!
> (*Giggles behind fan*)

PITTI-SING (*Singing*):
> Life is a joke that's just begun!
> (*Giggles behind fan*)

YUM-YUM, PEEP-BO *and* PITTI-SING (*Singing*):
> Three little maids from school!
> (*They dance.*)
> Three little maids who, all unwary,
> Come from a ladies' seminary,
> Freed from its genius tutelary—
> (*Suddenly demure*)
> Three little maids from school!

YUM-YUM (*Stepping forward, singing*):
> One little maid is a bride, Yum-Yum—

PEEP-BO (*Singing*):
> Two little maids in attendance come—
> (PEEP-BO *and* PITTI-SING *step forward and stand beside* YUM-YUM.)

PITTI-SING (*Singing*):
> Three little maids is the total sum.

YUM-YUM, PEEP-BO *and* PITTI-SING (*Singing*):
> Three little maids from school!

YUM-YUM (*Singing*):
> From three little maids take one away—
> (*Backs upstage*)

PEEP-BO (*Singing*):
>Two little maids remain, and they—

PITTI-SING (*Singing*):
>Won't have to wait very long, they say—
>(PITTI-SING *and* PEEP-BO *smile coquettishly at* NOBLES.)

YUM-YUM, PEEP-BO, *and* PITTI-SING (*Singing*):
>Three little maids from school!
>(*They dance.*)
>Three little maids who, all unwary,
>Come from a ladies' seminary,
>Freed from its genius tutelary—
>(*Suddenly demure*)
>Three little maids from school!
>(PEEP-BO, PITTI-SING *and* SCHOOLGIRLS *titter and make eyes at* NOBLES, *then run off up center.* NOBLES *follow, at first sedately, then quickly breaking into a fast trot.* YUM-YUM *remains behind. She is about to exit down right when* NANKI-POO *enters up left and calls softly to her.*)

NANKI-POO: Yum-Yum!

YUM-YUM (*Turning*): Nanki-Poo! (*They rush toward each other and meet center.*)

NANKI-POO: I have sought you night and day for a month, because I believed that Ko-Ko had been beheaded. Now I find you are to be married to the very same gentleman this afternoon!

YUM-YUM: Alas, yes!

NANKI-POO: Why don't you refuse him?

YUM-YUM: What good would that do? He's my guardian, and he wouldn't let me marry you. A wandering minstrel who plays the second trombone outside tea houses is hardly a fitting husband.

NANKI-POO (*Dramatically*): What if I told you that I am really no musician?

YUM-YUM: There! I knew you were no musician the moment I heard you play.

NANKI-POO: What if I told you that I am no other than the son of His Majesty the Mikado?

YUM-YUM (*Amazed*): The son of the Mikado! But why is Your Highness disguised? What has Your Highness done?

NANKI-POO: Last year I had the misfortune to attract the attention of Katisha, an elderly lady at Court. Under my father's law, she claimed me in marriage, and my father ordered me to marry her within a week or perish on the scaffold. I fled the Court and assumed the disguise of a wandering minstrel. And then I met you. (*Reaches out to take her hand*)

YUM-YUM (*Coyly retreating*): If you please, I think Your Highness had better not come too near. The laws against flirting are excessively severe. (*Sits on left platform*)

NANKI-POO: Ah, yes, if it were not for the law, we should now be sitting side by side—like this. (*Sits beside her*)

YUM-YUM: Instead of being obliged to sit half a mile apart—like this. (*Crosses and sits at other end of stage*)

NANKI-POO: We should be gazing into each other's eyes—like this. (*Crosses and kneels, gazing up at her ardently*)

YUM-YUM: Breathing sighs of unutterable love—like this. (*Sighs and gazes lovingly at him, then suddenly jumps to her feet and moves away*) But as it is, we can't do anything of the kind! (*Apologetically*) Being engaged to Ko-Ko, you know.

NANKI-POO (*Rising*): If it weren't for that, how happy we might be!

YUM-YUM (*Sadly*): Happy indeed!
(*They start off in opposite directions*—YUM-YUM, *left;* NANKI-POO, *right. They stop, turn and face each other across stage, sighing heavily in unison.* YUM-YUM *takes flower from her hair and tosses it to* NANKI-POO, *who picks it up and presses it to his lips.*)

NANKI-POO: Oh, sorrow, sorrow! (*Exits with bowed head.* YUM-YUM *sadly watches him go, then exits just as* KO-KO *enters down right.*)

KO-KO (*Looking off after* YUM-YUM): There she goes! To think how entirely my future happiness is wrapped up in that little parcel! Oh, matrimony! (PISH-TUSH *enters down right, waving a letter;* POOH-BAH *follows. Crossly*) What is it now? Can't you see I'm soliloquizing?

PISH-TUSH: A letter has just arrived from His Majesty the Mikado.

KO-KO (*Taking it reverently*): A letter from the Mikado! What in the world can he have to say to me? (*Reads letter*) Dear, dear! The Mikado is much displeased because no executions have taken place in Titipu for a year. He decrees that unless somebody is beheaded within one month, the post of Lord High Executioner shall be abolished, and the town of Titipu reduced to the rank of a village.

PISH-TUSH (*Moaning*): We will all be ruined!

KO-KO: I shall have to execute somebody. The only question is, who shall it be?

POOH-BAH: Well, as you are already under sentence of death for flirting, everything seems to point to *you*.

KO-KO: To *me?* I can't execute myself.

POOH-BAH: Why not?

KO-KO: It would be extremely difficult to cut off my own head, and besides, it would be suicide, and suicide is a capital offense.

PISH-TUSH: I can see no other way, unless a substitute can be found.

KO-KO (*Brightening*): A substitute? Nothing easier! Pooh-Bah, I appoint you Lord High Substitute.

POOH-BAH (*Bowing*): I should be delighted. Such an appointment would realize my fondest dreams. But no!—I must set a limit to my insatiable ambition! I must regretfully decline.

PISH-TUSH: And so do I.

POOH-BAH *and* PISH-TUSH (*As they bow themselves out; reciting*):

    To sit in solemn silence in a dull dark dock,
    In a pestilential prison, with a life-long lock,
    Awaiting the sensation of a short, sharp shock,
    From a cheap and chippy chopper on a big black block!
(*They exit.*)

KO-KO: This is simply appalling! I am required to die within a month, if I can't find a substitute. (NANKI-POO *enters. Rope with hangman's noose is around his neck. In surprise*) What are you going to do with that rope?

NANKI-POO: Hang myself.

KO-KO: Nonsense! What for?

NANKI-POO: Because you are going to marry the girl I adore.

KO-KO: I won't permit it! Are you aware, sir, that, in taking your life, you are committing a crime which is—which is—oh! (*Struck by an idea*) Substitute! (KO-KO *dances a jig of pleasure.*)

NANKI-POO: What's the matter?

KO-KO: If you are absolutely resolved to die, don't spoil it by committing suicide. Have yourself beheaded handsomely at the hands of the Lord High Executioner!

NANKI-POO: I don't see how that will benefit me.

KO-KO: You don't? Observe: you'll have a month to live, and you'll live like a nobleman at my expense. When the day comes, there will be a procession—a funeral march—bells tolling —all the girls in tears, especially Yum-Yum—

NANKI-POO: I should be sorry to cause Yum-Yum pain. (*Pauses*) I have a plan. I'll tell you how we'll manage it. Let me marry Yum-Yum tomorrow, and in a month you may behead me.

KO-KO: No, no—I draw the line at Yum-Yum!

NANKI-POO: All right, if you can draw the line, so can I. (*Goes upstage and throws loose end of rope over a cross-beam of the pagoda arch*)

KO-KO: Stop! (*Grabs rope and drags* NANKI-POO *away from arch*) Be reasonable! How can I consent to your marrying Yum-Yum if I'm going to marry her myself?

NANKI-POO: My good friend, she'll be a widow in a month, and you can marry her then.

KO-KO (*Pondering this*): That's true. After all, it's only putting off my wedding for a month. Very well, I agree. (NANKI-POO *removes noose from around neck.* POOH-BAH *and* PISH-TUSH *enter.*) Congratulate me, gentlemen. I've found a volunteer! It's Nanki-Poo!

POOH-BAH: I think he'll do.

PISH-TUSH: Yes, yes, he'll do!

KO-KO: He promises to let me execute him in a month, if I permit him to marry Yum-Yum first. It's not an easy decision, for I love Yum-Yum passionately. However, I love myself more. (YUM-YUM, PITTI-SING *and* PEEP-BO *enter.* KO-KO *leads* NANKI-POO *to* YUM-YUM. *Glumly*) Take her—she's yours. (NANKI-POO *and* YUM-YUM *joyfully embrace.* KO-KO *exits.*)

NANKI-POO (*To* YUM-YUM):
The threatened cloud has passed away,

YUM-YUM:
And brightly shines the dawning day;

NANKI-POO:
What though the night may come too soon,

YUM-YUM:
We'll have at least a honeymoon!

PITTI-SING: Come, let us be merry! (*All begin to dance. Suddenly* KATISHA *enters up center. She is a grim, domineering, elderly woman, with grotesque makeup that suggests a Kabuki mask. She strikes melodramatic pose.*)

KATISHA: Your revels cease! Assist me, all of you! I claim my perjured lover, Nanki-Poo! (*All draw back in fear.*)

NANKI-POO (*Aside to* YUM-YUM): It's Katisha! She's the elderly lady I am betrothed to! (*Starts to go*)

KATISHA (*Boldly*): No! You shall not go! (*Walks toward* NANKI-POO *with outstretched arms*) These arms shall yet enfold you! (*He ducks under* KATISHA'S *arms. She confronts him angrily.*) Fool—to flee my undying love! (*To* YUM-YUM) Pink cheek—your doom is nigh!

PITTI-SING (*Coming forward; to* KATISHA): Away with you! Nanki-Poo is going to marry Yum-Yum! (*Sings*)
For he's going to marry Yum-Yum!

ALL (*Singing*):
>Yum-Yum!

PITTI-SING (*Singing*):
>Your anger pray bury,
>For all will be merry—
>I think you had better succumb!

ALL (*Singing*):
>Cumb-cumb!

PITTI-SING (*Singing*):
>And join our expressions of glee.
>On this subject we pray you be dumb!

ALL (*Singing*):
>Dumb-dumb!

PITTI-SING (*Singing*):
>You'll find there are many
>Who'll wed for a penny—
>The word for your guidance is "mum"!

ALL (*Singing*):
>Mum-mum!

PITTI-SING (*Singing*):
>There's lots of good fish in the sea!

KATISHA (*Pointing finger accusingly at* NANKI-POO; *reciting*):
>Oh, faithless one, this insult you shall rue!
>In vain for mercy on your knees you'll sue.
>I'll tear the mask from your disguising!
(*To others*)
>Prepare yourselves for new surprising!
>No minstrel he, despite bravado!
>He is the son of your—
(*All interrupt* KATISHA, *shouting Japanese words to drown her voice.*)

ALL: *O ni! Bikkuri shakkuri to!*

KATISHA:

> In vain you interrupt with this tornado!
> He is the only son of your—

ALL (*Shouting*): *O ni! Bikkuri shakkuri to!*

KATISHA:

> I will spoil your gay gambado!
> He is the son—the only son—

ALL (*Shouting*): *O ni! Bikkuri shakkuri to! Oya! Oya!*

KATISHA: Do your worst, you haughty lords and ladies! I'm going to the Mikado to demand retribution! My wrongs shall be avenged! (*She rushes furiously upstage and exits center. Fast curtain.*)

* * * * *

SCENE 2

SETTING: *Ko-Ko's garden. Painted backdrop of Japanese landscape. In foreground is an arched bridge spanning a stream. Trellises are right and left stage. There is garden armchair on platform up center. Bench is down right. Willow tree is down left. Japanese lanterns are hung overhead.*

AT RISE: NANKI-POO *and* YUM-YUM *are strolling about garden.* YUM-YUM *is carrying an open parasol.*

YUM-YUM (*Leaning her head on* NANKI-POO'S *shoulder*): Today I'm to be married to the man I love best, and I'm the happiest girl in all Japan (*Sighing*)—even though my husband is to be beheaded in a month.

NANKI-POO (*Cheerfully*): What's a month? These divisions of time are purely arbitrary. We'll call each second a minute— each hour a day—and each day a year. At that rate, we've about thirty years of married happiness before us!

YUM-YUM (*Smiling*): How time flies when one is thoroughly enjoying oneself! (KO-KO *enters*.)

KO-KO (*To* YUM-YUM, *dolefully*): Oh, my poor child—my little bride that was to have been!

YUM-YUM (*Delighted*): *Was* to have been?

KO-KO: Yes—I've just learned that, according to the Mikado's law, when a married man is beheaded, his wife is buried alive.

YUM-YUM *and* NANKI-POO: Buried alive!

YUM-YUM (*Singing*):
    Here's a how-de-do!
    If I marry you,
    When your time has come to perish,
    Then the maiden whom you cherish
    Must be slaughtered too!
    Here's a how-de-do!

NANKI-POO (*Singing*):
    Here's a pretty mess!
    In a month, or less,
    I must die without a wedding!
    Let the bitter tears I'm shedding
    Witness my distress—
    Here's a pretty mess!

KO-KO (*Singing*):
    Here's a state of things!
    To her life she clings!
    Matrimonial devotion
    Doesn't seem to suit her notion—
    Burial it brings!
    Here's a state of things!

ALL (*Speaking together*): Here's a pretty how-de-do! (YUM-YUM *exits, weeping*.)

KO-KO (*To* NANKI-POO): My poor boy, I'm really very sorry for you. But you shan't be cheated out of a wedding—you shall come to mine.

NANKI-POO (*Shaking his head mournfully*): No—I can't live without Yum-Yum. This afternoon I shall hang myself.

KO-KO: Hang it all, you can't do that! You're under contract to be executed in a month's time. If you kill yourself, I shall have to be executed in your place.

POOH-BAH (*Entering*): The Mikado will be here in a few minutes!

KO-KO (*Shuddering*): The Mikado! He's coming to see if his orders have been carried out!

NANKI-POO: Well, then—behead me. (*Kneels and lays his head on bench*)

KO-KO (*Starting to cry*): I *can't* kill you! I can't kill anybody! Why, I never even killed a *horsefly!* (*Sits, sobbing*)

NANKI-POO (*Affably, rising*): Come, my poor fellow, if I don't mind, why should you? Remember, sooner or later, it must be done.

KO-KO (*Springing to his feet*): Must it? I'm not so sure about that! Why should I kill you when a certificate saying you've been executed will do just as well? (*Pointing to* POOH-BAH) Here are plenty of witnesses—the Lord Chief Justice, Lord High Admiral, Commander-in-Chief, Secretary of State, First Lord of the Treasury, and Chief Commissioner of Police.

NANKI-POO: But life without Yum-Yum—

KO-KO (*Exasperated*): Oh, bother Yum-Yum! (*To* POOH-BAH) Commissioner, go and fetch Yum-Yum. (POOH-BAH *exits.*)

Take Yum-Yum and marry Yum-Yum, only go away and never come back again. (POOH-BAH *re-enters with* YUM-YUM.) Yum-Yum, have you five minutes to spare?

YUM-YUM: Yes.

KO-KO: Then go along with his Grace the Archbishop of Titipu (*Indicating* POOH-BAH)—he'll marry you to Nanki-Poo at once. Don't ask any questions, just do as I tell you! (*He hustles them all off and wipes his brow.*) Phew! That was a close call! Here comes the Mikado! (*He exits quickly. Procession of* GUARDS, *carrying spears, enters down aisle to music of Mikado's March.* MIKADO *follows, preceded by two* GUARDS *holding banner depicting Rising Sun. At end of procession comes* KATISHA. *When all are onstage,* MIKADO *and* KATISHA *stand center and sing to audience.*)

MIKADO (*Singing*):
> From every kind of man
> Obedience I expect;
> I'm the Emperor of Japan—

KATISHA (*Singing*):
> And I'm his daughter-in-law elect!
> He'll marry his son
> (He's only got one)
> To his daughter-in-law elect.
> Bow—bow—
> To his daughter-in-law elect!

GUARDS (*Singing*):
> Bow—bow—
> To his daughter-in-law elect!

MIKADO (*Singing*):
> In a fatherly kind of way
> I govern each tribe and sect,

KATISHA (*Singing*):
>All except his daughter-in-law elect!
>As tough as a bone,
>With a will of her own,
>Is his daughter-in-law elect!
>Bow—bow—
>To his daughter-in-law elect!

GUARDS (*Singing*):
>Bow—bow—
>To his daughter-in-law elect!

MIKADO (*Singing*):
>My object all sublime
>I shall achieve in time—
>To let the punishment fit the crime,
>The punishment fit the crime...

GUARDS (*Singing as they exit*):
>His object all sublime
>He shall achieve in time—
>To let the punishment fit the crime,
>The punishment fit the crime.

(MIKADO *sits in garden chair;* KATISHA *stands beside him.* POOH-BAH, KO-KO *and* PITTI-SING *enter and kowtow to* MIKADO. POOH-BAH *hands certificate to* KO-KO.)

KO-KO (*To* MIKADO): Your Majesty, the execution has taken place.

MIKADO: Oh, you've had an execution, have you? (KO-KO *hands certificate to* MIKADO, *who glances at it and then passes it to* KATISHA.) This is very interesting, but we came about a totally different matter. A year ago, my son bolted from our Imperial Court and is now masquerading in this town, disguised as a Second Trombone. He goes by the name of Nanki-Poo.

KATISHA (*Reading certificate*): See here—his name—Nanki-Poo —beheaded this morning! (*Wailing*) Oh, where shall I find another? (KO-KO, POOH-BAH *and* PITTI-SING *prostrate themselves before* MIKADO.)

MIKADO (*Rising; to* KO-KO): My poor fellow, you have beheaded the heir to the throne of Japan! (*Turning to* KATISHA) I forget the punishment that fits the crime in this case. Something lingering, I think—with boiling oil. (*Groans from* KO-KO, POOH-BAH *and* PITTI-SING.) Or is it melted lead? (*Louder groans*) Come, come, don't fret—I'm not a bit angry. Now, about your punishment—will after luncheon suit you? Can you all wait until then?

KO-KO, POOH-BAH *and* PITTI-SING (*Miserably; together*): Oh, yes—we can wait.

MIKADO: Then we'll make it after luncheon. (*He exits with* KATISHA.)

POOH-BAH (*To* KO-KO, *as they all rise*): A nice mess you've got us into!

KO-KO: Well, there's only one thing to be done—Nanki-Poo must come to life again. (NANKI-POO *and* YUM-YUM *enter*.) Nanki-Poo, I have good news for you—you've been reprieved.

NANKI-POO: It's too late. I'm a dead man, and I'm off on my honeymoon with Yum-Yum.

KO-KO: Nonsense! It seems you're the son of the Mikado. Your father is here—with Katisha!—and he wants you particularly.

POOH-BAH: So does she.

NANKI-POO (*Putting arm around* YUM-YUM): I can't marry Katisha because I'm married already. She will insist on my execution, and if I'm executed, my wife will have to be buried alive. (*Clapping hand on* Ko-Ko's *shoulder*) There's only one chance for you, Ko-Ko. *You* must marry Katisha. Then she would have no claim on me.

Ko-Ko (*Staggering back in horror*): I marry Katisha? She's something appalling!

Nanki-Poo: It comes to this—while Katisha is single, I prefer to be a disembodied spirit. When Katisha is married, existence will be as welcome as the flowers in spring.

Ko-Ko (*Singing*):
>The flowers that bloom in the spring, tra la,
>Have nothing to do with the case.
>I've got to take under my wing, tra la,
>A most unattractive old thing, tra la,
>With a caricature of a face.
>And that's what I mean when I say, or I sing,
>"Oh, bother the flowers that bloom in the spring!"

All (*As they exit; singing*):
>Tra la la la la la, tra la la la la la,
>The flowers that bloom in the spring!
>(Katisha *enters, walking slowly, overcome with grief.*)

Katisha (*Sinking onto bench*): Ah, me! How can I live without Nanki-Poo? He is lost to me forever. (Ko-Ko *enters timidly. He falls on his knees before* Katisha.)

Ko-Ko: Katisha—mercy!

Katisha (*Rising; wrathfully*): See here, you! You have slain my love. Where shall I find another? It takes years to train a man to love me. Oh, where shall I find another?

Ko-Ko (*Leaping to his feet and spreading his arms*): Here! Here, darling!

Katisha: You dare to address such words to me?

Ko-Ko: I do! Accept my love, or I perish on the spot!

Katisha (*Scornfully*): Balderdash! Who knows better than I that no one has ever yet died of a broken heart?

Ko-Ko: Ah, but you are wrong. (*Walks to willow tree and sings with intense feeling*)

> On a tree by a river a little tom-tit
> Sang "Willow, titwillow, titwillow!"
> And I said to him, "Dicky-bird, why do you sit,
> Singing 'Willow, titwillow, titwillow'?"
> He sobbed and he sighed, and a gurgle he gave,
> Then he plunged himself into the billowy wave,
> And an echo arose from the suicide's grave—
> "Oh, willow, titwillow, titwillow!"

(*During this song* Katisha *has been deeply affected, and at the end is in tears.*)

Katisha (*Sobbing into her handkerchief*): Did he really die of love?

Ko-Ko: He really did. I knew the bird intimately.

Katisha: Poor little chap! And if I refuse you, will you go and do the same thing?

Ko-Ko: Immediately.

Katisha: No, no, you mustn't! I will marry you. (*Throws herself into his arms*)

Ko-Ko *and* Katisha (*Singing as they do a grotesque dance together*):

> If that is so,
> Sing derry down derry!
> It's evident, very,
> Our tastes are one!
> Away we'll go,

And merrily marry,
Nor tardily tarry
Till day is done!

(*They exit, dancing. Fanfare.* MIKADO *re-enters, attended by* PISH-TUSH, NOBLES, GUARDS, *and* SCHOOLGIRLS. MIKADO *sits in chair.*)

MIKADO (*To* PISH-TUSH): Now then, we've had a capital lunch, and we're quite ready. Produce the unfortunate gentleman and his two well-meaning accomplices. (KATISHA, KO-KO, POOH-BAH *and* PITTI-SING *enter and prostrate themselves before* MIKADO.)

KATISHA: Mercy! Mercy for Ko-Ko! Mercy for Pitti-Sing! Mercy even for Pooh-Bah! (*Rising*) My husband that was to be is dead and I am going to marry this miserable object. (*Indicates* KO-KO)

MIKADO: But he has slain the heir to the throne!

NANKI-POO (*Entering with* YUM-YUM): The heir is *not* slain!

MIKADO: Bless my heart, my son!

YUM-YUM (*Shyly*): And his daughter-in-law elected! (*Kneels*)

KATISHA (*Yanking* KO-KO *to his feet and shaking him*): Traitor! You have deceived me!

KO-KO: Your Majesty—Your Majesty—the death certificate makes everything all right!

KATISHA (*Releasing* KO-KO): What do you mean?

KO-KO: It's like this: When Your Majesty says, "Let a thing be done," it's as good as done—because Your Majesty's will is law. Your Majesty says, "Kill a gentleman," he is as good as dead—so why not a certificate saying he is dead?

MIKADO: I see. Nothing could possibly be more satisfactory!

PITTI-SING (*Singing*):
>   For he's gone and married Yum-Yum—

ALL (*Singing*):
>   Yum-Yum!

PITTI-SING (*Singing*):
>   Your anger pray bury,
>   For all will be merry,
>   I think you had better succumb—

ALL (*Singing*):
>   Cumb-cumb!

PITTI-SING (*Singing*):
>   And join our expressions of glee!

YUM-YUM *and* NANKI-POO (*Singing*):
>   The threatened cloud has passed away,
>   And brightly shines the dawning day;
>   What though the night may come too soon,
>   We've years and years of afternoon!

ALL (*Singing*):
>   Then let the throng our joy advance,
>   With laughing song and merry dance,
>   With joyous shout and ringing cheer,
>   Inaugurate our new career!

(*Curtain*)

THE END

Production Notes

THE MIKADO

Characters: 6 male; 4 female; as many male and female extras as desired for Schoolgirls, Nobles, and Guards.

Playing Time: 40 minutes.

Costumes: Female characters, colorful kimonos, ballet slippers; wigs or elaborate hairdos, decorated with combs and ornaments. All except Nanki-Poo, Go-To, and Guards carry fans (actors should practice snapping fans open and shut until action becomes second nature). Katisha should be overdressed and over-made-up. Ko-Ko, Pooh-Bah, Pish-Tush, and Nobles wear kimonos over wide trousers, ceremonial caps, and carpet slippers. Pooh-Bah carries large fan. Nanki-Poo wears short, ragged coat, harlequin trousers, coolie hat, and sandals. Mikado, formal court robes with wide sleeves, billowing full trousers, ceremonial cap, carpet slippers. Go-To, boy's kimono and sandals, hair in top-knot. Guards are dressed as Japanese warriors and carry spears.

Properties: Two scrolls, one very long; brush and ink; guitar; sheets of paper tied together with string, for ballads (Nanki-Poo); coins; sword in sheath; parasol; letter; long rope with noose; spears; banner with emblem of Rising Sun; certificate; handkerchief.

Setting: Scene 1, Courtyard of Ko-Ko's palace, in Titipu (Japan). There are low platforms on each side of stage, with taborets and cushions placed on them. Down left are a low table and cushion. Screens right and left are painted to suggest sliding panels. Main entrance is upstage center through pagoda arch beyond which part of garden is seen. Porcelain pottery and vases of flowers are set about stage. Scene 2, Ko-Ko's garden. There are trellises twined with flowers right and left stage. An ornamental garden armchair is on platform up center. Bench is down right. Willow tree is down left. In foreground is an arched bridge spanning a stream. Japanese lanterns are hung overhead about stage. Backdrop shows Japanese landscape, with Mt. Fuji in background. Note: Instead of backdrop, reverse side of screens used in Scene 1 may be substituted.

Lighting: No special effects.

Sound: Fanfare, as indicated in text.

Music for songs on following pages.

69

IF YOU WANT TO KNOW WHO WE ARE

Nobles

If you want to know who we are,_____ We are gentlemen of Ja-pan:_____ On many a vase and jar,_____ On many a screen and fan,_____ We figure in lively paint: Our at-ti-tude's queer and quaint. You're wrong if you think it ain't, Oh!_____ If you think we are worked by strings__ Like a Japanese mario-nette_____ You don't understand these things:__

70

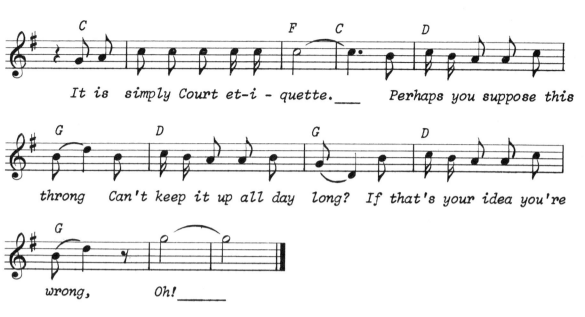

It is simply Court et-i - quette.___ Perhaps you suppose this throng Can't keep it up all day long? If that's your idea you're wrong, Oh!_____

A WANDERING MINSTREL I

Nanki-Poo

A wand'ring minstrel I   A thing of shreds___ and

patches,   Of ballads, songs and snatches, And   dreamy   lulla-

by!____   My   cat-a-logue is long   Thru ev'ry   pas - sion

ranging,   And   to your humors changing   I   tune   my   supple

song!____

73

Wafted by a fav'ring gale, As one sometimes is in
trances, To a height that few can scale, Save by long and
weary dances; Surely never had a male
Under such like circum - stances So ad-ven - turous a
tale, Which may rank with most ro - man - ces.

I'VE GOT A LITTLE LIST

Ko-Ko

There's the pesti-lential nuisances who write for auto-

graphs, All people who have flabby hands and irritating laughs, All

children who are up in dates and floor you with 'em flat, All persons who
in

shaking hands shake hands with you like that, That singular anomaly the

girl who's not been kissed, I don't think she'd be missed I'm sure she'd
not be

Nobles

missed! He's got her on his list, he's got her on his list, And I'm

sure she'll not be missed! Etc.

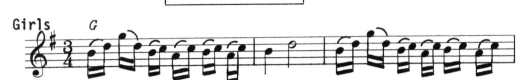

SCHOOLGIRLS WE

Schoolgirls we eighteen and under From scholastic trammels free And we wonder how we wonder, We wonder how we wonder what on earth the world can be.

THREE LITTLE MAIDS FROM SCHOOL ARE WE

Yum-Yum,
Peep-Bo, Pitti-Sing

Three little maids from school are we Pert as a

schoolgirl well can be, Filled to the brim with girlish glee___

Yum-Yum

Three little maids from school. Every - thing is a source of fun,

Peep-Bo   Pitti-Sing

Nobody's safe for we care for none!   *Life is a*

All

joke that's just be - gun!   *Three little maids from school!*

Three little maids who all unwary, Come from a ladies' sem-i-na-ry,

Freed from its genius tu-te - la - ry, Three little maids from school!

One little maid is a bride, Yum-Yum, Two little maids in attendance come

Three little maids is the total sum Three little maids from school.

From

three little maids take one a-way, Two little maids remain and they

Won't have to wait very long, they say, Three little maids from school!

Three little maids who all unwary, Come from a ladies' semina -ry,

Freed from its genius tu-te - la-ry, Three little maids from school!

Three little maids__ from school!

FOR HE'S GOING TO MARRY YUM-YUM

Pitti-Sing E — All Pitti-Sing

For ____ he's going to marry Yum-Yum! Your
Yum-Yum!

B — E

anger pray bury, For all will be merry, I think you had better
suc-

B All Pitti-Sing F#7 — B — E

cumb And join our expressions of glee. On this subject I
cumb cumb

All Pitti-Sing — B

pray you be dumb You'll find there are many Who'll wed for a
dumb dumb
penny. The

E — B All Pitti-Sing F#7 — B

word for your guidance is mum! There's lots of good fish in the sea!
mum mum!

HERE'S A HOW-DE-DO

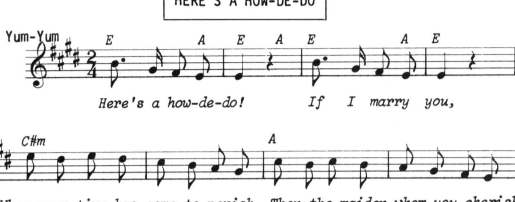

Yum-Yum

Here's a how-de-do! If I marry you,

When your time has come to perish, Then the maiden whom you cherish

Must be slaughtered too! Here's a how-do - do!

Nanki-Poo

Here's a pretty mess! In a month or less,

I must die with-out a wedding! Let the bitter tears I'm shedding

Witness my distress, Here's a pretty mess!

Ko-Ko

Here's a state of things! To her life she clings!

80

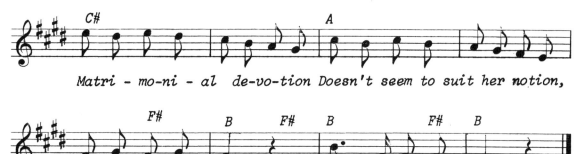

Matri - mo-ni - al de-vo-tion Doesn't seem to suit her notion,

Buri - al it brings! Here's a state of things!

FROM EVERY KIND OF MAN

Mikado C

From ev-'ry kind of man O - be-dience I___ ex-

Katisha

pect; I'm the Em-p'ror of Ja-pan, And I'm his daughter-in-law e-

Am Em   Am Em   Am Em   D7

lect! He'll marry his son He's only got one To his daughter-in-law e-

G   C   G7   C   G7

lect.___   Bow_____ Bow__ To his daughter-in-law e - lect.

Guards C   G7   C   G7   C Mikado

Bow___   Bow__ To his daughter-in-law   e - lect. In a

Katisha

fatherly kind of way I govern each tribe___ and sect,   All

Am Em   Am

except his daughter-in-law e - lect! As tough as a bone With a

82

will of her own Is his daughter-in-law e - lect.   Bow____

Bow___ To his daughter-in-law e - lect.   Bow_____

Bow___ To his daughter-in-law e - lect!

MY OBJECT ALL SUBLIME

Mikado

My object all sublime____   I shall achieve in

time,   To let the punishment fit the crime, The

punishment fit the crime!

THE FLOWERS THAT BLOOM IN THE SPRING

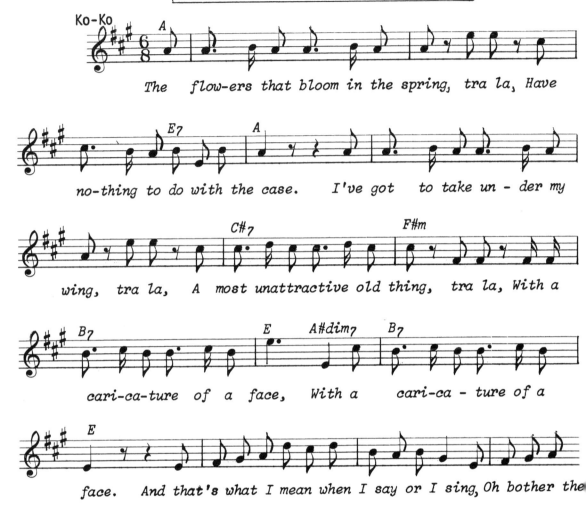

The flow-ers that bloom in the spring, tra la, Have

no-thing to do with the case. I've got to take un - der my

wing, tra la, A most unattractive old thing, tra la, With a

cari-ca-ture of a face, With a cari-ca - ture of a

face. And that's what I mean when I say or I sing, Oh bother the

flowers that bloom in the spring, Oh bother the flowers of spring!

ON A TREE BY A RIVER

Ko-Ko

On a tree by a riv-er a little tomtit Sang

Willow, titwillow, titwillow! And I said to him "Dicky-bird,

why do you sit Singing Willow, titwillow, titwillow?" He

sobbed and he sighed and a gurgle he gave Then he plunged himself into the

billow-y wave And an ech-o a-rose from the suicide's grave, "Oh,

willow, titwillow, tit-willow!"

IF THAT IS SO

Ko-Ko &
Katisha

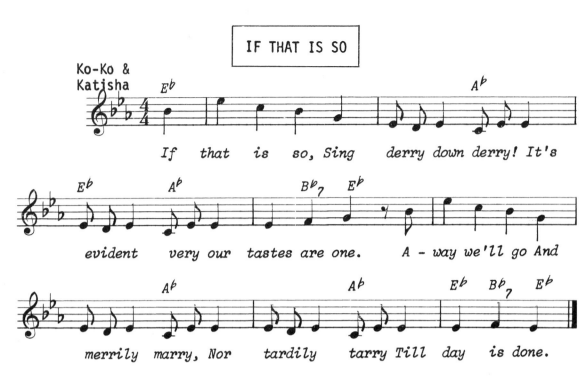

If that is so, Sing derry down derry! It's evident very our tastes are one. A - way we'll go And merrily marry, Nor tardily tarry Till day is done.

FOR HE'S GONE AND MARRIED YUM-YUM

For he's gone and married Yum-Yum Your anger pray
Yum-Yum
bury For all will be merry I think you had better succumb And
cumb cumb
join our expressions of glee. The threatend cloud has passed a-
way, And brightly shines the dawning day; What tho' the night may
come too soon, We've years and years of afternoon! Then let the
throng Our joy ad-vance With laughing song and merry dance, With
laughing song And merry dance With joyous shout and ringing

cheer, In - au - gu - rate in-au - gu - rate their new ca-

reer!

THE PIRATES OF PENZANCE

The story of

THE PIRATES OF PENZANCE

On the rocky coast of Cornwall, a band of pirates are celebrating the coming of age of Frederic, a young pirate who has joined the band through a mistake of his nurse, Ruth. Frederic's parents told her to apprentice him to a "pilot," but, being hard of hearing, she thought they had said "pirate." The Pirate King sings of the pleasures of piracy; then the pirates leave to make ready their ship for sailing. The daughters of Major-General Stanley enter and are about to go wading when Frederic appears. He tells the startled maidens that he's through with piracy, now that it is his twenty-first birthday, and that he intends to devote himself henceforth to fighting pirates. He pleads for their sympathy, and Mabel, one of the daughters, declares she will help him regain his position in the civilized world. General Stanley enters; he is "the very model of a modern Major-General." Suddenly the pirates surround the party and are about to capture them when the General sadly begs the pirates to spare him because he is "an orphan boy." Being kindhearted pirates, they won't attack orphans, so they spare the General and his daughters.

In the second act, Frederic is preparing to lead a squad of policemen on an expedition to arrest the pirates. Ruth and the Pirate King come to tell him that he was born on February 29 in a leap year and so, although he is twenty-one, he has had only *five* birthdays and is still indentured to the pirates. Now that he is a pirate again, Frederic's sense of duty obliges him to tell his companions that General Stanley is not an orphan and never was. Indignantly the pirates plan to attack him, but when the Police Sergeant orders them to yield in Queen Victoria's name, the pirates loyally obey. Ruth then informs everyone that the pirates are not pirates at all, but noblemen who have gone wrong. So the pirates and General Stanley's daughters embrace and Frederic marries Mabel.

THE PIRATES OF PENZANCE

Or, The Slave of Duty

Characters

THE PIRATE KING
SAMUEL, *his lieutenant*
FREDERIC, *the pirate apprentice*
RUTH, *pirate maid-of-all-work*
MAJOR-GENERAL STANLEY
MABEL
EDITH
KATE } *General's daughters*
ISABEL
POLLY
OTHER DAUGHTERS
SERGEANT OF POLICE
PIRATES
POLICE

SCENE 1

TIME: *Bright summer morning.*

SETTING: *A rocky seashore on the coast of Cornwall, England, near the town of Penzance. Rocks of various sizes are scattered about. A large wine cask is at right. Entrance to a cave is at left. A painted backdrop shows a ship, flying the skull-and-crossbones, riding at anchor in the bay.*

AT RISE: PIRATE KING *and* PIRATES *are sitting on rocks, laughing and drinking from golden goblets, while* RUTH, *the maid-of-all-work, goes among them refilling their goblets from a golden flagon.* FREDERIC *is sitting at left in a despondent attitude.*

91

PIRATES (*Singing lustily*) :
> Pour, oh pour the pirate sherry;
> Fill, oh fill the pirate glass;
> And, to make us more than merry,
> Let the pirate bumper pass.

PIRATE KING (*Coming to center and raising his goblet*) : Here's good luck to Frederic, our bold junior pirate, who is twenty-one years old today. At twelve o'clock his long apprenticeship will end and then he will be a full-fledged member of our band.

PIRATES (*Raising goblets to* FREDERIC) : Hurrah!

FREDERIC (*Rising*) : My friends, I thank you for all your kindly wishes. I'm sorry that I cannot repay them as they deserve.

KING: What do you mean?

FREDERIC: Today I must leave you forever. (PIRATES *exchange looks of surprise.*)

KING: Leave! How can you think of leaving when you have learned your trade so well? There never was a keener hand at scuttling a sailing ship!

FREDERIC: I've done my best for you. It was my duty—and I am a slave of duty. But my apprenticeship was a mistake.

KING: A mistake! What mistake?

FREDERIC: I cannot tell you. (*Turning to* RUTH) It would reflect upon my dear Ruth.

RUTH (*Coming forward*) : Master Frederic, you have shielded me long enough. (*To* KING) It was *my* mistake, sir. This is how it happened. (*Singing*)
> When Frederic was a little lad, he proved so brave and
> daring,

His father thought he'd 'prentice him to some career
    seafaring.
I was, alas, his nurserymaid, and so it fell to *my* lot
To take and bind the promising boy apprentice to a
    pi-lot;
Mistaking my instructions, which within my brain
    did gyrate,
I took and bound this promising boy apprentice to a
    pi-rate!

(*Contritely*) Oh, Frederic, forgive me! The words pilot and
pirate are so much alike.

FREDERIC (*Patting her shoulder reassuringly*): Yes, they *are*
alike, and I forgave you, dear Ruth, years ago. (*To* PIRATES)
But you see, my mates, although I like you, one by one, my
duty makes me determined to exterminate you as a band of
pirates.

KING: Well, my lad, if you feel it's your duty to destroy us, then
you must.

SAMUEL: Besides, we don't seem to make piracy pay. I'm sure I
don't know why.

FREDERIC: *I* know why, but I mustn't tell you. It wouldn't be right.

KING: Why not, my boy? (*Looks at his big gold watch on chain*)
It's only half-past eleven. You're one of my men until twelve.

SAMUEL: So until that time you are bound to protect our interests.

PIRATES (*Shouting*): Hear, hear!

FREDERIC: Very well. The reason you don't make any money is because you are too tenderhearted. For instance, you never attack a weaker party than yourselves, and when you attack a
stronger party, you are always beaten.

KING: Hm-m-m. That's true.

FREDERIC: And another thing—you make a point of never harming an orphan.

SAMUEL (*Offended*): Of course! We are orphans ourselves.

FREDERIC: Yes, but it has gotten about, and now everyone we capture says he's an orphan. The last three ships we took turned out to be manned entirely by orphans, and we had to let them go.

SAMUEL: Hang it all! You wouldn't want us to be absolutely merciless, would you?

FREDERIC: Until twelve o'clock I would—after twelve I wouldn't. Was ever a man placed in so delicate a situation?

RUTH (*Piteously*): And what about me, Master Frederic—faithful Ruth, your old nurse? What's to become of me?

KING: Oh, he'll take you with him. (*Delivers* RUTH *to* FREDERIC)

FREDERIC: Ruth, you're the only woman I've known in all my years as a pirate. I *think* yours must be a pretty face. Is it?

RUTH: It is, oh, it is!

KING (*Discreetly*): Er—Ruth has the *remains* of a handsome woman.

FREDERIC: In that case, I can't be so selfish as to take her from you. (*Returns* RUTH *to* KING)

KING: No, Frederic. We are rough men, but we are not so utterly heartless as to deprive you of your doting nanny. (*To* PIRATES) Am I right in saying that there is not one of us here who would rob Frederic of (*Indicating* RUTH) this priceless treasure?

PIRATES (*Loudly; together*): Not one!

KING: I thought there wasn't. So keep her, Frederic, keep her! (*Hands* RUTH *back to* FREDERIC)

FREDERIC: You are too kind—*you* keep her! (*Hands* RUTH *back to* KING)

KING: No, I insist—she's yours! (*Shoves* RUTH *at* FREDERIC)

FREDERIC: *I* insist! She's *yours!* (*They push* RUTH *back and forth between them*)

RUTH (*Breaking away*): *Stop!* I'm not an India-rubber ball to be bounced between the two of you! Let me alone! (*Flounces away and sits on a rock with her back to them*)

KING: Well, it's the top of the tide and we must be off. Farewell, Frederic.

FREDERIC (*Wistfully*): How nice it would be if I didn't have to exterminate you. Why don't you return to civilization with me?

KING: No, Frederic, I shall live and die a Pirate King (*Sings*)
> Oh, better far to live and die
> Under the brave black flag I fly,
> Than play a sanctimonious part,
> With a pirate head and a pirate heart.
> Away to the cheating world go you,
> Where pirates all are well-to-do;
> But I'll be true to the song I sing,
> And live and die a Pirate King.

(*Spoken*) For I am a Pirate King!

PIRATES (*Shouting*): You are! Hurrah for our Pirate King! (KING *and* PIRATES *exit left.* RUTH *goes to* FREDERIC.)

RUTH (*Pleadingly*): Oh, Frederic, take me with you! I cannot live if I am left behind.

FREDERIC: Ruth, I must be frank. You are very dear to me, as you know. But I am only twenty-one, and you are forty-seven. I should look for a wife of seventeen.

RUTH: A wife of seventeen! You will find me one wife in a thousand!

FREDERIC: Tell me honestly, Ruth, compared with other women— how are *you?*

RUTH: All right, thank you—except for a slight cold.

FREDERIC: I'm sorry about your cold, but I mean, are you beautiful?

RUTH (*Bashfully*): I have been told so.

FREDERIC: Lately?

RUTH: Oh, no, years and years ago. (*Quickly*) But I'm still a fine-looking woman.

FREDERIC: Well, Ruth, I want to do the right thing, and if—I say *if*—you are really a fine-looking woman, your age shall be no obstacle to our marriage. (*Voices of General's daughters are heard from off right, in the distance.*) Listen! What are those voices?

RUTH (*Aside to audience*): Confusion! They are the voices of young girls! If he sees them, I am lost.

FREDERIC (*Looking off right*): By all that's marvelous, a bevy of beautiful maidens! And Ruth told me *she* was beautiful! (*Turning to* RUTH, *angrily*) You told me you were fair as gold!

RUTH (*Wildly*): And, master, am I not so?

FREDERIC: And now I see you're plain and old.

RUTH: I'm sure I'm not a jot so!

FREDERIC: I trusted you, Ruth, and you have deceived me! Be gone! (RUTH *bursts into tears and runs off left. Voices of General's daughters are heard as if coming nearer.*) What shall I do? I dare not show myself before these gentle maidens dressed as a pirate. They would be scared out of their wits. (*Looks about*) I'll hide in this cave. (*Hurries into cave at left. General's daughters enter right.* KATE *holds an open parasol;* EDITH *has a butterfly net;* ISABEL *and* POLLY *carry a large picnic basket between them.* OTHER DAUGHTERS *carry daisy chains.*)

KATE: What a charming spot! I wonder where we are.

EDITH: And I wonder where Papa is. We have left him ever so far behind.

ISABEL: Oh, he'll catch up presently.

POLLY: Remember, Papa isn't as young as we are. (*They set down picnic basket.*)

EDITH: The sea is as smooth as glass. Suppose we take off our shoes and stockings and go wading.

DAUGHTERS (*Ad lib*): Yes, yes! The very thing! What fun! (*Etc. They start to take off shoes.* FREDERIC *steps out of cave.*)

FREDERIC: Stop, ladies, I pray!

DAUGHTERS (*Hopping about, and holding shoes in hands*): A man!

EDITH: Who are you, sir?

FREDERIC: I am a pirate.

DAUGHTERS (*Hopping away in terror*): A pirate! Horrors!

FREDERIC: Wait, ladies, please! I am renouncing my wild profession after dinner. I need your advice. (*They scream and retreat.*) Is there not one maiden here who will help me?

DAUGHTERS (*Emphatically*): No, not one!

FREDERIC (*In despair*): Not one?

MABEL (*Entering right*): Yes, there is one! *I* will help you.

KATE: It's Mabel!

MABEL: For shame, sisters! We must have a sense of duty. I'll take pity on him. (*Goes to* FREDERIC)

ISABEL (*Aside; to her other sisters*): The question is—if he hadn't been so good-looking, would her sense of duty have been so strong? (*They giggle and put on their shoes.*)

MABEL (*Singing to* FREDERIC):
Poor wandering one!
If such poor love as mine
Can help thee find
True peace of mind—
Why, take it, it is thine!
(MABEL *and* FREDERIC *sit at left, holding hands and gazing fondly at each other.* EDITH *beckons to others, who form a semicircle about her, at right.*)

EDITH: What should we do? Propriety says we ought to stay, but sympathy entreats us to leave them alone together.

KATE: Let's compromise. We'll turn our backs and talk about the weather. (*They turn away, occasionally stealing glances at* MABEL *and* FREDERIC, *who converse happily.*)

EDITH:
How beautifully blue the sky!

KATE:
The sun today seems very high.

ISABEL:
Continue fine I hope it may.

POLLY:
And yet it rained but yesterday.

KATE:
Tomorrow it may pour again.

POLLY:
I hear the country needs some rain.

ISABEL:
But people say, I don't know why,
That we shall have a warm July.

FREDERIC (*Suddenly jumping to his feet*): Young ladies, you must leave this place at once, for I hear the sounds of the pirate band returning! (*They squeal and scramble about, picking up their things.*)

POLLY (*Indignantly*): Pirates—nice companions for young ladies!

ISABEL: Let's go! (*They start to exit right, just as* PIRATES *rush in left and seize them. In the confusion,* FREDERIC *and* MABEL *hide in cave.*)

PIRATE KING (*Holding* EDITH): What a lovely bundle of wives we have found! (MAJOR-GENERAL STANLEY *enters unnoticed and stands watching.*)

PIRATES (*Chanting together*):
Here's a first-rate opportunity
To get married with impunity
By a doctor of divinity
Who resides in this vicinity.

MABEL (*Coming out of cave followed by* FREDERIC): Hold, monsters! Before you proceed to marry us against our will, bear in mind that our father is a Major-General.

SAMUEL (*Cowed*): Oh—their father is a Major-General. (PIRATES *release girls, who scurry away.* MAJOR-GENERAL STANLEY *steps forward.*)

MAJOR-GENERAL (*In a booming voice*): Yes, I am a Major-General. (*Sings*)
  I am the very model of a modern Major-General,
  I've information vegetable, animal and mineral;
  I know the kings of England, and I quote the fights
   historical,
  From Marathon to Waterloo, in order categorical.
  I'm very good at integral and differential calculus,
  I know the scientific names of beings animalculous;
  In short, in matters vegetable, animal and mineral,
  I am the very model of a modern Major-General.

ALL: Hurrah for the Major-General!

MAJOR-GENERAL: Now that I've introduced myself, I should like to know what is going on here.

SAMUEL: Permit me, sir, to explain in two words: we propose to marry your daughters.

MAJOR-GENERAL: That's six words. But, dear me, I'm not familiar with your picturesque uniforms. Who are you?

KING: We are all single gentlemen, sir.

EDITH: Don't believe him, Papa! They're the Pirates of Penzance!

MAJOR-GENERAL: My, my, I've heard of them.

MABEL: All except Frederic here, who was a pirate, but now leads a blameless life.

MAJOR-GENERAL (*Clicking his tongue in disapproval*): Tsk, tsk! I object to pirates as sons-in-law.

KING: We object to Major-Generals as fathers-in-law—but we're willing to overlook it.

MAJOR-GENERAL (*Aside*): Hah! An idea! (*To* PIRATES, *pathetically*) Do you really mean to rob me of my daughters, my only comfort in my old age? Have you ever known what it is to be—an *orphan?*

KING (*Disgusted*): Oh, dash it all! Here we go again!

MAJOR-GENERAL: Have pity on my lonely state—I am an orphan boy.

PIRATES (*Together*): He is an orphan boy—how sad! (*They sigh heavily*)

MAJOR-GENERAL: These children are all that I have. If you take them away from me, I shall be absolutely and *destitutely* alone.

PIRATES (*Sobbing*): *Poor* fellow, *poor* fellow!

KING: As you can see, sir, we are not altogether without feeling. You and your daughters are free to go. (*Girls squeal with pleasure.*) And to honor our new-found friendship, you are elected an honorary member of our band.

SAMUEL (*Cheering*): For he is an orphan boy!

PIRATES: He *is!* Hurrah for the orphan boy! (KING *holds up a black flag with skull-and-crossbones.* MAJOR-GENERAL *holds up a Union Jack. They exchange flags amid the cheers and applause of* PIRATES *and girls. Curtain.*)

* * * * *

SCENE 2

TIME: *Midnight.*

SETTING: *A ruined chapel on the estate of* MAJOR-GENERAL STAN-
LEY. *Moonlight shines on Gothic arches up center and at left.
Between arches there are niches with crumbling statues of
medieval lords and ladies in reverent attitudes, and stained-
glass windows at right. Under windows there is a tomb with
a carved reclining figure in armor, holding a shield. There is
a stone bench center. Columns are downstage right and left.*

AT RISE: MAJOR-GENERAL *is sitting on bench, weeping into a
large handkerchief.* MABEL *and* FREDERIC *enter down left.*

MABEL: See how he weeps! Oh, Frederic, can't you say something
that will relieve Papa of his sorrow?

FREDERIC: I'll try. What is his sorrow? Have you any idea?

MABEL: None whatever. (*They go to* MAJOR-GENERAL.)

FREDERIC: Come, sir, you shouldn't sit here in this drafty old ruin.
You'll catch your death of cold.

MABEL: It's almost midnight, Papa. You should be in bed. We're
all so worried. Why do you come here, night after night?

MAJOR-GENERAL (*Abjectly*): I come to atone for having told a
terrible lie.

MABEL: What lie, Papa?

MAJOR-GENERAL: To rescue my daughters from the pirates'
clutches, I told them I was an orphan, and, heaven help me,
I am no orphan. So I come here to humble myself before the
tombs of my ancestors, and to implore their pardon for having brought them dishonor.

FREDERIC: But, sir (*Indicating statues*)—these are not your ancestors. You only bought the property a year ago.

MAJOR-GENERAL (*Rising*): They *are* my ancestors! When I bought the property, I bought the ancestors, too, and I shudder to think that their descendant by purchase should have brought disgrace upon them by telling a lie.

FREDERIC: You have done nothing dishonorable, sir. Your lie saved your daughters from marrying the pirates. I have an expedition marching against the scoundrels at midnight. They shall be swept from the face of the earth—(*Taking* MABEL'S *hand*)—and then, dear Mabel, you will be mine!

MAJOR-GENERAL: What is this expedition?

FREDERIC: I have called on the local police for help. (*Sound of marching feet is heard from off right.*) Ah, here they come now! (POLICE *enter through arch up center, high-stepping in single file, led by* SERGEANT. *They form a line and sing.*)

SERGEANT (*Singing*):
When the foeman bares his steel,

POLICE (*Singing, using their clubs as trumpets*):
Tarantara! Tarantara!

SERGEANT (*Singing*):
We uncomfortable feel,

POLICE (*Singing*):
Tarantara!

SERGEANT (*Singing*):
And we find the wisest thing,

POLICE (*Singing*):
Tarantara! Tarantara!

SERGEANT (*Singing*):
Is to slap our chests and sing—

SERGEANT *and* POLICE (*Singing*):
   Tarantara!

SERGEANT (*Singing*):
   When the adversary shoots,

POLICE (*Singing*):
   Tarantara! Tarantara!

SERGEANT (*Singing*):
   And your heart is in your boots,

POLICE (*Singing*):
   Tarantara!

SERGEANT (*Singing*):
   There is nothing brings it round
   Like the trumpet's martial sound,

SERGEANT *and* POLICE (*Singing*):
   Tarantara! Tarantara!
   Tarantara, ra-ra-ra-ra!

MABEL: Go, ye heroes, go to glory!

SERGEANT *and* POLICE (*Without moving*): Yes, yes, we go!

MAJOR-GENERAL: Why do you stay? Why this delay?

SERGEANT *and* POLICE (*Still without moving*): All right, we go!

MAJOR-GENERAL (*Exasperated*): But you *don't* go!

SERGEANT *and* POLICE: We go, we go! Forward on the foe! Tarantara! (*They exit up stage and left, running like Keystone cops.*)

FREDERIC (*Laughing*): At last they really go—and so must I, to lead them to the pirates' den. (*Embracing* MABEL) Good night, my love. Tomorrow we will be married. (MABEL *and*

MAJOR-GENERAL *exit left.* FREDERIC *faces audience and draws his cutlass.*) Now to do my duty—to exterminate the scourge of the seas—the Pirates of Penzance! (PIRATE KING *and* RUTH *enter upstage, armed with pistols.*)

KING: Young Frederic!

FREDERIC (*Looking about*): Who calls?

KING: Your late commander.

RUTH: And I, your little Ruth! (*They advance on* FREDERIC, *covering him with their pistols.*)

FREDERIC (*Shaking his cutlass at them*): How dare you face me? You know I've sworn to exterminate you! (KING *and* RUTH *hold their pistols to his ears.*)

KING: Listen to what we have to say before slaughtering us.

FREDERIC: I shouldn't listen, but I'll be merciful. What is it? (*They put away their weapons.*)

RUTH: After you left, we tried to raise our spirits with riddles, quibbles and quips, but it was no use, until someone thought of a paradox—a most ingenious paradox! We knew you'd enjoy it, so we've come to tell it to you.

FREDERIC: Go ahead—I'm interested.

KING: Well, it concerns the month of February. Usually February has twenty-eight days, but every fourth year it has twenty-nine. You, Frederic, were born in a leap year on the twenty-ninth of February.

FREDERIC: So?

KING: So—though you have lived twenty-one years, if we go by birthdays, you're only five years old.

FREDERIC: That *is* a paradox! Who would think to look at me that I'm a little boy of five? (*They laugh.*)

RUTH: Now you can't exterminate us. You're still a pirate.

FREDERIC: What? I was apprenticed only until I reached my twenty-first year.

KING: No—until you reached your twenty-first *birthday*. And, going by birthdays, you are only five and a little over.

FREDERIC: Do you intend to hold me to that?

KING: We just leave it to your strong sense of duty.

FREDERIC (*Sighing*): Alas, my duty is only too clear—I must resume my piratical career. (*Suddenly exclaims*) Oh, good grief!

KING: What's the matter?

FREDERIC (*Pacing about*): Ought I to tell you? No, I can't. But as a pirate, it is my duty. Well, then, I must. General Stanley, father of my beloved Mabel. . . . (*Pauses, overcome with remorse*)

KING *and* RUTH: Yes, yes, go on!

FREDERIC: He escaped from you by saying he was an orphan. It breaks my heart, but I must tell you he is no orphan—and he never was one!

KING (*Furious*): The blackguard! He tricked us out of our brides! We were merciful because of a monstrous lie! We will attack his castle tonight and the traitor will die! (KING *and* RUTH *dash out up right, brandishing pistols.* FREDERIC *sits on bench dejectedly*)

MABEL (*Entering down left*): Frederic, why are you still here? The police are ready for your orders. Surely you haven't lost courage.

FREDERIC (*Rising and taking her hands*) : No, Mabel, it's not that. I've just learned that I was born in a leap year and so I won't reach my twenty-first birthday for another sixty-four years. I am still bound to the pirates! (*She stares at him in surprise*) Farewell, Mabel. I'll return for you in sixty-four years. Wait for me! (*Kisses her hand and exits quickly upstage.*)

MABEL (*Calling after him*) : I'll wait for you, Frederic, I swear it! (*Faces audience*) It will be a long wait. In sixty-four years I'll be (*Adding up on fingers*)—eighty-one! (*Shrugs*) Oh, well! (*Turns to call off left.*) Sergeant! Come here! (SERGEANT *enters and salutes.*) There's been a change in plans. Frederic cannot lead you against the pirates. He has become one of them again.

SERGEANT: Shame!

MABEL (*Loftily*) : You know nothing about it. He has done his duty. Now go and do yours. (*She exits down left.* SERGEANT *blows police whistle and* POLICE *march in with exaggerated high steps.*)

SERGEANT: My men, I have bad news for you. Frederic has rejoined his old comrades and left us to capture the pirates alone. (*Sings*)
When a felon's not engaged in his employment,

POLICE (*Singing*) :
His employment,

SERGEANT (*Singing*) :
Or maturing his felonious little plans,

POLICE (*Singing*) :
Little plans,

SERGEANT (*Singing*) :
His capacity for innocent enjoyment,

POLICE (*Singing*):
'Cent enjoyment,

SERGEANT (*Singing*):
Is just as great as any honest man's.

POLICE (*Singing*):
Honest man's.

SERGEANT (*Singing*):
Our feelings we with difficulty smother,

POLICE (*Singing*):
'Culty smother,

SERGEANT (*Singing*):
When constabulary duty's to be done,

POLICE (*Singing*):
To be done,

SERGEANT (*Singing*):
Ah, take one consideration with another,

POLICE (*Singing*):
With another,

SERGEANT (*Singing*):
A policeman's lot is not a happy one.

SERGEANT *and* POLICE (*Singing*):
Ah! When constabulary duty's to be done, to be done,
A policeman's lot is not a happy one, happy one.
(PIRATES *are heard off right.* POLICE *listen, trembling in fear.*)

PIRATES (*Offstage, singing*):
A rollicking band of pirates we,
Who, tired of tossing on the sea,

Are trying their hand at burglaree,
With weapons grim and gory.

SERGEANT: The pirates are coming! We must hide! (POLICE *try to conceal themselves at left in niches and behind columns. FREDERIC, SAMUEL, KING, RUTH and PIRATES enter cautiously upstage and tiptoe downstage.*)

PIRATES (*Speaking very loudly*):
So stealthily the pirate creeps
While all the household soundly sleeps.

FREDERIC (*Gesturing frantically*): *Sh-h-h-h-h!*

POLICE (*Softly*): Tarantara! Tarantara!

FREDERIC (*Looking off down left*): I see a light inside! The Major-General comes—hide! (PIRATES, KING, RUTH, SAMUEL *and* FREDERIC *conceal themselves at right behind tomb and columns.* MAJOR-GENERAL *enters in dressing gown and stocking cap, carrying a lighted candle.*)

MAJOR-GENERAL: I thought I heard a noise.

PIRATES *and* POLICE (*Whispering*): He thought he heard a noise. Ha, ha!

MAJOR-GENERAL (*Looking out arches at back*): No, all is quiet. (MABEL, EDITH, KATE, ISABEL, POLLY, *and* OTHER DAUGHTERS *enter down left, wearing white nightgowns and frilly nightcaps.*)

EDITH: What is Papa doing here at this time of night?

KATE: He always goes to bed at half-past ten. (KING, FREDERIC *and* SAMUEL *come out of hiding.*)

KING: Seize the General! (FREDERIC *and* SAMUEL *do so. Girls shriek and scatter.*)

MAJOR-GENERAL: Save me, Frederic! Call your policemen!

FREDERIC: I would if I could, sir, but I can't.

KING: That's right, he can't—so prepare to die, false General Stanley! (*Draws sword*)

MABEL (*Running to* FREDERIC): Oh, spare him, Frederic, for my sake! (POLICE *jump out of their hiding places at the same time as* PIRATES. *They struggle together.* KING *and* SERGEANT *scuffle. Girls watch, squealing at fight. Finally,* PIRATES *force* POLICE *to ground and stand over them.* KING *pins* SERGEANT *to floor with his sword.*)

SERGEANT: You have won for now, but it won't last long.

KING: Don't say you are orphans. We know that game.

SERGEANT: We have a stronger claim. (*Drawing small Union Jack from his pocket*) We charge you to yield in Queen Victoria's name!

KING (*Baffled*): You do?

POLICE: We do! (*They also hold up flags.* POLICE *get to their feet and* PIRATES *kneel.*)

KING: We yield at once, because, with all our faults, we love our Queen!

MAJOR-GENERAL: Away with them and lock them up in jail! (RUTH, *who has been lurking in the background, now comes forward.*)

RUTH: One moment! (*All turn to her.*) These pirates are not common thieves. They are all noblemen, British peers who have gone wrong!

DAUGHTERS (*With delight*): British peers!

MAJOR-GENERAL: Well, with all our faults, we love our House of
Peers, so (*Reciting*)—

> I pray you pardon me, ex-Pirate King,
> Peers will be peers, and youth will have its fling.
> Resume your ranks and legislative duties,
> And take my daughters, all of whom are beauties.

(*Each* PIRATE *takes a* DAUGHTER *as partner, and they begin
a lively dance, to music from offstage.* FREDERIC *dances with*
MABEL, *and* MAJOR-GENERAL *with* RUTH. POLICE *and* SER-
GEANT *stand in semicircle upstage, using their clubs as trumpets.*)

POLICE *and* SERGEANT (*Shouting in time to music*) : Tarantara!
Tarantara! Tarantara-a-a! (*Curtain*)

THE END

Characters: 5 male; 6 female; 4 or more Police; 4 or more Pirates; 4 or more Other Daughters.

Playing Time: 30 minutes.

Costumes: General's daughters wear summer dresses and hats in late 1870s style; in Scene 2 they re-enter wearing nightgowns and frilly nightcaps. Major-General wears full dress uniform: red tunic, trimmed with gold braid; navy blue trousers; cocked hat with drooping feathers in the crown; white gloves. He has a Union Jack flag concealed inside his uniform. Frederic, Pirate King, Samuel and Pirates are dressed in traditional pirate costumes and head-gear, and have shoes with buckles. The Pirate King wears a sword, and has a black flag with skull-and-crossbones on it concealed in a pocket. Frederic wears a cutlass in Scene 2. Ruth wears a blouse with laced bodice, full skirt with panniers, and dust cap. Sergeant and Police wear English "Bobby" uniforms, helmets with chin straps, and have Union Jack flags concealed inside their uniforms.

Properties: Wine cask; golden goblets and flagon; swords and pistols (Pirates); gold watch and chain; small pirate flag; parasol; butterfly net; large picnic basket; daisy chains; military medals and decorations; sword; small British flag, rolled up and stuck in belt; handkerchief; candle in candlestick (General Stanley). Cutlass (Frederic). Police whistle (Sergeant). Billyclubs; miniature British flags (Sergeant and Police).

Setting: Scene 1, rocky seashore, with cave at left; Scene 2, ruined chapel on the Stanley estate.

Lighting: Moonlight, Scene 2, as indicated in text of play.

Music for songs on following pages.

POUR, O POUR THE PIRATE SHERRY

Pirates

Pour, O pour the pirate sherry; Fill, O fill the pirate

glass; And, to make us more than merry, Let the pirate bumper

pass!

113

WHEN FREDERIC WAS A LITTLE LAD

Ruth

1. When Fred'ric was a___ little lad he__ proved so
brave and daring, His father thought he'd 'prentice him to
some career sea - faring. I__ was a - las his nurs-'ry
2. Mis-tak-ing my in - structions,

maid and so it fell to my lot To take and bind the
which with - in my brain did gyrate, I took and bound this

promising boy ap - prentice to a pi-lot.
promising boy ap - prentice to a pi-rate.

OH, BETTER FAR TO LIVE AND DIE

Oh, better far to live and die Under the brave black

flag I fly Than play a sancti - monious part with a pirate head and a

pirate heart. A-way to the cheating world go you Where pirates all are

well to do; But I'll be true to the song I sing And live and die a

Pi-rate King!

POOR WANDERING ONE!

Mabel

Poor wan-d'ring one!____ If such poor love as mine____ Can help thee find True peace of mind-- Why, take__ it, it___ is thine!_____

116

I AM THE VERY MODEL OF A MODERN MAJOR-GENERAL

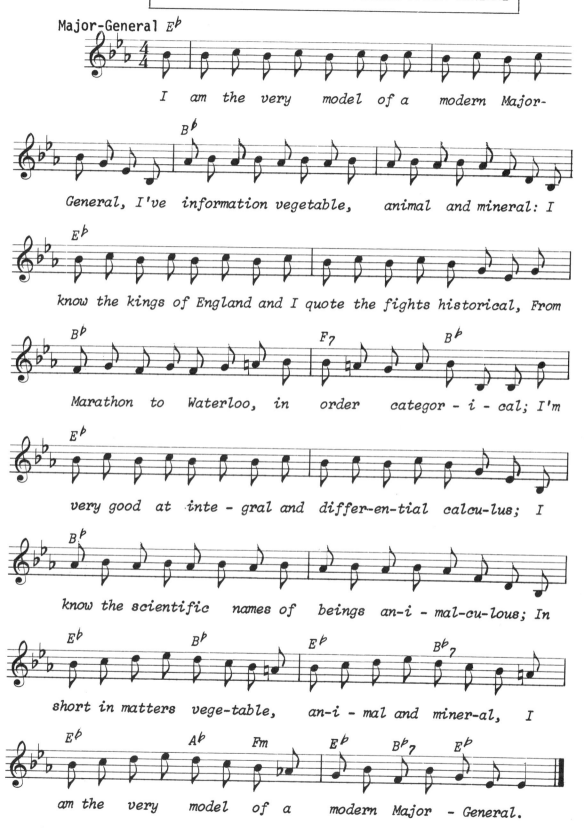

WHEN THE FOEMAN BARES HIS STEEL

Sergeant C

Police

When the foe-man bares his steel

Taran-ta - ra, taran-ta-

Sgt.

Pol.

Sgt.

We un-com-fort-a - ble feel

And we

ra!

Taran - ta - ra!

Pol.

Sgt.

find the wisest thing

Is to

Taran - ta - ra, taran - ta -ra!

slap our chests and sing Taranta - ra!

When the ad-ver-sar-y

Pol.

Sgt.

F

shoots

And your heart is in your

Taran-ta - ra, taran - ta-ra!

Pol.

C

Sgt.

G7

C

boots,

There is nothing brings it round Like the

Taran-ta - ra!

G7

C

G

D7

G All

G7

trumpet's martial sound Like the trumpet's martial sound, Taranta-

Am7

G7

C

ra, ta-ran-ta - ra!

WHEN A FELON'S NOT ENGAGED IN HIS EMPLOYMENT

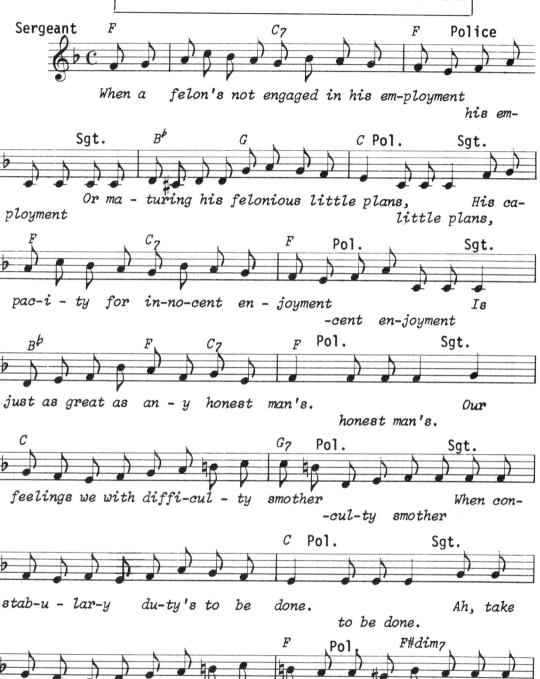

Sergeant | F | C7 | F | Police

When a felon's not engaged in his em-ployment
his em-

Sgt. | B♭ | G | C Pol. | Sgt.

Or ma - turing his felonious little plans,
ployment
little plans,

F | C7 | F | Pol. | Sgt.

pac-i - ty for in-no-cent en - joyment
-cent en-joyment
Is

B♭ | F | C7 | F | Pol. | Sgt.

just as great as an - y honest man's.
honest man's.
Our

C | G7 | Pol. | Sgt.

feelings we with diffi-cul - ty smother
-cul-ty smother
When con-

C | Pol. | Sgt.

stab-u - lar-y du-ty's to be done.
to be done.
Ah, take

F | Pol. | F#dim7

one consid-er - a -tion with an - oth-er,
with an-oth-er,
A po-

119

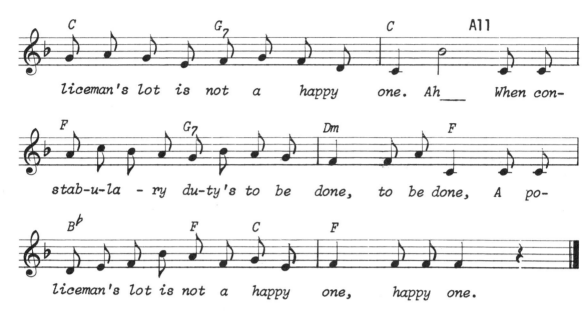

liceman's lot is not a happy one. Ah___ When con-

stab-u-la - ry du-ty's to be done, to be done, A po-

liceman's lot is not a happy one, happy one.

A ROLLICKING BAND OF PIRATES WE

Pirates (a cappella)

A rollicking band of pirates we, Who, tired of tossing

on the sea, Are trying their hand at a burglaree, With weap - ons

grim and gor - y.

TRIAL BY JURY

The story of

TRIAL BY JURY

In a London Court of Justice, Edwin is being sued by Angelina for breach of promise; he promised to marry her, and now no longer wishes to. The usher instructs the jury to rid itself of all prejudice in the case, but when Edwin enters and attempts to explain why he does not wish to marry Angelina, the jurymen have no sympathy for him, and shake their fists at him.

The judge, a self-made man and proud of it, is enraptured when beautiful Angelina comes in with her bridesmaids. He sends her a romantic note through the usher which she reads and then kisses as she waves ecstatically to the judge. While Angelina's counsel pleads on her behalf, she falls sobbing into the arms of the foreman of the jury. This pathetic scene so moves the jurymen that they heap imprecations on Edwin and call for substantial damages. All is confusion, until the judge can stand it no more and settles the matter by deciding to marry Angelina himself.

TRIAL BY JURY

A Dramatic Cantata

Characters

THE LEARNED JUDGE
ANGELINA, *the plaintiff*
EDWIN, *the defendant*
COURT USHER
COUNSEL FOR THE PLAINTIFF
ATTORNEYS
FOREMAN OF THE JURY
FIRST BRIDESMAID
OTHER BRIDESMAIDS, *4*
JURYMEN, *11*
PUBLIC
OFFSTAGE VOICE

TIME: *Late nineteenth century.*

SETTING: *Courtroom in Hall of Justice, London. Judge's bench is on a raised platform up center. In front of platform is a long table with pitcher and glass of water, and chairs behind it for Counsel and Attorneys. Plaintiff's chair is right of table. Left of table is witness stand. Jury box is stage right against wall. At left there is a double row of seats for Public. Exits are down left, leading outside; down right, leading to jury room; and up right, leading to Judge's chambers.*

AT RISE: PUBLIC *enters down left;* COURT USHER *directs them to back row of seats at left. When* PUBLIC *is seated,* JURYMEN *file in down right and take places in jury box.* COUNSEL FOR PLAINTIFF *and* ATTORNEYS *enter up right, carrying law books, and sit at table. Sound of clock striking ten is heard from offstage.*

123

CHORUS OF JURYMEN, COUNSEL, ATTORNEYS *and* PUBLIC (*Reciting together*):

> Hark, the hour of ten is sounding:
> Hearts with anxious fears are bounding,
> Hall of Justice crowds surrounding,
> Breathing hope and fear—
> For today in this arena,
> Summoned by a stern subpoena,
> Edwin, sued by Angelina,
> Shortly will appear.

(USHER *crosses to stand before* JURYMEN, *and motions for them to sit, which they do, sitting down exactly together.*)

USHER (*Singing*):

> Now, Jurymen, hear my advice—
> All kinds of vulgar prejudice
> I pray you set aside:
> With stern judicial frame of mind
> From bias free of every kind,
> This trial must be tried.

JURYMEN (*Nodding vigorously and singing*):

> From bias free of every kind,
> This trial must be tried!

USHER (*Speaking*): Precisely! You are not to be prejudiced in any way. You have only to look at the face of the broken-hearted plaintiff to sympathize with her distress. As for the defendant, what *he* may say, you needn't mind. (*Sings*)

> From bias free of every kind,
> This trial must be tried!

(PUBLIC *applauds enthusiastically.* USHER *pounds staff on floor.*) Silence in court! (*Goes to stand up left on platform beside* JUDGE'S *bench.* EDWIN *enters down left, carrying cane.*)

EDWIN: Is this the courtroom?

ALL (*Together*): It is! Who are you?

EDWIN: I am the defendant!

JURYMEN (*Rising, shaking their fists; together*): Monster! Beware our fury! We are the jury!

EDWIN (*Crossing to center*): Hear me, hear me, if you please! Would you condemn me without a hearing? These are very strange proceedings, I must say! (*Recites*)
>   For—permit me to remark—
>   On the merits of my pleadings
>   You're at present in the dark.
(EDWIN *beckons to* JURYMEN. *They leave box and gather around him.*)

JURYMEN (*Reciting together*):
>   That's a very true remark—
>   On the merits of his pleadings
>   We're completely in the dark!
(*To* EDWIN) Enlighten us!

EDWIN (*Singing*):
>   When first my old, old love I knew,
>   My bosom welled with joy;
>   My riches at her feet I threw—
>   I was a love-sick boy!
>   No terms seemed too extravagant
>   Upon her to employ—
>   I used to mope, and sigh, and pant,
>   Just like a love-sick boy!
(*Pantomimes playing banjo with his cane, as he sings.*)
>   Tink-a-tank, tink-a-tank, tink-a-tank,
>   Tink-a-tank, tink-a-tank, tink-a-tank!
>   I used to mope, and sigh, and pant,
>   Just like a love-sick boy!
(*Speaking to* JURYMEN) But alas! Soon the joy turned to boredom—the flame of love burned out—and so I became the love-sick boy of someone else.

JURYMEN (*Clucking tongues disapprovingly*): Tsk, tsk, tsk! He became the love-sick boy of someone else!

FOREMAN OF JURY (*Reciting*):
Oh, I was like that when a lad!
A shocking young scamp of a rover,
I behaved like a regular cad!

JURYMEN (*To each other*): So did I! So did I! So did I!

FOREMAN: But that sort of thing is all over. I am now a respectable chap.

JURYMEN (*Together*): So am I!

FOREMAN *and* JURYMEN (*Together*): And, therefore, I haven't a scrap of sympathy for the defendant! (*They return to jury box.*)

USHER (*Pounding staff on floor*): Defendant, take the witness stand! (EDWIN *steps onto witness stand.*) All rise! (*All stand.*) His honor, the Judge! (JUDGE *enters up right, carrying gavel and papers, and crosses to bench.*)

ALL (*Together, extending arms toward* JUDGE): All hail, great Judge! All hail! (*All sit.*)

JUDGE (*Bowing elaborately*): Thank you, thank you, good people and associates. We have a Breach of Promise suit to try today. But before I hear the case, I wish to tell you how I came to be a Judge.

ALL (*Together, nodding to each other*): He'll tell us how he came to be a Judge!

JUDGE: I'll tell you how—

ALL (*Together*): He'll tell us how—

JUDGE: Let me speak!

ALL: Let him speak!

JUDGE (*Bellowing*): Let me speak!

ALL (*Together in hushed voices*): Let him speak! He'll tell us how he came to be a judge. (JUDGE *crosses to center stage.*)

JUDGE (*Singing*):
> When I, good friends, was called to the bar,
> I'd an appetite fresh and hearty,
> But I was, as many young barristers are,
> An impecunious party.
> I soon got tired of third-class journeys,
> And dinners of bread and water;
> So I fell in love with a rich attorney's
> Elderly, ugly daughter.

ALL (*Singing together*):
> So he fell in love with a rich attorney's
> Elderly, ugly daughter.

JUDGE (*Singing*):
> The rich attorney, he jumped with joy,
> And replied to my fond professions:
> "You shall reap the reward of your pluck, my boy,
> At the Bailey and Middlesex Sessions.
> You'll soon get used to her looks," said he,
> "And a very nice girl you'll find her!
> She may very well pass for forty-three
> In the dusk, with a light behind her!"

ALL (*Singing, together*):
> She may very well pass for forty-three
> In the dusk, with a light behind her!

JUDGE (*Speaking*): Well, to make a long story short, the rich attorney was as good as his word, and cases came to me thick and fast. (*Muses*) Ah, yes! I restored many a burglar to his friends and relations—*if* he could afford my fee. At last I became as rich as the rich attorney himself and I threw over his elderly, ugly daughter. (*Laughs. All murmur approval as* JUDGE *returns to sit on bench.*) And now, if you please, I'm ready to try this Breach of Promise of Marriage. (*Proudly*) For I am a Judge!

ALL (*Together*): And a good Judge, too!

JUDGE: Yes, I am a Judge!

ALL (*Together*): And a good Judge, too!

JUDGE (*Reciting*):
>Though all my law is fudge,
>Yet I'll never, never budge,
>But I'll live and die a Judge!

ALL (*Together*): And a good Judge, too! (JUDGE *pounds gavel.*)

JUDGE: Court is in session! (COUNSEL *rises.*)

COUNSEL (*To* USHER): Swear in the jury!

USHER (*Coming forward to center*): Kneel, Jurymen, kneel! (JURYMEN *kneel in jury box.* USHER *raises right hand.*)
>Oh, will you swear by yonder skies,
>Whatever question may arise,
>'Twixt rich and poor, 'twixt low and high,
>That you will well and truly try?

JURYMEN (*Together, raising their hands high*):
>To all of this we make reply
>That we will well and truly try.

(JURYMEN *rise and seat themselves again, except one who remains standing.*)

USHER (*In a hoarse, loud whisper*): *Sit down!* (JURYMAN *sits, embarrassed.*)

COUNSEL (*To* USHER): Where is the plaintiff? Let her be brought in.

USHER (*Cupping hand to mouth, calling offstage*): An-gel-*eee*-na!

VOICE (*From offstage echoing*): An-gel-*eee*-na!

USHER (*Calling to left side of stage, but speaking last syllable in deep voice*): An-gel-eee-*na*! (*Cups hand to ear and listens for answer.*)

VOICE (*From offstage*): An-gel-eee . . . (VOICE *is unable to get down to bass note.*)

USHER (*Smiling slyly; in deep voice*): . . . *na*! (USHER *crosses to stand next to* JUDGE'S *bench.* BRIDESMAIDS *enter down left and file into front row of public seats. Each carries a long garland of roses.*)

BRIDESMAIDS (*Singing, together*):
>Comes the broken flower—
>Comes the cheated maid—
>Though the tempest lower,
>Rain and cloud will fade.
>Take, oh maid, these posies:
>Though thy beauty rare
>Shame the blushing roses,
>They are passing fair!
>Wear the flowers till they fade;
>Happy be thy life, oh maid!

(*While* BRIDESMAIDS *are singing,* JUDGE *catches* 1ST BRIDESMAID'S *eye, waves to her, then quickly writes note which he gives to* USHER, *who gives it to* 1ST BRIDESMAID. *She reads it, waves ecstatically to* JUDGE, *kisses note and tucks it into neckline of dress.* ANGELINA *enters in bridal gown, and crosses to center.* JUDGE *looks at her admiringly.*)

ANGELINA (*Singing*):
>O'er the season vernal,
>Time may cast a shade;

Sunshine, if eternal,
Makes the roses fade;
Time may do his duty;
Let the thief alone—
Winter hath a beauty
That is all his own.
Fairest days are sun and shade:
I am no unhappy maid!
(JUDGE *whispers to* USHER, *who nods, crosses to* 1ST BRIDES-
MAID, *and holds out his hand.* BRIDESMAID *pretends not to
understand, then throws note on floor, and as* USHER *at-
tempts to pick it up, she stamps on his fingers.* USHER *finally
takes note to* ANGELINA, *who reads it, waves to* JUDGE, *kisses
note rapturously, and tucks it into neckline of dress.*)

JUDGE (*Leaning far out over his desk, gazing at* ANGELINA):
     Oh, never, never, *never*, since I joined the human race,
     Have I seen so exquisitely fair a face.

JURYMEN (*Together, shaking fingers at him*): Ah, sly dog! Sly
     dog!

JUDGE (*To* JURYMEN): How say you—is she not designed for cap-
     ture? (FOREMAN *consults with* JURYMEN.)

FOREMAN (*To* JUDGE): We've but one word, m'lord, and that is—
     rapture!

ANGELINA (*Curtsying*): Your kindness, gentlemen, quite over-
     powers!

JURYMEN (*Together, extending both arms to* ANGELINA): We
     love you dearly, and would make you ours!

BRIDESMAIDS (*Together, shaking fingers at* JURYMEN): Ah, sly
     dogs! Sly dogs! (COUNSEL *leads* ANGELINA *to plaintiff's
     chair. She sits.*)

COUNSEL (*To* JUDGE) : May it please you, m'lord! (*To* JURYMEN)
    Gentlemen of the jury! (*Sings*)
              With a sense of deep emotion,
              I approach this painful case;
              For I never had a notion
              That a man could be so base,
    (*Points to* EDWIN)
              Or deceive a girl confiding,
              Vows, etcetera, deriding.

ALL (*Singing*) :
              He deceived a girl confiding,
              Vows, etcetera, deriding.

JURYMEN (*Shaking fists at* EDWIN) :
              Monster! Monster! Dread our fury!
              There's the Judge and we're the Jury!
              Come! Substantial damages!
              Damages! Damages! Dam—

USHER (*Pounding staff on floor*) : Silence in court!

COUNSEL (*Singing*) :
              See my interesting client,
              Victim of a heartless wile!
    (ANGELINA *nods.*)
              See the traitor all defiant
              Wear a supercilious smile!
    (EDWIN *looks up, timidly.*)
              Sweetly smiled my client on him,
              Coyly wooed and gently won him.

ALL (*Singing*) :
              Sweetly smiled his client on him,
              Coyly wooed and gently won him.
    (COUNSEL *moves to stand by* ANGELINA.)

COUNSEL (*Singing*):
Picture, then, my client naming,
And insisting on, the day;
Picture him excuses framing—
Going from her far away;
Doubly criminal to do so,
For the maid had bought her trousseau!

ALL (*Singing together*):
Doubly criminal to do so,
For the maid had bought her trousseau!
(ANGELINA *collapses, sobbing, into* COUNSEL'S *arms.*)

COUNSEL (*Comforting her*): Cheer up, my pretty—oh, cheer up!

JURYMEN (*Together*): Cheer up, cheer up, we love you!

FOREMAN (*Holding out his arms, leaning over rail of jury box*):
If you're feeling faint, recline on me. (ANGELINA *leaves*
COUNSEL, *goes to jury box rail, and falls sobbing into* FORE-
MAN's *arms.* JUDGE *stands.*)

JUDGE (*Holding out his arms*): Or, if you'd rather, recline on *me!*
(ANGELINA *runs up onto bench, sits in* JUDGE's *lap and sobs
on his shoulder.*)

COUNSEL (*Handing* JUDGE *glass of water from table*): Give her
a drink of water! (JUDGE *takes glass, drinks water himself
and returns empty glass to* COUNSEL. *Then he takes from his
pocket a large red bandanna handkerchief, with which he
dabs* ANGELINA's *lips.*)

JURYMEN (*Together, shaking fists at* EDWIN):
Monster! Monster! Dread our fury!
There's the Judge, and we're the Jury!
Come! Substantial damages!
Damages! Dam—

USHER (*Pounding staff on floor*): Silence in court! (ANGELINA
descends from JUDGE's *lap, and* USHER *leads her back to*

plaintiff's chair. She sits, as EDWIN *leaves witness stand, walks to center and addresses* JURYMEN.)

EDWIN: Gentlemen, let me speak in my own defense. It is true that I have broken my engagement to Angelina, but only because I obey the laws of nature, and nature is constantly changing. A young fellow is very apt to love this lady today and that lady tomorrow. (*Sings*)

> You cannot eat breakfast all day,
> Nor is it the act of a sinner,
> When breakfast is taken away,
> To turn his attention to dinner.
> And it's not in the range of belief,
> To look upon him as a glutton
> Who, when he is tired of beef,
> Determines to tackle the mutton.
> But this I am willing to say,
> If it will appease her sorrow,
> I'll marry *this* lady (*Indicating* ANGELINA) today,
> And I'll marry *that* lady (*Indicating* 1ST BRIDESMAID)
>   tomorrow!

JUDGE (*To* COUNSEL, *reciting*):

> That seems a reasonable proposition,
> To which, I think, your client may agree.

COUNSEL:

> But, I submit, m'lord, with all submission,
> To marry two at once is burglary!

(*Refers to law book*)

> In the reign of James the Second,
> It was generally reckoned
> As a rather serious crime
> To marry two wives at a time.

(*Hands book up to* JUDGE, *who looks at it*)

JUDGE (*Looking up*):

> A nice dilemma we have here,
> That calls for all our wit.

COUNSEL:
>   And at this stage, it doesn't appear
>   That we can settle it.

(ANGELINA *runs to* EDWIN *and throws her arms around him.*)

ANGELINA: Though he has broken my heart, still I love him! I adore him! (*Addresses* JURYMEN) See what happiness I've lost, and remember it when you assess the damages Edwin must pay.

EDWIN (*Furiously pushing her away*): Nonsense! She wouldn't be able to endure me even for a day! (*Recites*)
>   I'm sure I should thrash her—
>   Perhaps I should kick her!
>   I am such a very bad lot!

(*To* JURYMEN) Remember *that* when you assess the damages I must pay.

JUDGE: He says when angry he would thrash and kick her. Let's make him angry, gentlemen, and find out!

COUNSEL: I object!

EDWIN: I *don't* object!

ALL (*Together*): We *do* object!

JUDGE (*Exasperated, tossing his books and papers into air*):
>   All the legal furies seize you!
>   No proposal seems to please you!
>   I can't sit up here all day,
>   I must shortly get away.
>   Barristers, and you, attorneys,
>   Set out on your homeward journeys;
>   Put your briefs upon the shelf—
>   I will marry her myself!

(*He comes down from bench and embraces* ANGELINA. *All cheer and applaud.*)

ALL (*Together*):
>
> For he is a Judge,
> And a good Judge, too!

JUDGE:
>
> Yes, I am a Judge,
> And a good Judge, too!
> Though homeward as you trudge,
> You declare my law is fudge,
> (*Pinches* ANGELINA'S *cheek*)
> Yet of beauty I'm a Judge!

ALL (*Together*): And a good Judge, too! (JUDGE *escorts* ANGE-LINA *to bench, where they stand together in a fond embrace. Two cardboard cupids in long white powdered wigs are lowered from ceiling over their heads.* COUNSEL *stands up center in front of table.* BRIDESMAIDS *give him one end of flower garlands to hold while they hold other ends and fan out, facing upstage, in a semicircle on apron of stage.* EDWIN *stands in witness box, smiling broadly.* JURYMEN, ATTORNEYS *and* PUBLIC *wave handkerchiefs and scarves.* USHER *waves staff. Curtain*)

THE END

Trial by Jury

Characters: 5 male; 6 female; as many extras, male or female, as desired for Attorneys, Jurymen, Public, Offstage Voice.

Playing Time: 25 minutes.

Costumes: Late nineteenth century. Angelina wears bridal gown and veil and carries bouquet. Bridesmaids' gowns are in pastel colors and they wear circlets of flowers on their heads. Edwin is dressed as a fashionable young man-about-town of the period. Jurymen wear conservative suits. Judge, Counsel and Attorneys wear long white powdered wigs and black legal robes. Court Usher wears a black suit, grey vest and high collar. Public are dressed in costumes of the period.

Properties: Gavel, law books, pitcher and glass of water, large red bandanna handkerchief, legal papers in leather folders, staff, cane, garlands (lengths of heavy drapery cord twined with artificial roses), bride's bouquet, two cardboard cupids with white powdered wigs to be lowered from ceiling as indicated in text.

Setting: Courtroom. There is a desk on a raised platform upstage center for Judge's bench. In front of platform there is a long table with a pitcher and glass of water on it, and chairs behind it for Counsel and Attorneys. Plaintiff's chair is right of table. Left of table is a chair on a platform for witness stand. There are 12 chairs with a railing around them for jury box. Stage left there is a double row of chairs for Public. The public entrance is down left. A door down right leads to jury room. Another door up right leads to Judge's chambers.

Lighting: No special effects.

Sound: Clock striking ten, as indicated in text.

Music for songs on following pages.

NOW, JURYMEN, HEAR MY ADVICE

Usher

Now, Jury - men, hear my ad-vice--

All kinds of vulgar preju-dice I pray you set a-side, I pray you

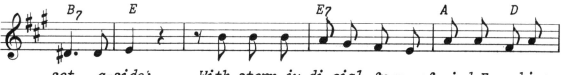

set a-side: With stern ju-di-cial frame of mind From bias

free of ev-'ry kind, This trial must be tried. From bias

free of ev - 'ry kind, This trial must be tried!

WHEN FIRST MY OLD, OLD LOVE I KNEW

Edwin

When first my old, old love I knew, My bosom welled wit.

joy;   My riches at her   feet I threw,   I was a lovesick

boy!   No terms seemed too ex-tra-va-gant Up - on her to em-

I used to mope and sigh and pant Just like a lovesi

ploy_____

boy__ Tink-a-tank, tink-a-tank, Tink-a-tank, tink-a-tank, tink-a-

tank, Tink-a-tank, tink-a-tank!

138

WHEN I, GOOD FRIENDS, WAS CALLED TO THE BAR

Judge

When I, good friends, was called to the bar I'd an

appetite fresh and heart-y; But I was as many young bar-ris-ters

are, An im-pe-cu-nious party. But I soon got tired of

third class journeys and dinners of bread and water; So I fell in

love with a rich at-tor-ney's Elder-ly, ug-ly daughter. So he

fell in love with a rich attorney's Elder-ly, ug-ly daughter. The

rich at-tor-ney he jumped with joy and re-plied to my fond profes-

sions: "You shall reap the reward of your pluck, my boy, At the Bailey and
Middlesex

Sessions.   You'll soon get used to her looks," he said "and a very nice

girl you'll find her. She may very well pass for forty-three In the

dusk with a light behind her!" She may   very well pass for   forty-

three In the dusk with a light behind her!

COMES THE BROKEN FLOWER

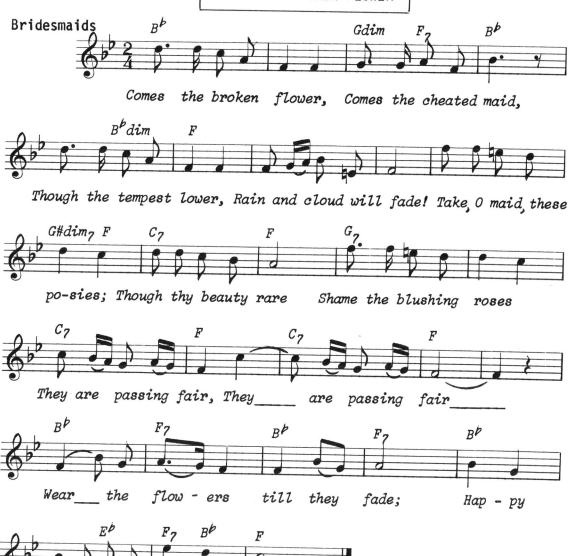

Comes the broken flower, Comes the cheated maid,

Though the tempest lower, Rain and cloud will fade! Take, O maid, these

po-sies; Though thy beauty rare Shame the blushing roses

They are passing fair, They_____ are passing fair_____

Wear___ the flow - ers till they fade; Hap - py

happy be thy life, O maid!

O'ER THE SEASON VERNAL

Angelina

O'er the season vernal Time may cast a shade;

Sunshine if e - ter-nal, Makes the roses fade: Time may do his

duty; Let the thief a-lone, Winter hath a beauty

That is all his own, That___ is all his own._____

Fair - est days are sun and shade: I am

no un - hap - py maid!

WITH A SENSE OF DEEP EMOTION

Counsel

With a sense of deep e - motion I approach this painful case; For I never had a notion That a man could be so base, Or de-ceive a girl con-fid - ing, Vows, et - ce-te - ra, de-rid-ing. He deceived a girl con-fiding, Vows, et - ce-te - ra, de-rid-ing. See my in-ter-esting client, Victim of a heartless wile! See the traitor all de-fi - ant Wear a su-per-cil - ious smile!

143

Sweetly smiled my client on him, Coy-ly wooed and gently
won him. Sweetly smiled his client on him, Coy-ly wooed and
gently won him. Picture then my client naming,
and insisting on the day: Picture him excuses framing
Going from her far a-way; Doubly crimi-nal to do so,
For the maid had bought her trousseau. Doubly crimi-nal to
do so, For the maid had bought her trousseau!

OH, GENTLEMEN, LISTEN, I PRAY

Edwin

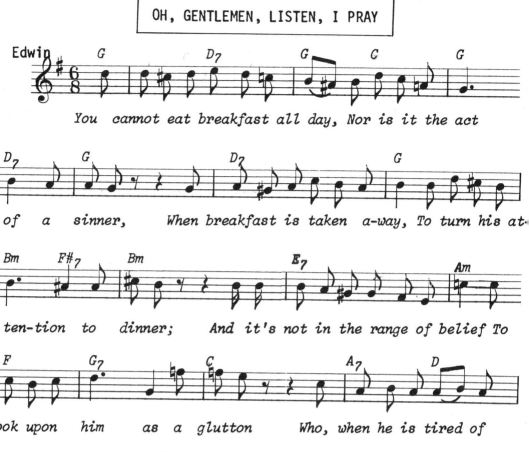

You cannot eat breakfast all day, Nor is it the act

of a sinner, When breakfast is taken a-way, To turn his at-

ten-tion to dinner; And it's not in the range of belief To

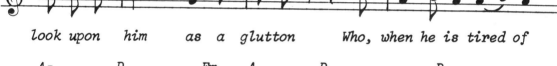

look upon him as a glutton Who, when he is tired of

beef, Determines to tackle the mutton. Ah!___ But

this I am willing to say, If it will appease her sorrow, I'll

marry this lady to-day And I'll marry that lady to-mor-row!

THE GONDOLIERS

The story of

THE GONDOLIERS

Two handsome gondoliers, Marco and Giuseppe, are adored by all the flower girls of Venice. They find it difficult to choose brides from such a bevy of charming ladies, so they have themselves blindfolded, and each catches a girl—Tessa is caught by Giuseppe and Gianetta by Marco. As the couples hurry off to be married, the Duke of Plaza-Toro, a Spanish nobleman, arrives, accompanied by the Duchess, their daughter, Casilda, and their attendant, Luiz, who is Casilda's secret love.

The Duke informs Casilda that when she was a baby, she was married by proxy to the infant son of the King of Barataria. The baby prince was in turn kidnapped by Don Alhambra, the Grand Inquisitor, and brought to Venice, where he was placed in the home of a worthy gondolier, who had a son the same age. Unfortunately, the gondolier mixed up the two boys, who are the just-married Marco and Giuseppe. Now the throne of Barataria is vacant, but no one knows which gondolier is the rightful King.

It is decided that Marco and Giuseppe will reign in Barataria as joint monarchs until it is ascertained which is which. Inez, the rightful King's old nurse (and the mother of Luiz) has been sent for to make the identification. Marco and Giuseppe enjoy their joint rule enormously, even though Don Alhambra has made them leave their new wives behind in Venice. They set up a monarchy in which there are no social distinctions and everybody is equal. However Don Alhambra soon arrives at court with Casilda and her parents and breaks the news that the true King is already married to Casilda. There is great consternation when Tessa and Gianetta, who suddenly appear to join their husbands, realize that one of them is married to a bigamist. However, the old nurse sets everything to rights by revealing that when Don Alhambra came to kidnap the prince, she substituted her own son to be carried off to Venice. Thus Luiz, raised as her son, is in reality the King of Barataria. To everyone's satisfaction, Casilda and Luiz are reunited, and Marco and Giuseppe are allowed to return to Venice with their wives and to the uncomplicated life of gondoliers.

THE GONDOLIERS

Or, The King of Barataria

Characters

DUKE OF PLAZA-TORO, *Grandee of Spain*
DUCHESS OF PLAZA-TORO
CASILDA, *their daughter*
LUIZ, *Duke's attendant*
DON ALHAMBRA DEL BOLERO, *the Grand Inquisitor*
MARCO PALMIERI }
GIUSEPPE PALMIERI } *Venetian gondoliers*
INEZ, *the King's foster mother*
ANTONIO }
FRANCESCO }
GIORGIO } *gondoliers*
ANNIBALE }
GIANETTA }
TESSA }
FIAMETTA } *Italian country girls (contadine)*
VITTORIA }
GIULIA }
BOATMAN }
TWO GUARDS } *non-speaking roles*
TWO PAGES }
GONDOLIERS
COUNTRY GIRLS

SCENE 1

TIME: *1750.*

SETTING: *Plaza outside the palace of the Duke of Venice. Backdrop represents a scene on the Grand Canal with boats and Venetian buildings in the distance. Up center is a raised landing with an iron railing and steps right and left leading down to stage level. Mooring posts for gondolas are at back of landing. Entrance to palace is through arch at right. Exits to street are at left between columns. Benches are down right and left.*

AT RISE: GIANETTA, TESSA, FIAMETTA, VITTORIA, GIULIA, *and other* COUNTRY GIRLS *are gathered in plaza, some seated on benches, others on landing steps and railing, tying bouquets of red and white roses which they take from baskets scattered about stage. As they sing, they make appropriate gestures with roses, as if they were characters.*

GIRLS (*Singing*):
> List and learn, ye dainty roses,
> Roses white and roses red,
> Why we bind you into posies
> Ere your morning bloom has fled.
> By a law of maiden's making,
> Accents of a heart that's aching,
> Even though that heart be breaking,
> Should by maiden be unsaid:
> Though they love with love exceeding,
> They must seem to be unheeding—
> Go ye then and do their pleading,
> Roses white and roses red!

(*During song,* ANTONIO, FRANCESCO, GIORGIO, ANNIBALE *and other* GONDOLIERS *enter in pairs and small groups and mingle with* GIRLS.)

FRANCESCO: Good morrow, pretty maids! Are you making those bouquets for us?

FIAMETTA: No, they are for Marco and Giuseppe Palmieri—the two handsomest gondoliers in all Venice.

GIULIA: They're coming here today to choose their brides.

ANTONIO: Do you all love them?

GIRLS: Passionately!

ANNIBALE: But what about us? We make our living as gondoliers, too. We're as good as those conceited Palmieri boys!

GIORGIO: And you know we adore you!

FIAMETTA: Marco and Giuseppe must first make their choice. After they have picked two of us, you may have what's left!

VITTORIA (*Pertly*): Till then, enjoy yourselves!

ANTONIO (*Bowing*): With pleasure. (GIRLS *move to landing and left side of stage as if to exit, but turn back as* ANTONIO *starts to sing,* GONDOLIERS *joining in.*)

ANTONIO *and* GONDOLIERS (*Singing*):
> For the merriest fellows are we, tra la,
> That ply the emerald sea, tra la;
> With loving and laughing,
> And quipping and quaffing,
> We're happy as happy can be, tra la—
> As happy as happy can be!

FIAMETTA (*On landing, pointing off left*): See! Here they come— Marco and Giuseppe!

GIRLS: Viva! (*Gondola crosses stage at back of landing with* MARCO *and* GIUSEPPE *standing.* NOTE: *See Production Notes. They disembark off right, then enter on landing. Each has a guitar slung across his back. As they come down steps to center stage, they exchange greetings with* GIRLS *in the exaggerated manner of Italian opera.*)

MARCO *and* GIUSEPPE: Good day, ladies!

GIRLS (*Demurely; curtsying*): We are only peasant girls.

MARCO *and* GIUSEPPE (*Bowing*): Your most humble servants!

MARCO: Why all these flowers?

GIRLS: They are for you, dear gondoliers! (GIRLS *present bouquets to* MARCO *and* GIUSEPPE, *who have difficulty holding so many.*)

MARCO: Ladies, we love you! (*They toss bouquets back to* GIRLS *and throw them kisses.*)

GIUSEPPE: And we serenade your beauty!

MARCO *and* GIUSEPPE (*Singing, accompanying themselves on guitars*):
> We're called *gondolieri*,
> But that's a vagary,
> It's quite honorary
> The trade that we ply.
> For gallantry noted
> Since we were short-coated,
> To beauty devoted.
> Giuseppe/Marco and I.

MARCO (*Speaking*): And now to choose our brides! (GIRLS *flirt with them to attract attention.*)

GIUSEPPE: It won't be easy. All the ladies are young and fair and very amiable.

MARCO: We will let Fate make the choice—by playing blindman's-buff. (*Turning to* GIRLS) And we will marry any two of you we catch! Now blindfold us. (FIAMETTA *and* VITTORIA *tie scarves over eyes of* MARCO *and* GIUSEPPE.)

FIAMETTA (*To* MARCO): Is it tight enough?

VITTORIA (*To* GIUSEPPE): Can you see anything? (MARCO *and* GIUSEPPE *slyly uncover one eye.*)

GIRLS (*Pointing fingers accusingly*): They're peeking!

GIULIA: You can spy, sir!

VITTORIA: Shut your eye, sir!

FIAMETTA: You may use it by-and-by, sir!

TESSA: You can see, sir!

GIANETTA: Don't tell me, sir!

GIULIA: That will do—now let it be, sir!
    (MARCO *and* GIUSEPPE *replace blindfolds.*)

GIRLS (*Chanting*):
                My papa, he keeps three horses,
                Black and white and dapple grey, sir;
                Turn three times, then take your courses,
                Catch whichever girl you may, sir!
    (MARCO *and* GIUSEPPE *turn around as directed and try to
    catch* GIRLS, *who have scattered and skip about just out of
    reach. Finally* MARCO *catches* GIANETTA, *and* GIUSEPPE
    catches TESSA. *They pass their hands lightly over their faces
    to discover their identity.*)

GIUSEPPE (*Guessing*): It's Tessa! (*Removing blindfold*) How
    very fortunate!

MARCO: And I've captured Gianetta! (*Removing blindfold*) Just
    the girl I wanted!

GIANETTA *and* TESSA (*Curtsying*): Gallant gondoliers, we thank
    you.

GIUSEPPE (*Taking* TESSA's *hand*): Now each gondolier has his
    bride! We'll all go to the nearest church and be married!
    (MARCO *and* GIANETTA *take hands, other* GIRLS *and* GONDO-
    LIERS *pair off, and all exit left, dancing. Pause; then roll on
    drum offstage right is heard. Gondola crosses behind landing*

from right to left. In the prow, opposite BOATMAN, *is* LUIZ,
vigorously beating drum. In center of gondola are DUKE *and*
DUCHESS OF PLAZA-TORO *and* CASILDA, *all three staring
haughtily into space.* LUIZ *continues beating drum offstage
left, then enters on landing, followed by* DUKE, DUCHESS *and*
CASILDA. *They walk unsteadily to railing, grip it for support,
and sing, facing audience.* LUIZ *gives a roll on drum at end
of each solo line.*)

DUKE (*Singing*):
> From the sunny Spanish shore—(*Drum-roll*)
> The Duke of Plaza-Tor'—(*Drum-roll*)

DUCHESS (*Singing*):
> And His Grace's Duchess true—(*Drum-roll*)

CASILDA (*Singing*):
> And His Grace's daughter, too—(*Drum-roll*)

LUIZ (*Singing*):
> And His Grace's private drum—(*Drum-roll*)
> To Venetia's shores have come:—(*Drum-roll*)

DUKE, DUCHESS, CASILDA *and* LUIZ (*Singing*):
> And if ever, ever, ever they get back to Spain,
> They will never, never never cross the sea again!
> (*Drum-roll, as* DUKE, DUCHESS *and* CASILDA *come down steps
> to center.*)

DUKE (*Speaking pompously*): At last we have arrived at our des-
tination. (*Indicating*) This is the Ducal Palace where the
Grand Inquisitor resides. I regret that I am unable to pay
my state visit in style. I should have preferred to ride through
the streets of Venice on a horse, but (*Gesturing toward canal*)—the streets are full of water. An unusually wet season,
I presume. Where is our suite?

LUIZ (*Coming forward*): Your Grace, I am here. (*Beats drum*)

DUCHESS (*Frowning*) : Luiz, you should kneel when you address His Grace. (LUIZ *kneels and beats another tattoo on drum.*)

CASILDA (*Contemptuously*) : Our servant is presumptuous. He has no appreciation of the respect due from a menial to a Castilian nobleman. He should be whipped until he knows his place.

DUKE: Casilda, my child, you are too hard on our suite. Rise, Luiz. Where is the brass band that was to have met us here and announced our arrival to the Grand Inquisitor?

LUIZ: The band required to be paid in advance.

DUCHESS: That's so like a band!

DUKE (*Disappointed*) : Even one trumpet would be something. Luiz, can you tootle like a trumpet?

LUIZ: Alas, no, Your Grace! But I can imitate a barnyard.

CASILDA (*Sneering*) : That wouldn't help us in the least! We're not a parcel of farmers come to market, you dolt!

DUKE (*Protesting mildly*) : My dear, our servant's feelings! (*Takes large calling card from pocket*) Luiz, be so good as to inform the Grand Inquisitor that (*Reading from card*) His Grace, the Duke of Plaza-Toro, Count Montadoro, Baron Picadoro—

DUCHESS: And party—

DUKE: And party—have arrived in Venice and seek—

CASILDA: Desire—

DUCHESS: *Demand!*

DUKE: And demand an audience. (*Gives card to* LUIZ *who tucks it in his belt*)

LUIZ: Your Grace has but to command, and I obey! (LUIZ *executes a complicated roll on drum, comes to attention, about-faces twice, then marches to palace entrance and exits, beating drum in time to his march.*)

DUKE (*Turning to* CASILDA): And now, my dear, prepare yourself for a magnificent surprise. It is my agreeable duty to reveal to you a secret which should make you the happiest young lady in Venice!

CASILDA: A secret?

DUKE: Yes! When you were only six months old, you were married by proxy to the infant son and heir of the King of Barataria.

CASILDA: Married! Was I consulted? (DUKE *shakes his head.*) Then he took a most unpardonable liberty!

DUKE: Consider his extreme youth (*Pantomimes rocking baby in his arms*)—and forgive him. Shortly after your wedding, your father-in-law, the King, for some unaccountable reason, changed from being a kind and just ruler to a tyrannical despot.

CASILDA: What happened then?

DUKE: Well, the Grand Inquisitor of Spain feared that harm would come to the infant Prince, so he had him smuggled out of Barataria and brought to Venice. Two weeks ago, the King and all his court were killed in a revolution, and we have come to this city to find your husband. He will be crowned the new King, and *you*, Casilda, will be the reigning Queen of Barataria!

DUKE *and* DUCHESS (*Kneeling*): Your Majesty!

CASILDA (*Bursting into tears*): How can I be a queen? I've nothing to wear! We're practically penniless!

DUKE (*Rising with* DUCHESS): That point has not escaped me, and I have formed a company, to be called "The Duke of Plaza-Toro, Limited." Shares will be sold to everyone who wishes to buy them—and though we're now as poor as church mice, we shall soon be rolling in wealth.

CASILDA: My father turned into a public company? How degrading!

DUKE (*Boastfully*): My child, the Duke of Plaza-Toro does not *follow* fashions—he *leads* them. I've always led everybody. When I was in the army, I led my regiment. Sometimes I led them *into* action, but most of the time, I led them *out* of it. (DUCHESS, CASILDA *and* LUIZ—*who enters from palace, beating drum—line up behind* DUKE *and pantomime his army. All face right and march forward as* DUKE *sings with military bravado.*)

DUKE (*Singing*):
  In enterprise of martial kind,
  When there was any fighting,
  I led my regiment from behind—
(DUKE *marches to end of line*)
  I found it less exciting.
  But when away my regiment ran,
("*Army*" *faces left and runs forward, forcing* DUKE *to back up*)
  My place was at the fore, O!—
(*All come to a halt and* DUKE *faces audience*)
  This celebrated, cultivated, underrated nobleman,
  The Duke of Plaza-Toro!

DUCHESS, CASILDA *and* LUIZ (*Facing audience and singing*):
  In the first and foremost flight, ha, ha!
  You always found that knight, ha, ha!
  That celebrated, cultivated, underrated nobleman,
  The Duke of Plaza-Toro!

DUKE (*Singing*):
>When, to evade Destruction's hand,
>To hide they all proceeded,

(*All hide behind columns left stage;* DUKE *leans out toward audience as he continues to sing*)

>No soldier in that gallant band
>Hid half as well as I did.
>I lay concealed throughout the war,
>And so preserved my gore, O!—
>This unaffected, undetected, well-connected warrior,
>The Duke of Plaza-Toro!

DUCHESS, CASILDA *and* LUIZ (*Coming out from behind columns and marching downstage, singing*):
>In every doughty deed, ha, ha!
>He always took the lead, ha, ha!
>That unaffected, undetected, well-connected warrior,
>The Duke of Plaza-Toro!

LUIZ (*Speaking to* DUKE): Your Grace, the Grand Inquisitor is waiting to receive you.

DUKE (*Offering arm to* DUCHESS): Come, my dear. (*They exit into palace. As soon as they have disappeared,* LUIZ *lays aside his drum and embraces* CASILDA.)

LUIZ: My darling! At last we are alone and can express our true feelings for each other.

CASILDA: Oh, Luiz, forgive my cold disdain when my parents are with us. You know it is only a mask I must wear to hide my love for you.

LUIZ: How much longer must we keep up this masquerade? Marry me today, Casilda, and then we can reveal our love to all the world.

CASILDA (*Drawing away from him*): Alas, I can never be yours! I have just learned that I was married in babyhood to the son of the King of Barataria.

LUIZ (*Amazed*): What! The child who was stolen in infancy by the Inquisition? Why, my mother was his nurse!

CASILDA: Well, he has been found, and my father has brought me here to claim his hand. (*Voices are heard off right.* LUIZ *and* CASILDA *quickly separate,* LUIZ *hurrying to get his drum from bench and retire upstage.* DUKE *and* DUCHESS *enter, followed by* DON ALHAMBRA DEL BOLERO, *the Grand Inquisitor.*)

DUKE (*To* CASILDA): My child, allow me to present to you His Distinction Don Alhambra del Bolero, the Grand Inquisitor of Spain. It was this gentleman who so thoughtfully stole your infant husband and brought him to Venice.

DON ALHAMBRA: So th's is the little lady who is to be the Queen of Barataria. And a very pretty little lady, too! (*Bowing*) Your Majesty. (CASILDA *returns his bow coldly.*)

DUCHESS: If I'm not mistaken, Your Excellency, there seems to be some doubt as to the young King's whereabouts.

DON ALHAMBRA: A doubt? Oh, mercy, no! He's here in Venice, plying the picturesque trade of a gondolier. Listen, and I will tell you about it. (DUKE *and* DUCHESS *sit on bench, right;* CASILDA *sits on bench, left.* DON ALHAMBRA *sings.*)
> I stole the Prince, and brought him here,
> And left him gaily prattling
> With a highly respectable gondolier,
> Who promised the royal babe to rear,
> And teach him the trade of a timoneer [*helmsman*]
> With his own beloved bratling.
>
> Both of the babes were strong and stout,
> And, considering all things, clever.
> Of *that* there is no manner of doubt—
> No probable, possible shadow of doubt—
> No possible doubt whatever.

But owing, I'm much disposed to fear,
To his terrible taste for tippling,
That highly respectable gondolier
Could never declare with a mind sincere
Which of the two was his offspring dear,
And which the royal stripling!

Which was which he could never make out
Despite his best endeavor.
Of *that* there is no manner of doubt—
No probable, possible shadow of doubt—
No possible doubt whatever.

DUKE (*Rising*): But surely the two boys knew which was which!

DON ALHAMBRA (*Shaking his head*): No, they looked enough alike to be brothers, and when the old gondolier died, they followed his trade. So it is quite certain—beyond all probable, possible shadow of a doubt—that the King of Barataria is a Venetian gondolier.

CASILDA (*Haughtily, rising*): Do you mean to tell me I am married to one of two gondoliers, but nobody knows *which?*

DON ALHAMBRA: Be reassured, Your Majesty—we have a way of finding out. The mother of that drummer of yours, Luiz, was once nurse to the royal child. *She* can establish the King's identity beyond all question. (DON ALHAMBRA *turns to* LUIZ.) Young man, you will set off at once to fetch your mother from the mountains near Cordova. She will return with you and identify the rightful King. (*Pounds walking stick on ground three times.* TWO GUARDS *enter from palace and lead* LUIZ *to landing.* DON ALHAMBRA *exits into palace, accompanied by* DUKE *and* DUCHESS. *After exchanging a despairing look with* LUIZ, CASILDA *follows.* LUIZ *and* GUARDS *exit right on landing. Brief pause—then* GIUSEPPE *and* TESSA, MARCO *and* GIANETTA *enter from left, the two couples with their arms about each other's waists. Garlands of flowers are on their heads and around their necks.*)

TESSA *and* GIANETTA (*Singing as they enter*):
> When a merry maiden marries,
> Sorrow goes and pleasure tarries;
> Every sound becomes a song,
> All is right, and nothing's wrong!

GIUSEPPE: Now our lives are going to begin in real earnest!

MARCO: What a delightful institution is marriage!
(*Couples break into spontaneous dancing which is interrupted by entrance of* DON ALHAMBRA *from palace.*)

DON ALHAMBRA: Good afternoon! Is some sort of celebration going on here?

GIANETTA: Yes! I've just been married to Marco!

TESSA: And I, to Giuseppe!

DON ALHAMBRA (*Aghast*): Married? To the Palmieri brothers? How extremely awkward!

GIANETTA: You don't mind, do you?

TESSA (*Coquettishly*): You weren't thinking of either of us for yourself, were you?

DON ALHAMBRA (*Indignantly*): No, of course not! (TESSA *and* GIANETTA *giggle and sit together on bench left.*)

GIUSEPPE (*Slapping* DON ALHAMBRA *on back*): Now, my man, if your curiosity is satisfied, you can go.

DON ALHAMBRA (*Wincing at this familiarity*): You mustn't call me "your man." I don't think you know who I am.

GIUSEPPE: We don't care who you are, for we hold all men to be equal. As we despise oppression, we despise kings.

MARCO: We hate a monarchy and love a republic. We are republicans, heart and soul—the sons of the patriot, Baptisto Palmieri, who led the last revolution!

DON ALHAMBRA (*Chuckling slyly*): *One* of you may be Baptisto's son, but the other one is the son of the late King of Barataria, and the new King of that country. (TESSA *and* GIANETTA *squeal with delight.*)

GIUSEPPE: One of us a *king!*

MARCO: But which is it?

DON ALHAMBRA (*Shrugging*): What does it matter? Since both of you detest kings, naturally you'll abdicate at once. Good afternoon. (*Starts to walk away*)

GIUSEPPE: Wait! When I say that we detest kings, I mean only *bad* kings! Now I can picture a king that would be absolutely unobjectionable. He would abolish taxes and make everything cheap—except gondola rides, of course.

MARCO: And he would give free entertainments to gondoliers.

GIUSEPPE: I would be such a king!

MARCO: And so would I!

GIUSEPPE: The two of *us* would rule Barataria in an ideal way.

MARCO: A monarchy that would be tempered with equality for all.

DON ALHAMBRA: I'm glad to find your objections are not insuperable.

GIUSEPPE: Oh, they're not insuperable!

MARCO: Besides, we are open to being convinced by you.

GIUSEPPE: Yes, indeed! Our views may have been hastily formed on insufficient grounds. We've a very poor opinion of the politician who is not open to being convinced.

DON ALHAMBRA: Then we'll consider it settled, and until I can find out which of you is King, you will reign together.

MARCO: As one individual? (DON ALHAMBRA *nods.*)

GIUSEPPE: Like this? (GIUSEPPE *and* MARCO *strike "one-individual" pose. With a little jump, each places outstretched arm on other's shoulder, raises outside leg with knee bent and pointed out to side, toe of foot touching floor. They assume this position from now on whenever their royalty is referred to.*)

DON ALHAMBRA (*After studying pose*): Er—something like that.

MARCO: May we take our friends with us and give them positions in the court?

DON ALHAMBRA: Certainly—that's always done. (MARCO *and* GIUSEPPE *break pose and shake hands.*) Your country is now in a state of revolt, so it's imperative that you take over the government right away. There's a ship sailing to Barataria in an hour.

GIANETTA (*Rising from bench with* TESSA): We'll just run home and pack a few things—(*They start to leave.*)

DON ALHAMBRA: Stop! Ladies are not admitted to the court of Barataria! (*Exclamations of dismay from both couples.*)

GIUSEPPE: Are you going to separate us from our wives?

DON ALHAMBRA: Just for a little while. As soon as the King's old nurse determines which of you is the rightful monarch, your wives may come and join you. (DON ALHAMBRA *tips his hat and bows to* TESSA *and* GIANETTA, *then exits into palace.*)

GIANETTA (*Speaking to* MARCO *and* GIUSEPPE, *who look dejected*):
Oh, do cheer up! We won't be parted long, and when it's finally settled which one of you is King, then one of *us* (*Putting arm around* TESSA)—will be *Queen*! (*Sings.*)
>   Then one of us will be Queen,
>   And sit on a golden throne,
>   With a crown instead of a hat on her head,
>   And diamonds all her own!

TESSA (*Singing*):
>   With a beautiful robe of gold and green,
>   I've always understood;
>   I wonder whether she'd wear a feather?
>   I rather think she would!

BOTH (*Singing*):
>   Oh, 'tis a glorious thing, I ween,
>   To be a regular Royal Queen!
>   No half-and-half affair, I mean,
>   But a right-down regular Royal Queen!

(*They dance a polka.* ANTONIO, FRANCESCO, GIORGIO, ANNIBALE, FIAMETTA, VITTORIA, GIULIA, *and other* GONDOLIERS *and* GIRLS *enter in couples and watch.*)

ANTONIO (*Calling out*): What is the reason for all this hilarity?

FRANCESCO: Have you fallen heir to a fortune?

MARCO *and* GIUSEPPE: Better than that! (*Assuming their "one-individual" pose*) We have fallen heir to a kingdom!

MARCO: We have just been summoned to Barataria—

GIUSEPPE: Where we are to rule jointly as King.

MARCO *and* GIUSEPPE: United we stand, united we reign, and united we invite all you gondoliers to come with us.

MARCO: There are posts at court for every one of you—

GIUSEPPE: With no differences in rank.

MARCO *and* GIUSEPPE: All shall be equal! (*They break pose.* GIRLS *ad lib excitedly.*)

MARCO (*Announcing loudly*): No ladies are allowed at court for the present! You will join us later. (GIRLS *and* GONDOLIERS *murmur disappointment.*)

GIUSEPPE (*Embracing* TESSA): Goodbye, my love. It breaks my heart to leave you behind.

MARCO (*Embracing* GIANETTA): Every hour will be a year until you come to me. (*Other couples bid each other farewell.*)

GIUSEPPE: We must be off! A ship is waiting in the harbor to take us to Barataria.

GIUSEPPE, MARCO *and* GONDOLIERS (*Singing*):
      Then away we go to an island fair
      That lies in a southern sea;
      We know not where, and we don't much care,
      Wherever that isle may be.
(GONDOLIERS *exit up aisle through auditorium, singing and waving their caps to* GIRLS, *who stand on stage waving their handkerchiefs. Curtains close.*)

* * * * *

SCENE 2

TIME: *Three months later.*
SETTING: *Pavilion in the Court of Barataria. At center back are two thrones on dais under a canopy, with end table set between thrones. Sofa, tea table and two chairs are left. Billiard table is against right wall. Two gilt stools are down left. A stake for hoop-tossing is down right. Entrances are right and left and on each side of the thrones.*
AT RISE: MARCO *and* GIUSEPPE, *elegantly dressed, are seated on thrones, busily polishing a crown and scepter.* ANTONIO,

FRANCESCO, GIORGIO, ANNIBALE *and other* GONDOLIERS—
some dressed as courtiers, others as servants—are playing
games: billiards, checkers, marbles, tossing wooden hoops
onto stake, etc. After a moment, ANNIBALE *blows a whistle.*

ANNIBALE: Play hour is over! It's time to attend to our duties!
(GONDOLIERS *grumble and beg to play longer.*) No, no! Remember, this is a monarchy of absolute equality. Equal play,
equal work! (GONDOLIERS *put away games and playthings.*
ANNIBALE *turns to* MARCO *and* GIUSEPPE.) I trust Your Majesties agree with me, and will work hard.

GIUSEPPE (*Rising with* MARCO, *both still polishing crown and*
scepter): Oh, yes, we quite understand that a man who holds
the position of King should do something to justify it. The
least we can do is to make ourselves useful about the palace.

MARCO: You know, of course, that we have taken over the servants' quarters and are living there in strict simplicity.
(*They put crown, scepter and polishing cloths on throne ta-*
ble and come down center.)

MARCO *and* GIUSEPPE (*Singing*):
> Rising early in the morning,
> We proceed to light the fire,
> Then our Majesty adorning
> In our work-a-day attire,
> We embark without delay
> On the duties of the day.

(*Following lines are spoken;* MARCO *and* GIUSEPPE *panto-*
mime action.)

MARCO: We dress our private valet—

GIUSEPPE: Write letters for our private secretary—

MARCO: Polish the coronation plate—

GIUSEPPE: Run errands for the Ministers of State.

MARCO *and* GIUSEPPE (*Singing*):
>   Then we go and stand as sentry
>   At the palace (private entry),
> (*They stand at attention, then march back and forth*)
>   Marching hither, marching thither, up and down and
>   to and fro,
>   While the warrior on duty
>   Goes in search of beer and beauty,
>   And it generally happens that he hasn't far to go.
> (*They stop marching.*)
>   He relieves us, if he's able,
>   Just in time to lay the table,
>   Then we dine and serve the coffee, and at half-past
>   twelve or one,
>   With a pleasure that's emphatic,
>   We retire to our attic,
> (*They lean against each other wearily*)
>   With the gratifying feeling that our duty has been
>   done!

MARCO, GIUSEPPE *and* GONDOLIERS:
>   Oh, philosophers may sing
>   Of the troubles of a King,
>   But of pleasures there are many and of worries there
>   are none;
>   And the culminating pleasure
>   That we/they treasure beyond measure
>   Is the gratifying feeling that our/their duty has been
>   done!
> (GONDOLIERS *exit as they sing;* MARCO *and* GIUSEPPE *remain
> on stage.*)

GIUSEPPE: It really is a very pleasant existence here.

MARCO: And yet, we're lacking just one thing to make us thoroughly comfortable, and that is—the dear little wives we left behind us three months ago.

GIUSEPPE: Yes, it *is* dull without female society. If we had that, we'd have everything. (*Excited voices and laughter are heard offstage.* TESSA *and* GIANETTA *enter and run to embrace* GIUSEPPE *and* MARCO. *They are followed onstage by* GIRLS *and* GONDOLIERS, *who enter in couples.*)

MARCO: What a happy surprise!

TESSA: Yes, we thought you'd like it. You see, we felt very bored and mopey after you left—and you *didn't* write! So at last I said to Gianetta, "I can't stand this any longer! Think of those poor men with nobody to mend their stockings or sew on their buttons. Let us all go and see how our husbands are getting on." And she said, "Done!"—and all the girls said, "Done!"—and we've crossed the sea, and, thank goodness, *that's* done!—and here we are, and—*I've* done!

GIANETTA: And now—which of you is King?

TESSA: And which of *us* is Queen?

GIUSEPPE: We won't know that until the nurse turns up. But in the meantime, what do you all say to a banquet and a dance? (GONDOLIERS *and* GIRLS *agree enthusiastically.*)

ANTONIO: Cheers for our King—whichever he may be!

ALL: Viva, Marco! Viva, Giuseppe! (*Cheering is interrupted by entrance, right, of* DON ALHAMBRA, *who looks about disapprovingly, scowling at* GIRLS.)

DON ALHAMBRA (*Sternly*): So! The ladies didn't wait for my permission before coming to court.

MARCO (*Nervously*): They—they just arrived, sir.

DON ALHAMBRA (*Waving them off imperiously*): Leave us! (GIRLS *and* GONDOLIERS *exit hurriedly.* TESSA *and* GIANETTA *pause in doorway at back of stage and listen to following dialogue.*) Tell me, Your Majesties, does your new employment please you? Is it more fun than gondoliering? Do you think your subjects like you?

GIUSEPPE: Yes, indeed! You see, we have remodeled the monarchy on democratic principles.

DON ALHAMBRA: What! (*Clutching at nearby chair, almost falling to floor*)

MARCO: All departments rank equally, and everybody is at the head of his department.

DON ALHAMBRA: But there are rules of etiquette in every court that *must* be observed! No, no, young men, this business of democracy will never work. Years ago there was a king who felt the same way as you do. (*Singing*)

> He wished all men as rich as he
> (And he was rich as rich could be),
> So to the top of every tree
> Promoted everybody.
> Lord Chancellors were cheap as sprats,
> And Bishops in their shovel hats
> Were plentiful as tabby cats—
> In point of fact, too many.
> Ambassadors cropped up like hay,
> Prime Ministers and such as they
> Grew like asparagus in May,
> And Dukes were three a penny.

(*Sings directly to audience*)

> In short, whoever you may be,
> To this conclusion you'll agree,
> When everyone is somebodee,
> Then no one's anybody!

(*Speaking to* MARCO *and* GIUSEPPE) And now, Your Majesties, I have some important news for you. The Duke and Duchess of Plaza-Toro, and their daughter, Casilda, will be here any moment.

MARCO: The Duke and Duchess mean nothing to us.

DON ALHAMBRA: Quite right—but their beautiful daughter—ah! Many years ago, when a baby, one of you was married to her.

MARCO: Married when a baby!

GIUSEPPE: But we were married three months ago!

TESSA *and* GIANETTA (*Coming forward*): They most certainly were!

DON ALHAMBRA: Have patience, ladies! The old woman who once nursed the royal child is now in the palace, waiting for me to interview her. As soon as possible, we shall clear up this affair. (*Exits left*)

GIANETTA (*Ready to cry*): Which of you is married to which of us, and what's to become of the other?

GIUSEPPE (*Facetiously*): It's quite simple. Marco and I have managed to acquire three wives: Tessa, Gianetta, and Casilda. That means two-thirds of a husband to each wife.

TESSA (*Sarcastically*): My good sir, one can't marry a common fraction!

GIUSEPPE: I resent being called a common fraction!

MARCO (*Intervening good-naturedly*): Come, come, we'll get nowhere fighting. Let's face the situation calmly. (*Doorbell rings.*) That's the visitors' bell. Someone is at the front door.

GIUSEPPE: It's probably the Duke and Duchess, and the one and only Casilda.

GIANETTA (*Fuming*): I'll teach her to marry the man of my heart!

TESSA: I'll pinch her and scratch her and send her away with a flea in her ear! (TESSA *and* GIANETTA *flounce over to sofa and sit with folded arms, glowering.* MARCO *and* GIUSEPPE *go to thrones. One puts on crown, the other takes up scepter; they stand on dais, facing front, and strike their "one-individual" pose.* DUKE, DUCHESS *and* CASILDA *enter right; all three are now dressed with the utmost magnificence.*)

DUKE: Ah! Their Majesties! (*Bows with great ceremony.* DUCHESS *and* CASILDA *curtsy.*)

MARCO *and* GIUSEPPE (*Speaking together*): The Duke of Plaza-Toro, I believe?

DUKE (*Correcting them*): The Duke of Plaza-Toro, *Limited!* (MARCO *and* GIUSEPPE *look amused and break out of pose.* DUKE *brings* CASILDA *forward.*) Allow me to present the young lady that one of you married—my daughter, Casilda. (TESSA *and* GIANETTA, *on sofa, snort in contempt.*) Take her, and may she make you happier than her mother has made me.

DUCHESS (*Outraged*): *Sir!*

DUKE (*Adding hastily*): If possible! (MARCO *and* GIUSEPPE *sit on thrones.*) And now, I have a complaint to make to Your Majesties. I come here in state, and what do I find? A guard of honor to receive me? No!

MARCO *and* GIUSEPPE (*Agreeing*): No.

DUKE: A royal salute fired? No!

MARCO *and* GIUSEPPE: No.

DUKE: The bells set ringing?

MARCO *and* GIUSEPPE: No.

DUKE (*Shouting indignantly*): Yes! *One!* The visitors' bell, and I rang it myself! Don't you know, Your Majesties, that you must be more observant of etiquette? Such things should never happen in a well-ordered court!

MARCO: But we can't help it. Our people want us to be plain and democratic. (*They discard crown and scepter, placing them on table.*)

DUKE: We'll have to change all that when my daughter becomes Queen. (*Offers arm to* DUCHESS) Come, my dear. (*They exit right.*)

GIUSEPPE (*To* MARCO, *as they come down center*): The old birds have gone away and left the chickens together. That's called tact.

CASILDA: Gentlemen, I must tell you quite honestly that although I may have been married to one of you in infancy, I am head over ears in love with somebody else!

GIUSEPPE: Our case exactly! *We* are in love with our wives!

CASILDA: Your wives! Then you are married?

TESSA *and* GIANETTA: Yes, they are! (*They run to husbands, who put arms around them.*)

CASILDA: It seems we are all sisters in misfortune. There's only one thing to do—we must reach a compromise.

GIANETTA: How can marriage be called a state of unity when husbands are bisected and wives are divisible by three?

GIANETTA, TESSA *and* CASILDA (*Speaking together*): One-third of myself is married to half of you or you! (*Pointing first to* MARCO, *then to* GIUSEPPE.)

MARCO *and* GIUSEPPE: And half of myself is married to two-thirds of you or you or you! (*Pointing to each girl in turn. Fanfare of trumpets is heard offstage.* DON ALHAMBRA, DUKE, DUCHESS, ANTONIO, FRANCESCO, GIORGIO, ANNIBALE, FIAMETTA,

VITTORIA, GIULIA *and other* GONDOLIERS *and* GIRLS *enter right and left.* DON ALHAMBRA *stands at center,* DUKE *and* DUCHESS *stand nearby with* MARCO, GIUSEPPE, CASILDA, TESSA *and* GIANETTA; *others are grouped at back and sides of stage.*)

DON ALHAMBRA: Good people, I have an important announcement to make! The King's foster mother has been found! She will declare the rightful King—and he will be crowned the sole, supreme sovereign of Barataria! (DON ALHAMBRA *goes off and politely leads in* INEZ *to center, where she stands in silence.*)

MARCO: Speak, woman, speak! Is Giuseppe the King? Or am I? (INEZ *remains silent.*)

ALL (*Shouting*): Speak, woman, speak!

INEZ (*Singing*):
>   The Royal Prince was by the King entrusted
>   To my fond care, ere I grew old and crusted!
>   When traitors came to steal his son reputed,
>   My own small boy I deftly substituted!
>   The villains fell into the trap completely—
>   I hid the Prince away—still sleeping sweetly:
>   I called him "son" with pardonable slyness—
>   His name, Luiz! Behold His Royal Highness!

DUKE: Do you mean that Luiz is King? (INEZ *points out front to aisle. Fanfare of trumpets is heard.* TWO GUARDS *enter, followed by* LUIZ, *crowned and robed as King, holding scepter and orb.* TWO PAGES *carry train of his robe. Procession goes up on stage and* LUIZ *ascends dais.*)

LUIZ: Casilda, my wife, come forward and be crowned my Queen! (LUIZ *gives his orb and scepter to* 1ST PAGE *to hold, then picks up other crown and scepter from table, gives scepter to* CASILDA *and places crown on her head. All cheer.* LUIZ *and* CASILDA *sit on thrones.*)

ALL (*Singing*):

> Then hail, O King of a Golden Land,
> And the high-born bride who claims his hand!
> The past is dead, and you gain your own,
> A royal crown and a golden throne!

MARCO, GIUSEPPE *and* GONDOLIERS (*Singing*):

> Once more *gondolieri*,
> Both skillful and wary,
> Free from this quandary,
> Contented are we.
> From Royalty flying,
> Our gondolas plying
> And merrily crying
> Our "premé," "stalì!" [*These are gondoliers' cries.*
> *Premé—push in or press down; stalì—stop or*
> *stand there!*]

GIANETTA, TESSA *and* GIRLS: Goodbye to Barataria!

ALL (*Singing*):

> So goodbye cachucha, fandango, bolero—
> We'll dance a farewell to that measure—
> Old Xeres, adieu—Manzanilla—Montero--
> We leave you with feelings of pleasure!

(MARCO *and* GIANETTA, GIUSEPPE *and* TESSA, GONDOLIERS *and* GIRLS *dance up aisle and exit at rear of auditorium. Characters remaining on stage dance until curtains close.*)

THE END

Production Notes

THE GONDOLIERS

Characters: 9 male; 8 female; 5 male for non-speaking roles; as many male and female as desired for Gondoliers and Girls.

Playing Time: 30 minutes.

Costumes: In the style of 1750. Don Alhambra wears black clerical outfit and black Spanish hat. He carries a walking stick. In Scene 1, Duke, Duchess, and Casilda wear shabby court dress. Luiz wears drummer's uniform. Marco, Giuseppe, Gondoliers, and Boatmen wear stocking caps, short colorful jackets and knee pants. In Scene 2, Duke, Duchess and Casilda wear rich court costumes. Luiz is dressed in royal robes. Marco, Giuseppe and Gondoliers wear court costumes (some Gondoliers are dressed as servants). Tessa, Gianetta and other girls wear peasant dress in bright colors. Inez wears dark dress and black mantilla. Guards and Pages wear appropriate court costumes. Duke and Don Alhambra wear wigs.

Properties: Baskets and bouquets of red and white roses; two guitars; two blindfolds; drum; large calling card; garlands of flowers; two crowns, two scepters; orb; polishing cloths; billiard balls and cues; checkers; wooden hoops; whistle; marbles.

Setting: Scene 1: The plaza outside the palace of the Duke of Venice. Backdrop represents scene of the Grand Canal in Venice, with boats and Venetian buildings in the distance. Up center is a raised landing with iron railing and steps right and left leading down to stage level. Mooring posts for gondolas are at back of landing. Gondola in which characters make their entrances is a cut-out on wheels, pulled across stage behind landing, but visible to audience. Actors walk along with cut-out so as to appear to be seated or standing in gondola. Entrance to palace is through arch at right. Exits to street are at left between columns. Benches are down right and left. Scene 2: Pavilion in the Court of Barataria. Up center are two thrones on dais under a canopy, with end table between thrones. Sofa, table and two chairs are left. Billiard table is against right wall. Two stools are down left. Stake for hoop-tossing is down right. Entrances are right and left and on each side of thrones.

Lighting: No special effects.

Sound: Offstage trumpet fanfares, doorbell.

Music for songs on following pages.

175

LIST AND LEARN

List and learn, list and learn, list and learn, ye dainty ro-ses, Roses white and ros-es red, Why we bind you into po-sies Ere your morning bloom has fled. By a law of maiden's making, Ac-cents of a heart that's ach-ing, Even tho' that heart is breaking Should by maiden be un-said. Tho' they love with love exceeding, They must seem to be un - heeding. Go ye then and do their pleading, Roses white and roses red!

176

Antonio &
Gondoliers

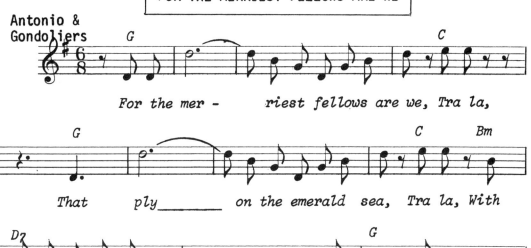

For the mer - riest fellows are we, Tra la,

That ply_____ on the emerald sea, Tra la, With

loving and laughing and quipping and quaffing We're happy as happy can

be, Tra la, As happy as happy can be!

Marco & Giuseppe

We're called____ gondo - lieri, But that's a va-

ga-ry-- It's quite honor - a - ry, The trade that we ply._____

For gal - lant-ry noted Since we were short-

coat-ed, To beauty de - voted, Giu - seppe and I!____
                                                    Mar - co and I!____

178

FROM THE SUNNY SPANISH SHORE

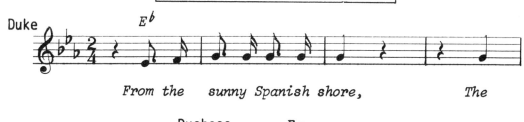

Duke

From the   sunny Spanish shore,   The

Duchess

Duke of Plaza - Tor'   And his Grace's Duchess true--

Casilda   Luiz

And his Grace's daughter too--   And his Grace's private

drum To Vene-tia's shores have come, To Ve-ne - tia's

shores have   come: And__ if ever ever ever They get

back to Spain, They will never never never Cross the sea again!

IN ENTERPRISE OF MARTIAL KIND

Duke

1. In enterprise of martial kind When there was any__
2. When to evade Destruction's hand To hide they all pro-

fighting, I led my reg'ment from behind I found it less ex-
ceeded, No soldier in that gallant band Hid half as well as

citing. But when away my reg'ment ran My place was at the
I did. I__ lay concealed thru-out the war And so preserved my

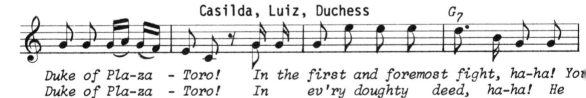

fore O! This celebrated, cultivat-ed, underrated nobleman, The
gore O! This unaffected, undetected, well-connected warrior, The

Casilda, Luiz, Duchess

Duke of Pla-za - Toro! In the first and foremost fight, ha-ha! You
Duke of Pla-za - Toro! In ev'ry doughty deed, ha-ha! He

always found that knight, ha-ha! That celebrat-ed, cultivated,
always took the lead, ha-ha! That unaffected, undetected,

underrated nobleman, The Duke of Pla - za - To - ro!
well-connected warrior, The Duke of Pla - za - To - ro!

180

I STOLE THE PRINCE

Don Alhambra Eb

1. I stole the Prince and I brought him here And
2. But owing I'm much dis-posed to fear To his

left him gaily prattling   With a   highly   respectable
terrible taste for tippling,   That   highly   respectable

gondolier, Who promised the royal   babe to rear, And teach him the
gondolier Could never declare with a mind sincere   Which of the

trade of a   timoneer With his own   beloved   bratling.
two was his offspring dear And which the royal   stripling!

Both of the babes were   strong and stout And considering all things
Which   was which he could never make out   Despite   his best en-

clever.   Of that there is no   manner of doubt No probable
deavor.   Of that there is no   manner of doubt No probable

possible   shadow of doubt No   possible doubt whatever.
possible   shadow of doubt No   possible doubt whatever.

WHEN A MERRY MAIDEN MARRIES

Gianetta & Tessa

When a merry maiden marries, Sorrow goes and pleasu

tarries; Ev-'ry sound becomes a song, All is

right and nothing's wrong!

ONE OF US WILL BE A QUEEN

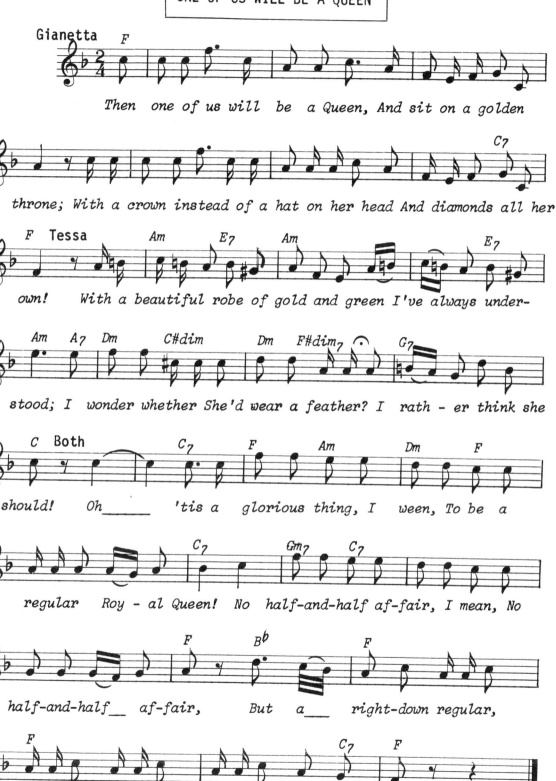

Then one of us will be a Queen, And sit on a golden throne; With a crown instead of a hat on her head And diamonds all her own! With a beautiful robe of gold and green I've always understood; I wonder whether She'd wear a feather? I rath - er think she should! Oh_____ 'tis a glorious thing, I ween, To be a regular Roy - al Queen! No half-and-half af-fair, I mean, No half-and-half_ af-fair, But a_ right-down regular, regular, regular, regular Roy-al Queen!

Giuseppe, Marco,
Gondoliers

Then a-way___ we go to an island fair__ That

lies in a southern sea; We know___ not where and we don't mu

care__ Wherever that isle may be.____

RISING EARLY IN THE MORNING

Giuseppe &
Marco

Rising early in the morning, We proceed to

light the fire; Then, our Majesty a-dorn - ing In its

workaday attire, We embark without de - lay On the

duties of the day. Then we go and stand as

sentry At the Palace (private entry) Marching hither, marching

thither, up and down and to and fro, While the warrior on

duty Goes in search of beer and beauty (And it gener-al - ly

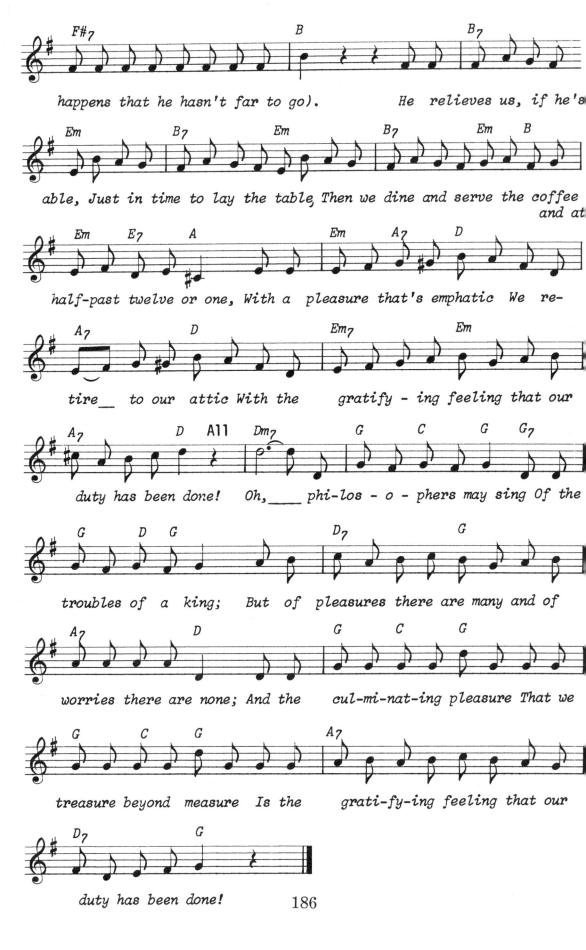

happens that he hasn't far to go). He relieves us, if he's

able, Just in time to lay the table, Then we dine and serve the coffee
and at

half-past twelve or one, With a pleasure that's emphatic We re-

tire__ to our attic With the gratify - ing feeling that our

duty has been done! Oh,____ phi-los - o - phers may sing Of the

troubles of a king; But of pleasures there are many and of

worries there are none; And the cul-mi-nat-ing pleasure That we

treasure beyond measure Is the grati-fy-ing feeling that our

duty has been done!

186

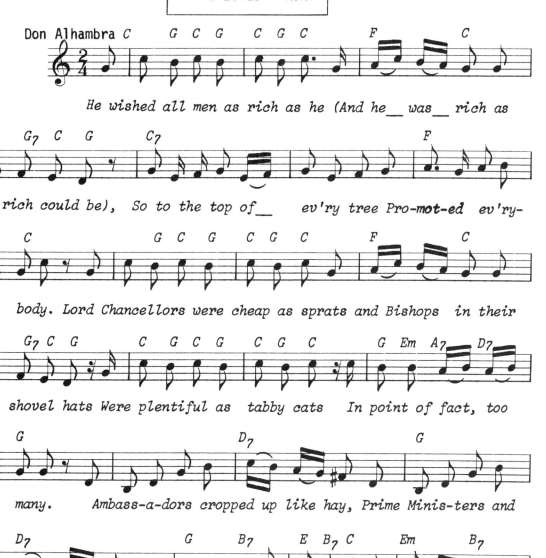

THERE LIVED A KING

Don Alhambra

He wished all men as rich as he (And he__ was__ rich as

rich could be), So to the top of__ ev'ry tree Pro-**mot-ed** ev'ry-

body. Lord Chancellors were cheap as sprats and Bishops in their

shovel hats Were plentiful as tabby cats In point of fact, too

many. Ambass-a-dors cropped up like hay, Prime Minis-ters and

such as__ they grew like aspara - gus in May and Dukes were three a

penny. In short whoever you may be, To this con-clusion

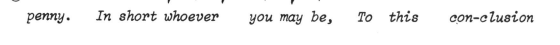

187

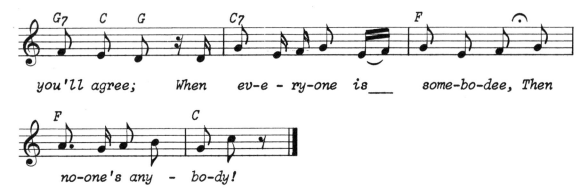

you'll agree; When ev-e - ry-one is___ some-bo-dee, Then

no-one's any - bo-dy!

THE ROYAL PRINCE

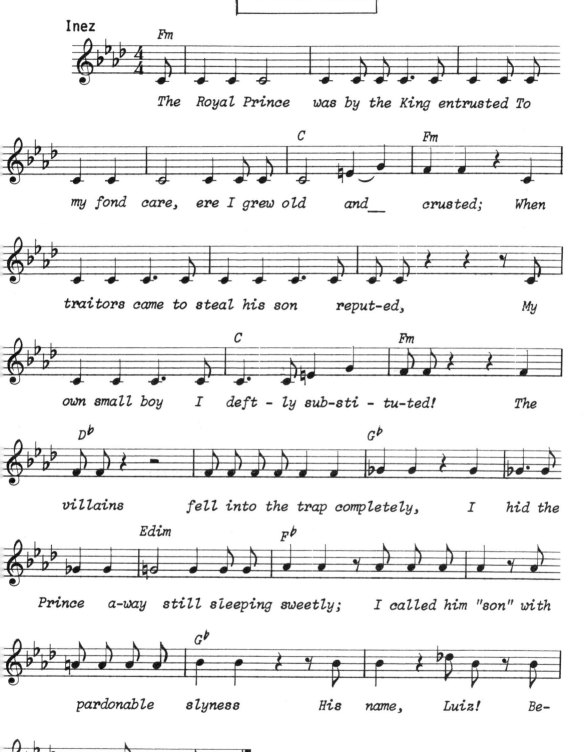

Inez

Fm

The Royal Prince was by the King entrusted To

C   Fm

my fond care, ere I grew old and__ crusted; When

traitors came to steal his son reput-ed, My

C   Fm

own small boy I deft - ly sub-sti - tu-ted! The

Db   Gb

villains fell into the trap completely, I hid the

Edim   Fb

Prince a-way still sleeping sweetly; I called him "son" with

Gb

pardonable slyness His name, Luiz! Be-

hold his Royal Highness!

189

HAIL, O KING OF A GOLDEN LAND

All

Hail, O King of a Gold-en Land, And the high-born bride who claims his hand. The past is dead, and you gain your own, A roy - al crown and a gold-en throne!__ Once more__ gondo-

Gondoliers

lieri Both skilful and wa-ry__ Free from this quan - da-ry, Con-tented are we.__ Ah_____

From roy - al-ty flying, Our gondolas

190

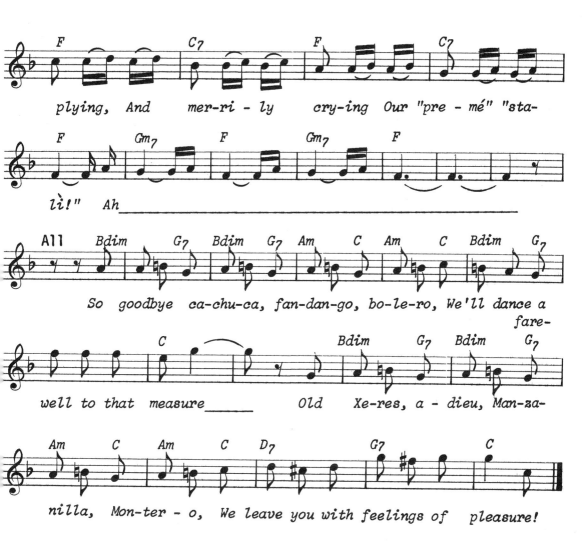

plying, And mer-ri-ly cry-ing Our "pre-mé" "sta-

lì!" Ah _____

All So goodbye ca-chu-ca, fan-dan-go, bo-le-ro, We'll dance a fare-

well to that measure _____ Old Xe-res, a-dieu, Man-za-

nilla, Mon-ter-o, We leave you with feelings of pleasure!

PATIENCE

The story of

PATIENCE

About 1880, London was caught up in an "aesthetic" craze. Young men grew their hair long and wore knee breeches, and young women dressed in flowing robes. They wrote poetry, idolized their favorite poets, and met for discussions of "High Art."

In this operetta, a number of young maidens are in love with Reginald Bunthorne, a most "aesthetic" poet, but he does not return their affection. Instead, Bunthorne's fancy has lighted on Patience, the village milkmaid, who admits that she has never been in love and questions its desirable qualities. The maidens find this difficult to understand, for they are always in love. A year ago, in fact, they were all engaged to Dragoons, whom they jilted for Bunthorne.

Bunthorne, left alone, confesses that he is an aesthetic sham—his affectation is born of a morbid craving for admiration. He makes poetic advances to Patience, who is not at all responsive. Later, however, Patience comes to the conclusion that love is a duty and must be completely unselfish; she decides she must fall in love at once. Just at this moment, Archibald Grosvenor, also a poet, appears, and Patience recognizes him as her childhood playmate of fifteen years ago. Although she wants to love Archibald, she decides it is her duty to marry Bunthorne, for whom she has no desire whatsoever, and so could love unselfishly. The Dragoons, meanwhile, make an unsuccessful attempt to become aesthetic in the hope of winning back the maidens, who now have fastened their affections on Archibald (all except one, Jane, who remains faithful to Bunthorne).

Bunthorne decides to reform and be a perfect being, free from vanities of any kind; whereupon Patience tells him that she cannot marry him because there would be nothing unselfish in loving such a perfect being. She can now marry Archibald, who discards his aesthetic ways to become a commonplace, matter-of-fact young man. The maidens find suitors among the Dragoons, even the faithful Jane, and that leaves nobody to be Bunthorne's bride.

PATIENCE

Or, Bunthorne's Bride

Characters

PATIENCE, *a dairy maid*
REGINALD BUNTHORNE, *a fleshly poet*
ARCHIBALD GROSVENOR, *an idyllic poet*
COLONEL CALVERLEY ⎫
MAJOR MURGATROYD ⎬ *officers of Dragoon Guards*
DUKE OF DUNSTABLE ⎭
LADY ANGELA ⎫
LADY SAPHIR ⎪
LADY ELLA ⎬ *rapturous maidens*
LADY JANE ⎭
DRAGOON GUARDS
RAPTUROUS MAIDENS

SCENE 1

TIME: *1880.*

SETTING: *Exterior of Bunthorne Castle and castle garden. A terraced walk extends across rear of stage with steps descending to garden. Formal shrubs and pedestals holding large vases of flowers are set about garden. Garden bench is down right and another is down left. Wrought-iron fence with arched gateway is at left. Entrance to castle is right through an arch.*

AT RISE: ANGELA, SAPHIR, ELLA, JANE *and other* MAIDENS, *dressed in Grecian costumes, are grouped about garden, posing like Greek statues. Some are playing lyres and mandolins, and all are in a mood of despair.*

MAIDENS (*Singing*):
> Twenty lovesick maidens we,
> Lovesick all against our will.

195

> Twenty years hence we shall be
> Twenty lovesick maidens still.
> All our love is all for one,
> Yet that love he heedeth not.
> He is coy and cares for none,
> Sad and sorry is our lot.
> Ah, miserie!

ANGELA (*Speaking to others*): How strange it is that there is no jealousy among us, though we all love the same man, Reginald Bunthorne.

ELLA (*Sighing*): That's because our love is as interesting to him as taxes.

SAPHIR: Would that it were! He pays his taxes.

ANGELA: And cherishes the receipts.

ELLA: He is a poet and lives in a world of poetic fancy. Love means nothing to him.

JANE: You're wrong. I've discovered that Bunthorne is wildly in love with Patience, the village milkmaid.

MAIDENS (*Aghast*): Patience! A milkmaid!

JANE: Yesterday I caught him in her dairy, eating fresh butter with a tablespoon. Today he is not well.

SAPHIR: But Patience boasts that she has never loved. Oh, he can't be serious! (PATIENCE *enters up left on terrace, swinging a milk pail.*)

ELLA (*Looking up*): It's Patience. Happy girl—loved by a poet!

PATIENCE: Your pardon, ladies—I intrude upon you.

ANGELA: No, pretty child, come here. (PATIENCE *descends steps to garden.*) Is it true that you have never loved?

PATIENCE: Most true. (*Singing*)

> I cannot tell what this love may be
> That cometh to all, but not to me.
> It cannot be kind as they'd imply,
> Or why do these ladies sigh?
> It cannot be joy and rapture deep,
> Or why do these gentle ladies weep?
> It cannot be blissful as 'tis said,
> Or why are their eyes so wondrous red?
> Though everywhere true love I see
> A-coming to all but not to me,
> I cannot tell what this love may be!
> For I am blithe and I am gay,
> While they sit sighing night and day.
> Think of the gulf 'twixt them and me,
> "Fa la la la!"—and "Miserie!"

ANGELA: Ah, Patience, if you have never loved, you have never known true happiness. (*Turning to* MAIDENS) Come, it is time to sing our morning carol outside Bunthorne's door.

PATIENCE: Wait—I have news for you! The Thirty-Fifth Dragoon Guards have halted in the village, and they are on their way here to see you.

SAPHIR (*Disdainfully*): We care nothing for Dragoons. They are dull and unpoetic.

PATIENCE: Bless me, you were all engaged to them a year ago!

ANGELA: A year ago, they suited us very well, but since then our tastes have changed. Come, ladies, let us go and waken Bunthorne with music. (MAIDENS *exit right into castle, singing refrain of* "Twenty Lovesick Maidens We," *accompanying themselves on their instruments.* PATIENCE *watches them go off, then laughs lightheartedly and exits left. Martial music is heard.* DRAGOON GUARDS *enter at rear of auditorium, led by* MAJOR MURGATROYD. *They march down aisle and up onto stage, where they fall into formation, marking time.*)

DRAGOONS (*Singing as they march*):
>   The soldiers of our Queen
>   Are linked in friendly tether;
>   Upon the battle scene
>   They fight the foe together.
>   There every mother's son
>   Prepared to fight and fall is;
>   The enemy of one
>   The enemy of all is!

MAJOR (*Barking command*): Halt! Make ready for inspection by Colonel Calverley. (DRAGOONS *adjust tunics, straighten hats, tighten sword belts, etc.* MAJOR *whips out handkerchief and, putting one foot and then the other on a bench, dusts his boots, blows his nose, and awaits the arrival of* COLONEL CALVERLEY. COLONEL *enters up right on terrace, comes downstage and inspects* DRAGOONS *with approval.*)

COLONEL: Ah, there's nothing like a Heavy Dragoon. There never was and there never will be. And *what* a mysterious mixture he is! (*Sings with vigor*)
>   If you want a receipt for that popular mystery,
>   Known to the world as a Heavy Dragoon,
>   Take all the remarkable people in history,
>   Rattle them off to a popular tune.
>   The pluck of Lord Nelson on board of the *Victory*—
>   Genius of Bismark devising a plan—
>   The humor of Fielding (which sounds contradictory)—
>   Force of Mephisto pronouncing a ban—
>   The science of Jullien, the eminent musico—
>   Wit of Macaulay, who wrote of Queen Anne—
>   The pathos of Paddy, as rendered by Boucicault—
>   Style of the Bishop of Sodor and Man—
>   The genius strategic of Caesar or Hannibal—
>   Skill of Sir Garnet in thrashing a cannibal—
>   Flavor of Hamlet—Othello, a touch of him—
>   Thomas Aquinas (but not very much of him)—

Tupper and Tennyson—Daniel Defoe—
Mr. Micawber and Madame Tussaud!
Take of these elements all that is fusible,
Melt them all down in a pipkin or crucible,
Set them to simmer and take off the scum,
And a Heavy Dragoon is the residuum!

DRAGOONS (*Singing*):
Yes! yes! yes! yes!
A Heavy Dragoon is the residuum!

COLONEL: Well, here we are once more on the scene of our former triumphs. But where's the Duke? (DUKE OF DUNSTABLE *enters listlessly through gateway left.*)

DUKE: Here I am. (*Sighs*)

COLONEL: Come, cheer up, Your Grace.

DUKE: How can I be cheerful when I have the misfortune to be a duke with an income of a thousand pounds a day? All my life I have known nothing but flattery and adulation. Great heavens, what is there to adulate in me?

DRAGOONS: Good lord, nothing!

DUKE: Am I particularly intelligent?

DRAGOONS: No!

DUKE: Or remarkably accomplished?

DRAGOONS: I should say not!

DUKE: Or excruciatingly witty?

DRAGOONS: Witty! (*Jeering laughter*) Ha, ha, ha!

COLONEL: You are about as commonplace a young man as ever I saw.

DUKE: That describes me to a T. Well, I couldn't stand it any longer, so I joined this second-class cavalry regiment.

DRAGOONS (*Outraged*) : What! (*They half-draw their swords.*)

DUKE (*Hastily*) : I figured that in the army I might be snubbed or even bullied, and that would be a welcome change—so, here I am.

COLONEL (*Looking toward castle*) : Yes—and here are the ladies. (ANGELA, SAPHIR, ELLA, JANE *and other* MAIDENS *enter from castle with* BUNTHORNE.)

MAJOR: But why are they dressed like that?

DUKE: And who is the odd-looking gentleman with them? (BUNTHORNE *is in the throes of composing a poem, writing in gold notebook with gold pencil. He clutches his brow, rolls his eyes upward, beats his chest, as he walks across stage and up onto terrace.* MAIDENS *trail after him with arms extended beseechingly, ignoring* DRAGOONS, *who react with surprise and indignation.*)

COLONEL: Angela! What is the meaning of this? What in the world has come over all of you?

ANGELA (*Pointing rapturously*) : Bunthorne! *He* has come over us! (BUNTHORNE *suddenly springs forward and grabs a handful of air.*)

BUNTHORNE: I have it! I've found the word I wanted! (*Writes feverishly*) Finis! My poem is finished at last! (*Staggers, as if overcome with the mental strain.* MAIDENS *support him.*)

ANGELA: Will you please read your poem to us, Reginald?

SAPHIR: This we supplicate. (MAIDENS *kneel.*)

BUNTHORNE: Shall I?

DRAGOONS (*Shouting*): *No!*

BUNTHORNE (*Jumping; startled*): It is a wild, weird, fleshly thing—yet very tender, very yearning. It is called "Oh, Hollow! Hollow! Hollow!" (*Recites with exaggerated passion*)
>
> What time the poet hath hymned
> The writhing maid, lithe-limbed,
> Quivering on amaranthine asphodel,
> How can he paint her woes,
> Knowing, as well he knows,
> That all can be set right with calomel?

(*Choked with emotion,* BUNTHORNE *exits up right.* MAIDENS *rise.*)

SAPHIR: How purely fragrant!

ELLA: How earnestly precious!

DUKE: It sounds to me like nonsense.

COLONEL (*Speaking to* MAIDENS): See here, you seem to forget that you are all engaged to us.

JANE: We *were* engaged—but now it can never be. Look at your uniforms—red and yellow! Primary colors! Unaesthetic and ordinary! Come, ladies. (MAIDENS *exit disdainfully up left.* DRAGOONS *watch in astonishment.*)

COLONEL: Gentlemen, this is an insult to the British uniform! (*He sings.*)
>
> When I first put this uniform on,
> I said, as I looked in the glass:
> "Now every beauty will feel it her duty
> To yield to its glamor and class.
> They will see that I'm freely gold-laced
> In a uniform handsome and chaste"—
> But the peripatetics of long-haired aesthetics
> Are very much more to their taste—
> Which I never counted upon,
> When I first put this uniform on!

DRAGOONS (*Singing*) :

>By a simple coincidence, few
>Could ever have counted upon,
>I didn't anticipate that,
>When I first put this uniform on!

(*All march off through gateway left.* BUNTHORNE *enters, and after looking about to make sure he is alone, his manner changes completely. He drops his aesthetic pose and reveals himself as an ordinary young man.*)

BUNTHORNE: Am I alone and unobserved? I am! Then let me own I'm an aesthetic sham! This air severe is but a mere veneer! I confess my manner is an affectation born of a morbid love of admiration. (*Sings*)

>If you're anxious for to shine in the high aesthetic line
>   as a man of culture rare,
>You must get up all the germs of the transcendental
>   terms, and plant them everywhere.
>You must lie upon the daisies and discourse in novel
>   phrases of your complicated state of mind,
>The meaning doesn't matter if it's only idle chatter of
>   a transcendental kind.
>And every one will say, as you walk your mystic way,
>"If this young man expresses himself in terms too
>   deep for *me*,
>Why, what a very singularly deep young man this
>   deep young man must be!"
>Then a sentimental passion of a vegetable fashion
>   must excite your languid spleen,
>An attachment à la Plato for a bashful young potato,
>   or a not-too-French French bean!
>Though the Philistines may jostle, you will rank as an
>   apostle in the high aesthetic band,
>If you walk down Piccadilly with a poppy or a lily in
>   your medieval hand.

(BUNTHORNE *illustrates by taking lily from buttonhole and walking mincingly with flower held in front of his nose*)

And every one will say, as you walk your flowery way,
"If he's content with a vegetable love which would
certainly not suit *me*,
Why, what a most particularly pure young man this
pure young man must be!"
(PATIENCE *enters, and* BUNTHORNE *quickly resumes his artificial mannerisms.*) Ah, Patience, come hither. (*She ap-
proaches cautiously.*) I am pleased with thee, for you are not
hollow. *Are* you?

PATIENCE: No, thanks, I have dined.

BUNTHORNE: Tell me, girl, do you ever yearn?

PATIENCE (*Misunderstanding him*): Oh, yes, sir! I earn my living.

BUNTHORNE (*Impatiently*): No, no! Do you know what it is to be
heart-hungry? To seek oceans and to find only puddles? That
is my case. (*Sinking tragically on bench*) Oh, I am a cursèd
thing!

PATIENCE (*Nervously*): If you please, sir, I don't understand
you. You frighten me.

BUNTHORNE (*Leaping to feet, seizing her hand*): I don't want to
frighten you. I only want to love you—and have you love me.
Would that be too hard for you?

PATIENCE (*Pulling her hand away*): I'm afraid it would. I have
never loved anyone but my great-aunt. She told me that love
must be unselfish, that it is the highest kind of duty. So I'm
quite sure that I couldn't possibly love *you*.

BUNTHORNE (*Melodramatically*): Very well. Life is henceforth
a blank. I don't care what becomes of me. Broken-hearted
and desolate I go. Farewell, Patience! (*He rushes into castle
with a sob.*)

PATIENCE (*Bewildered*): What on earth does it all mean? Everyone talks of love. If love *is* the highest form of duty, as my
great-aunt said, then it's my *duty* to fall in love. I'll go at
once and fall in love with—let me see—with—(*Stops as*
ARCHIBALD GROSVENOR *enters through archway.*) A
stranger!

GROSVENOR (*Removing hat, bowing and crossing to* PATIENCE;
singing):
>Prithee, pretty maiden—prithee, tell me true,
>(Hey, but I'm doleful, willow willow waly!)
>Have you e'er a lover a-dangling after you?
>Hey willow waly O!
>I would fain discover
>If you have a lover?
>Hey willow waly O!

PATIENCE (*Singing*):
>Gentle sir, my heart is frolicsome and free—
>(Hey, but he's doleful, willow willow waly!)
>Nobody I care for comes a-courting me—
>Hey willow waly O!
>Nobody I care for
>Comes a-courting—therefore,
>Hey willow waly O!

GROSVENOR (*Singing*):
>Prithee, pretty maiden, will you marry me?
>(Hey, but I'm hopeful, willow willow waly!)
>I may say, at once, I'm a man of propertee—
>Hey willow waly O!
>Money, I despise it;
>Many people prize it.
>Hey willow waly O!

PATIENCE (*Singing*):
>Gentle sir, although to marry I design—
>(Hey, but he's hopeful, willow willow waly!)

As yet I do not know you, and so I must decline,
Hey willow waly O!
To other maidens go you—
As yet I do not know you,
Hey willow waly O!

GROSVENOR: Patience, can it be that you don't recognize me? Have fifteen years so greatly changed me?

PATIENCE: Fifteen years? (*Peering into his face*) You're not—you can't be—

GROSVENOR: Archibald—Archibald Grosvenor, the friend of your childhood, your little playmate.

PATIENCE (*Delighted*): Archie! Is it possible? I thought we should never see each other again. How you've grown!

GROSVENOR: Yes, Patience, I am much taller than I was at the age of five.

PATIENCE: And how you've improved! You're very handsome.

GROSVENOR (*Sadly*): Alas, yes.

PATIENCE: Surely that doesn't make you unhappy? Why?

GROSVENOR: It is my fate to be loved at first sight by every woman I meet. And yet, for fifteen years I have loved only you.

PATIENCE: Oh, Archibald, until this moment I have been deaf to the voice of love—but now, to be loved by so beautiful a person—it is ecstasy! (*He starts to embrace her, but she holds him off as a sudden thought strikes her.*) Wait! Love should be unselfish. It would be pure selfishness on my part to take you from all the other women who adore you. My duty tells me it wouldn't be right—so we must part.

GROSVENOR: Oh, misery! If only I were a shade less beautiful than I am!

PATIENCE: But, Archibald, although I may not love you—for you are perfection—there's nothing to prevent you from loving *me*. I am quite plain. The love of such a man as you for such a girl as I would be totally unselfish.

GROSVENOR: That's true.

PATIENCE (*Singing*):
　　　Though to marry you would very selfish be—

GROSVENOR (*Singing*):
　　　Hey, but I'm doleful—willow willow waly!

PATIENCE (*Singing*):
　　　You may, all the same, continue loving me—

GROSVENOR (*Singing*):
　　　Hey willow waly O!

PATIENCE *and* GROSVENOR (*Singing*):
　　　All the world ignoring,
　　　You'll/I'll go on adoring—
　　　Hey willow waly O!
(*They exit, despairingly, in opposite directions.* ANGELA, ELLA, *and* SAPHIR *enter from castle, leading* BUNTHORNE *by rose garlands with which he is draped. Crown of roses is on his head. He carries a small table that holds a flowered top hat and cash box.* MAIDENS *follow, dancing classically and playing on their instruments.* JANE *brings up the rear with large cymbals which she clashes in time to the music.* COLONEL, MAJOR, DUKE *and* DRAGOONS *enter left, attracted by noise.*)

DRAGOONS (*Ad lib*): What does this mean? Why is the poet arrayed in that fashion? Is it a wedding? They can't *all* marry him! (*Etc.* PATIENCE *enters on terrace unobserved.*)

BUNTHORNE (*Setting down table, motioning for silence*): Gentlemen, I am a heartbroken man. My own choice, Patience, does not want me. These ladies do. So I've put myself up to be raffled off. The raffle tickets are in this hat. (*Shows tickets in top hat, giving them a shake, then opens cash box*) Come, dear ladies, pay half a guinea and you may win a husband! Pay half a guinea and you may draw him in a lottery! Such an opportunity may not occur again! (MAIDENS *crowd about* BUNTHORNE *to buy tickets.*)

PATIENCE (*On terrace, calling out*): Hold! Stop the lottery!

BUNTHORNE: She's changed her mind—she wants a ticket! (*Runs to* PATIENCE *with hat*) Take a dozen!

PATIENCE: I've thought it over, Mr. Bunthorne, and if you still desire me, I will be your bride.

MAIDENS (*Ad lib; angrily*): Brazen hussy! Shameless vixen! Bold-faced thing! (*Etc.*)

PATIENCE (*Speaking to* MAIDENS): Let me explain! True love must be unselfish! True love must not think of happiness for itself—that would be vanity. (*Turning to* BUNTHORNE) And so, Mr. Bunthorne, in marrying you, I have no thought of happiness or gain. I will simply devote myself to you in complete unselfishness. (BUNTHORNE *puts his arm around her and they exit up left.*)

ANGELA (*Philosophically, to* MAIDENS): Oh, well, we still have our old loves. (MAIDENS *gaze fondly at* DRAGOONS, *who clear their throats and straighten their uniforms. As* MAIDENS *move to* DRAGOONS, GROSVENOR *enters up right on terrace, reading a book of poetry. He takes no notice of others but comes down steps and sits on bench, right, still reading.* MAIDENS *are fascinated by him and gradually withdraw from* DRAGOONS.)

ANGELA: Who is this, whose godlike grace proclaims he comes of noble race?

GROSVENOR (*Lowering book*): I am a melancholy troubadour whose mind is aesthetic and whose tastes are poetic.

ANGELA: Aesthetic!

SAPHIR: And poetic!

MAIDENS (*In one voice and motion, kneeling*): Then, we love you!

GROSVENOR (*Rising*): Alas, my fatal beauty! (*Tries to walk away, but* MAIDENS *cling to his legs and feet.*)

MAIDENS: We love you, we love you!

DRAGOONS: They love him!

GROSVENOR: They love me!

DRAGOONS *and* GROSVENOR (*Exclaiming together*): Horror! Horror! Horror! (*Fast curtain*)

*   *   *   *   *

SCENE 2

TIME: *A few days later.*

SETTING: *The same as Scene 1. Lottery table, hat and cash box have been removed.*

AT RISE: JANE *is seated on bench, left, leaning thoughtfully against a cello.*

JANE: The fickle crew have deserted Reginald and sworn allegiance to his rival, Archibald. But I have not deserted him— and when he grows weary of that wishy-washy milkmaid, I shall reap my reward. But do not dally too long, Reginald, for my charms are fading. (*Sings, accompanying herself on cello*)

> Silvered is the raven hair,
> Spreading is the parting straight,
> Mottled the complexion fair,
> Halting is the youthful gait;

Stouter than I used to be,
Still more corpulent grow I—
There will be too much of me
In the coming by and by!

(JANE *sighs and goes into castle, carrying cello awkwardly in both arms.* GROSVENOR *enters up left on terrace, followed by* ANGELA, SAPHIR, ELLA *and* MAIDENS. *He is reading and pays no attention to them.*)

MAIDENS (*Singing as they follow* GROSVENOR *across terrace and down into garden*):
Turn, oh, turn in this direction,
Shed, oh, shed a gentle smile,
With a glance of sad perfection
Our poor fainting hearts beguile!

GROSVENOR (*Stopping and facing* MAIDENS): Ladies, it is best to speak plainly. I know that I am loved by you, but I can never love you in return, for my heart is given elsewhere. Remember the fable of the Magnet and the Churn. (*Singing*)
A magnet hung in a hardware shop,
And all around was a loving crop
Of scissors and needles, nails and knives,
Offering love for all their lives;
But for iron the magnet felt no whim,
Though he charmed iron, it charmed not him,
From needles and nails and knives he'd turn,
For he'd set his love on a silver churn!
His most aesthetic, very magnetic
Fancy took this turn—
"If I can wheedle a knife or needle,
Why not a silver churn?"
And iron and steel expressed surprise,
The needles opened their well-drilled eyes,
The pen-knives felt "shut up," no doubt,
The scissors declared themselves "cut out,"
The kettles they boiled with rage, 'tis said,
While every nail went off its head,

And hither and thither began to roam,
Till a hammer came up—and drove them home.
While this magnetic, peripatetic
Lover he lived to learn,
By no endeavor, can magnet ever
Attract a silver churn!

(GROSVENOR *speaks to* MAIDENS) Ladies, I am sorry to distress you, but you have been following me about ever since Monday, and this is Saturday. I should like the usual half-holiday, if you please. (*Sits on left bench and returns to his reading.* MAIDENS *reluctantly exit into castle.* GROSVENOR *sighs in relief.*) At last they're gone! (PATIENCE *enters up right on terrace and runs to* GROSVENOR.)

PATIENCE: Oh, Archibald, I wanted to see you so much—to ask you if you still love me as fondly as ever?

GROSVENOR (*Rising, seizing her hand*): Love you! If the devotion of a lifetime—

PATIENCE (*Indignantly, withdrawing her hand*): Sir, pray remember that I am another's! (*Tenderly*) But you *do* love me, don't you?

GROSVENOR: Madly, hopelessly, despairingly!

PATIENCE: That's right! I can never be yours—but that's right!

GROSVENOR: And do you love this Bunthorne?

PATIENCE: I am miserable with him—but I love him because it is my duty.

GROSVENOR: That's right! I can never be yours—but that's right!

BUNTHORNE (*Offstage, calling*): Patience! Where are you?

PATIENCE: It's Bunthorne! He mustn't find us together! (GROSVENOR *hurries off left, while* PATIENCE *runs into castle.* BUNTHORNE *and* JANE *enter on terrace.*)

BUNTHORNE: Patience! She's not here. She's probably off somewhere with that fellow Grosvenor. (*He comes downstage and sits on garden bench, complaining peevishly.*) Everything has gone wrong with me since that smug-faced idiot came here. Before that I was admired.

JANE (*Kneeling beside him*): No—adored!

BUNTHORNE: The damozels used to follow me everywhere—now they follow him!

JANE: Not all! I am still faithful to you.

BUNTHORNE (*Rising, crossing to center*): But I am not beaten yet! It's his confounded simplicity they like. Well, if they want insipid stuff, they shall have it! I'll meet this fellow on his own ground and prove I can be ten times as simple as he is!

JANE (*Briskly, joining* BUNTHORNE): And I will help you! (*Singing*)
> So go to him and say to him, with compliment ironical—

BUNTHORNE (*Singing, facing audience as if addressing* GROSVENOR *with contempt*):
> Sing "Hey to you—good day to you"—
> And that's what I shall say!

JANE (*Singing*):
> "Your style is much too sanctified—your cut is too canonical"—

BUNTHORNE (*Singing*):
> Sing "Bah to you—ha! ha! to you"—
> And that's what I shall say!

JANE (*Singing*):
> "I was the beau ideal of the morbid young aesthetical—

To doubt my inspiration was regarded as heretical—
Until you cut me out with your placidity emetical."

BUNTHORNE (*Singing*):
Sing "Booh to you—pooh, pooh to you"—
And that's what I shall say!

JANE *and* BUNTHORNE (*Singing*):
Sing "Hey to you, good day to you"—
Sing "Bah to you, ha! ha! to you"—
Sing "Booh to you, pooh, pooh to you"—
And that's what you/I shall say!
(BUNTHORNE *and* JANE *dance offstage together into castle.*
COLONEL, MAJOR *and* DUKE *enter through archway, carry-
ing respectively a sunflower, a poppy, and an orchid. They
have changed their uniforms for costumes similar to* BUN-
THORNE'S. *As they walk, they stop and pose, imitating with-
out much success* BUNTHORNE'S *aesthetic movements and
poses.*)

COLONEL: It's quite clear that our only chance of making a lasting
impression on these young ladies is to become as aesthetic as
Bunthorne and Grosvenor are. (*Striking ludicrous poses as
he speaks*)
You hold yourself like this—
(*Shields eyes with sunflower and looks right, leaning
forward at waist*)
Then you hold yourself like that.
(*Faces front, extends flower at arm's length with left
hand, right hand on heart*)
By hook and crook you try to look both angular and
flat.

MAJOR (*Posing with head thrown backward, gazing at poppy
dangling from his hand*): I wonder if this is effective enough
—at a distance.

DUKE (*Sitting on bench and posing, shoulders drooping, one hand
pressed to his bowed head*): I don't like it, I never did. I do
it—but I don't like it.

COLONEL: My good friend, it's not a question of whether *we* like it, but whether *they* do. (*Voices are heard off right.*) Oh, here they come! 'Ten-*shun!* (*All three carry out a change of posture with military precision:* COLONEL *points left toe forward, holds sunflower under chin with right hand, and lifts left hand, palm upward;* MAJOR *steps back and covers eyes with arm as if seeing an apparition;* DUKE *stands, raises one hand to heaven, holds out other hand appealingly, with an attempt at a look of love and tenderness.* ANGELA *and* SAPHIR *enter from castle.*)

ANGELA: Oh, Saphir, look! The immortal fire has descended on them and they are now converted to High Art.

SAPHIR (*Clasping hands in admiration*): Ah, yes! How utterly Botticellian they are, how intensely Fra Angelican! (*Officers are having difficulty maintaining strained attitudes.*)

COLONEL (*Apologetically*): I'm afraid we're not quite right.

ANGELA: Oh, it's extremely good—for beginners. (*Officers assume still more absurd postures:* COLONEL *places one hand on heart, other hand on brow, opens his eyes wide and stares overhead;* MAJOR *places index finger in front of lips and leans forward confidentially to poppy, held in other hand;* DUKE *stands on tiptoe, touches hands overhead to make large circle with arms, turns torso left and smiles.*)

COLONEL: Ladies, we are doing this in order to express our devotion to you. We hope our efforts are not in vain.

ANGELA: We are deeply touched—aren't we, Saphir?—and our hearts may—*may*, mind you!—once again be yours.

COLONEL (*As if giving a command*): By sections of three—rapture! (*Officers strike identical attitudes expressive of rapture: they go down on one knee, raise both hands in a big gesture of adoration, then clasp hands in front of chest, and smile ecstatically.* ANGELA *and* SAPHIR *applaud. Officers relax and rise.*)

MAJOR: The only question is, who will marry whom?

COLONEL: It's perfectly simple. Suppose the Duke chooses Angela and I take Saphir, then the Major takes nobody. Or suppose the Duke chooses Saphir and the Major takes Angela, then *I* take nobody. But if the Duke chooses neither, then I take Angela and the Major takes Saphir. It's as clear as day! (*All link arms and exit left, laughing.* BUNTHORNE *enters gloomily from castle.*)

BUNTHORNE: It's no use—I can't live without admiration. I must think of some way to win back the affection of my ladies. (GROSVENOR *enters left on terrace.*) Ah, there's my rival! (*Calling out*) Grosvenor! I want to speak to you!

GROSVENOR (*Coming down into garden*): Yes, Bunthorne, what is it?

BUNTHORNE: Ever since you came here, you have monopolized the attentions of my young ladies—*my* young ladies, do you hear?

GROSVENOR: My dear sir, your young ladies are the plague of my life. I'd give anything to escape their unwelcome attentions.

BUNTHORNE: I know how you can escape them.

GROSVENOR (*Shaking* BUNTHORNE'S *hand*): Tell me, old chap, and you'll have my everlasting gratitude!

BUNTHORNE: Very well, it's this: You must make a complete change—at once. You must cut your hair and stop reciting poetry. Your conversation must be perfectly matter-of-fact. In appearance and costume, you must be absolutely commonplace.

GROSVENOR (*Enthusiastically*): By all that's commonplace, I'll do it! (*Singing, as he performs some fancy steps*)
    A commonplace young man,
    A matter-of-fact young man,

A steady and stolid-y, jolly Bank-holiday,
Every-day young man! (*Dances off through arch-way*)

BUNTHORNE (*Rubbing hands together in glee*): Good! Now I shall be popular again! My ladies will return to me. (*Sings and dances exuberantly*)
A most intense young man,
A soulful-eyed young man,
An ultra-poetical, super-aesthetical,
Out-of-the-way young man!
(PATIENCE *enters up left on terrace and stares in astonishment at* BUNTHORNE.)

PATIENCE: Reginald! *Dancing?*

BUNTHORNE (*Bounding up steps to terrace*): Patience, I'm a new man! I have reformed! Henceforth I shall be amiable and cheerful. (*Assumes fixed smile*) I shall be pastoral. In short, I shall be a perfect being.

PATIENCE: Is it quite certain that you have reformed—that you are free from defect of any kind?

BUNTHORNE: I have sworn it.

PATIENCE: Then I cannot marry you, Reginald, because love must be unselfish—and to marry so perfect a being as you have become would be most selfish of me. (*She walks away into garden.* GROSVENOR, ANGELA, ELLA, SAPHIR, MAIDENS *and* DRAGOONS *enter from right and left in a happy mood.* GROSVENOR *has removed long-haired wig and wears bowler hat. He is dressed in ordinary suit.* ANGELA, ELLA, SAPHIR *and* MAIDENS *are dressed in fashionable dresses of the period.*)

GROSVENOR (*Singing*):
I'm a commonplace young man,
A matter-of-fact young man,
A steady and stolid-y, jolly Bank-holiday,
Every-day young man!

MAIDENS (*Singing*):
>   We're stylish, elite young girls,
>   We're popular, chic young girls,
>   We're prettily pattering, cheerily chattering,
>   Every-day young girls!

BUNTHORNE (*Speaking from terrace*): Angela—Ella—Saphir—
what does this mean? (JANE, *still in Grecian costume, enters
on terrace and stands to one side watching.*)

ANGELA: It means that if Archibald says it's the right thing to be
commonplace, then we will be commonplace, too.

PATIENCE: Archibald, is it quite, quite certain that you will *always* be a commonplace young man?

GROSVENOR: Always and forever.

PATIENCE: Why, then, there's nothing to prevent my loving you
with all the fervor at my command. (*Holding out arms*) My
Archie!

GROSVENOR: My Patience! (*They embrace.*)

BUNTHORNE (*Tragically*): Deserted by all! (JANE *goes to* BUN-
THORNE.)

JANE: I'm still here, Reginald. I have never left you and I never
will.

BUNTHORNE: Thank you, Jane. (*Putting arm around her waist*)
After all, there's no denying you're a fine figure of a woman.
(*Fanfare is heard.* COLONEL, DUKE *and* MAJOR *enter left;
they have changed back into their military uniforms.*)

COLONEL: Ladies, the Duke has finally decided to choose a bride.
(*General excitement.*)

DUKE: Dear ladies, in personal beauty, you have all that is necessary to make a woman happy. Therefore, I think it's only

fair that I should choose the one lady among you who is distinctly plain. (*Turning upstage, extends his hand.*) Lady Jane!

JANE: Oh, Your Grace! (*Without hesitation, she leaves* BUNTHORNE *and runs to* DUKE.)

BUNTHORNE (*Utterly disgusted*): Deserted again!

DUKE (*Singing*):
> After much debate internal,
> I on Lady Jane decide,
> Saphir now may take the Colonel,
> Angie be the Major's bride!

(SAPHIR *pairs off with* COLONEL, ANGELA *with* MAJOR, ELLA *with a* DRAGOON. OTHER MAIDENS *pair off with* DRAGOONS.)

BUNTHORNE (*Singing*):
> In that case unprecedented,
> Single I must live and die—
> I shall have to be contented
> With a tulip or li*ly!* [*Rhymes with "die"*]

(BUNTHORNE *takes lily from buttonhole and gazes at it affectionately.*)

ALL (*Singing*):
> He will have to be contented
> With a tulip or li*ly!*
> Greatly pleased with one another,
> To be married we decide,
> Each of us will wed the other,
> Nobody be Bunthorne's Bride!

(*All dance. Curtain*)

THE END

Characters: 5 male; 5 female; male and female extras for Dragoons and Maidens.

Playing Time: 30 minutes.

Costumes: Patience wears pretty hat and dress, suitable for country girl. Angela, Saphir, Ella, Jane and Maidens wear Grecian costumes until end of Scene 2, when all but Jane change into fashionable dresses and hats of the period. Bunthorne wears velvet jacket and knee-breeches, loose silk shirt with flowing tie, and has white lily in his buttonhole. His hair is long. Grosvenor is dressed much like Bunthorne, with long-haired wig and hat. At end of Scene 2, he appears in business suit, bowler hat and short hair. Colonel, Major, Duke and Dragoons wear appropriate military uniforms. In Scene 2, Colonel, Major and Duke change into costumes similar to Bunthorne's, with hats and long-haired wigs, then change back to uniforms.

Properties: Lyres, mandolins or guitars; cymbals; cello; milkpail; handkerchief; golden notebook and pencil, rose garlands and crown of roses; small table with top hat, raffle tickets and cash box; coins; book; sunflower, poppy, orchid, lily.

Setting: Exterior of Bunthorne Castle and castle garden. Terraced walk extends across rear of stage with steps descending to garden, which has formal shrubs and pedestals holding large vases of flowers and plants set about it. Garden benches are down right and left. Wrought-iron fence with an arched gateway is at left. Entrance to castle is right, through an arch. Entrances are also made from terrace.

Lighting: No special effects.

Sound: Fanfare, as indicated in text.

Music for songs on following pages.

218

Maidens

Twenty lovesick maidens we   Lovesick all against our

will.   Twenty years hence we shall be   Twenty   lovesick maidens

still.   All   our love is all for one,   Yet that love he heedeth

not,   He is   coy   and cares for none, Sad and   sor - ry is our

lot!   Ah,   Mi - se-rie!

I CANNOT TELL

Patience

I cannot tell what this love may be That cometh to

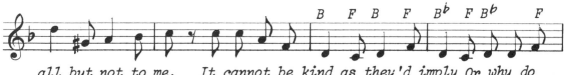

all but not to me.   It cannot be kind as they'd imply Or why do these

ladies

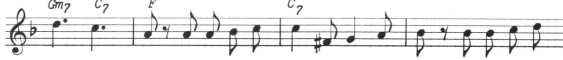

ladies   sigh? It cannot be joy and rapture deep, Or why do these

gentle ladies weep? It cannot be blissful as 'tis said or why are their

eyes   so_____ wondrous red?_____   Though ev - 'ry-

where true love I see   A-coming to all but not to me, I cannot tell

what this love   may   be!____   For I__ am blithe and I__ am

220

gay, while they sit sighing night and day. For I am blithe and I am

gay, Think of the gulf 'twixt them and me, Fal la la la

la and mi - se - rie!

THE SOLDIERS OF THE QUEEN

Dragoons

The soldiers of the Queen Are link'd in friendly

tether; Up - on the battle scene They fight the foe to-

gether. There ev-'ry mother's son___ Prepared to fight and

fall is; The en-e-my of one The en-e - my of all is!

IF YOU WANT A RECEIPT

Colonel

If you want a receipt for that pop-u-lar mys-te-ry,

Known to the world as a Heavy Dragoon, Take all the remarkable

People in histo-ry, Rattle them off to a popu-lar tune. ____

____ The pluck of Lord Nelson on board of the Victo-ry,

Genius of Bismarck devis-ing a plan; The humor of Fielding (which

sounds contradic-to-ry), Force of Mephisto pro-nouncing a ban, The

science of Jullien the em-i-nent musi - co, Wit of Macaulay, who

222

wrote of Queen Anne, The pathos of Paddy, as render'd by Boucicault,

Style of the Bishop of Sodor and Man, The genius stra-te-gic of

Caesar or Han-i-bal, Skill of Sir Garnet in thrashing a cannibal,

Flavor of Hamlet the Stranger a touch of him, Thomas Aquinas (but

not very much of him), Tupper and Tennyson, Daniel Defoe—

Mister Micawber and Madame Tussaud! Take of these elements

all that is fusible, Melt 'em all down in a pipkin or crucible—

Set 'em to simmer and take off the scum,_____ And a

Hea - vy Dra-goon is the re - si - du - um!

WHEN I FIRST PUT THIS UNIFORM ON

Colonel

When I first put this uniform on, I said as I

looked in the glass, Now e-ve-ry beauty will feel it her duty To

Yield to its glamor and class. They'll see that I'm freely gold-laced

In a

un-i-form handsome and chaste, But the per - i-pa-te - tics of

long-hair'd esthetics Are very much more to their taste. Which

I never counted up-on, When I first put this uniform on! By a sim - ple co - incidence few Could ever have reckoned up-on, I didn't an - ti-cipate that, When I first put this uniform on!

Bunthorne

If you're anxious for to shine__ in the high esthetic line As a man of culture rare, You must get up all the germs of the transcendental terms and plant them ev - 'rywhere. You must lie upon the daisies and discourse in novel phrases of your compli- cated state of mind, The meaning doesn't matter if it's only idle chatter of a transcenden-tal kind. And ev-'ry one will say, As you walk your mystic

way, If   this young man ex-presses himself in terms too deep for

me,   Why, what a   very   singularly deep young man this

deep young man must be!

PRITHEE, PRETTY MAIDEN

Grosvenor

Prithee, pretty maiden, prithee tell me true,

(Hey but I'm doleful, willow willow wa - ly!) Have you e'er a

lover a - dangling after you? Hey willow waly O!

I would fain discover If you have a lover! Hey____ wil-low

Patience

wa - ly O! Gentle sir, my heart is frolicsome and free

(Hey but he's doleful, willow willow waly!) Nobody I care for

comes a-courting me. Hey willow wa - ly O!

Nobody I care for Comes a-courting therefore, Hey__ willow

wa - ly O! Prithee, pretty maiden, will you marry me?

(Hey but I'm hopeful, willow willow waly!) I may say at once I'm a

man of pro-per-tee-- Hey willow wa - ly O!

Money I despise it, But many people prize it. Hey__ willow

wa - ly O! Gentle sir, although to marry I design

(Hey but he's hopeful willow willow wa-ly!) As yet I do not

know you and so I must decline, Hey wil-low

229

wa - ly O!   To other maidens go you,   As yet I do not

know you.   Hey__   willow   wa - ly O!

SILVERED IS THE RAVEN HAIR

Silver'd is the raven hair, Spreading is the part-ing straight, Mottled the complexion fair, Halting is the youthful gait. Stouter than I used to be, Still more corpulent grow I. There will be too much of me In the coming bye and bye! There will be too much of me In the com - ing bye and bye!

TURN, OH TURN

Turn, oh turn in this di - rec - tion, Shed, oh

shed a gentle smile; With a glance of sad per-

fec - tion, Our poor fainting hearts be - guile!

THE MAGNET AND THE CHURN

Grosvenor

A magnet hung in a hardware shop And all a-

round was a loving crop Of scissors and needles, nails and knives,

Offering love for all__ their lives, But for iron the magnet

felt no whim, Tho' he charmed iron, it charmed not him, From

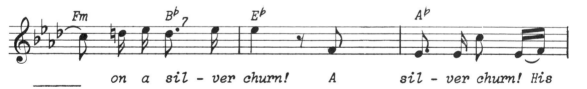

needles and nails and knives he'd turn, For he'd set his love____

____ on a sil - ver churn! A sil - ver churn! His

most es-the - tic, Very magne - tic Fan-cy took this

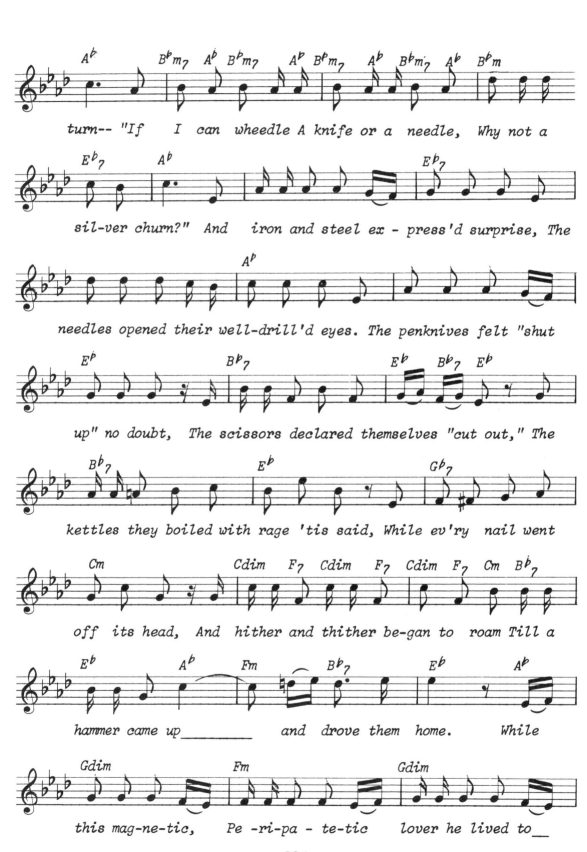

turn-- "If I can wheedle A knife or a needle, Why not a

sil-ver churn?" And iron and steel ex - press'd surprise, The

needles opened their well-drill'd eyes. The penknives felt "shut

up" no doubt, The scissors declared themselves "cut out," The

kettles they boiled with rage 'tis said, While ev'ry nail went

off its head, And hither and thither be-gan to roam Till a

hammer came up_____ and drove them home. While

this mag-ne-tic, Pe -ri-pa - te-tic lover he lived to__

learn, By no en - dea - vor Can mag-net e - ver At-

tract a sil-ver churn!

SO GO TO HIM

So go to him and say to him, with compli-ment i - ron - i-cal, Sing "Hey to you, good day to you" and that's what I shall say! "Your style is much too sanctified, your cut it too can-on - i - cal," Sing "Bah to you, ha! ha! to you" and that's what I shall say! "I was the beau i - de-al of the morbid young es - the-ti-cal, To doubt my in-spi - ra-tion was re - garded as he-

236

re - ti-cal, Un - til you cut me out with your pla-

ci - di - ty e - me - ti-cal." Sing "Booh to you, pooh,

pooh, to you" and that's what I shall say!

A COMMONPLACE YOUNG MAN

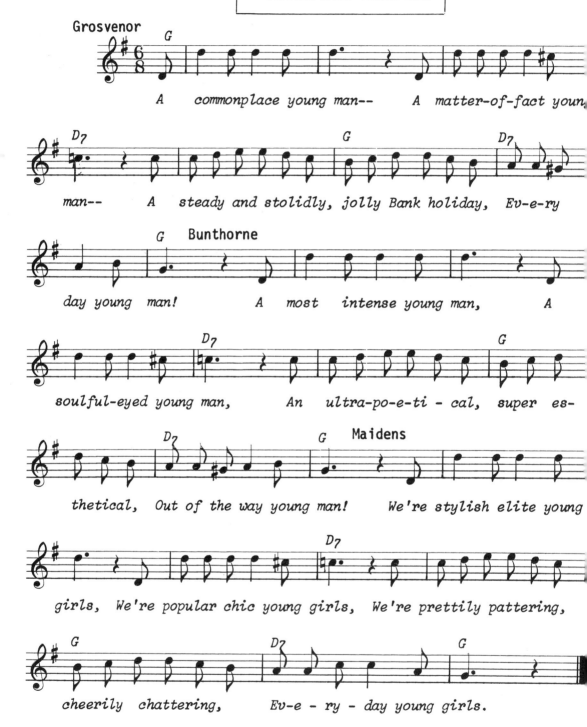

Grosvenor

A commonplace young man-- A matter-of-fact young man-- A steady and stolidly, jolly Bank holiday, Ev-e-ry day young man!

Bunthorne

A most intense young man, A soulful-eyed young man, An ultra-po-e-ti - cal, super es-thetical, Out of the way young man!

Maidens

We're stylish elite young girls, We're popular chic young girls, We're prettily pattering, cheerily chattering, Ev-e - ry - day young girls.

AFTER MUCH DEBATE INTERNAL

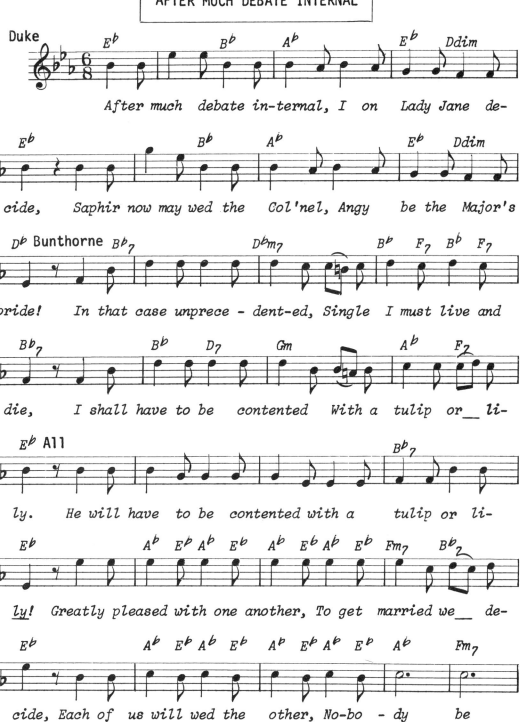

Duke

After much debate in-ternal, I on Lady Jane de-

cide, Saphir now may wed the Col'nel, Angy be the Major's

bride! In that case unprece - dent-ed, Single I must live and

die, I shall have to be contented With a tulip or_ li-

ly. He will have to be contented with a tulip or li-

ly! Greatly pleased with one another, To get married we_ de-

cide, Each of us will wed the other, No-bo - dy be

Bun - thorne's Bride!

THE YEOMEN OF THE GUARD

The story of

THE YEOMEN OF THE GUARD

Colonel Fairfax, scientist, is a prisoner in the Tower of London, condemned to death for sorcery. This is a false accusation made by his wicked cousin, who, if Fairfax dies unmarried, will inherit his estate and wealth. Fairfax asks the Lieutenant of the Tower, as a last favor, to find a woman who will marry him for the sum of one hundred crowns, so the cousin will be foiled. As Fairfax is to be executed immediately, the woman will at once become a rich widow and free to do as she pleases.

The Lieutenant persuades Elsie Maynard, a wandering singer, to become Fairfax's bride, and Jack Point, a jester to whom Elsie is betrothed, agrees to the marriage, since Fairfax is to die within the hour. Elsie is blindfolded, led into the Tower, and married to Fairfax, who is not told her identity.

Meanwhile, Sergeant Meryll of the Yeomen of the Guard, who knows Fairfax is innocent, plots with his daughter, Phoebe, to steal the keys to Fairfax's cell from Wilfred, the head jailor. Meryll releases Fairfax, disguises him in a Yeoman's uniform and introduces him to everyone as his son, Leonard, who is not known in London. Elsie falls in love with Fairfax, unaware that he is her husband and not Leonard Meryll. When the time for the execution arrives, there is no prisoner. Elsie, on learning that she is a wife and not a widow, faints into the arms of Fairfax. Later Dame Carruthers, housekeeper of the Tower, indicates to Fairfax (thinking him to be Leonard) that Elsie was married to the prisoner, and he is delighted to discover that Elsie is his bride.

In the meantime the jester, Jack Point, who loves Elsie and wants her to believe that Fairfax is dead, concocts a story, with the help of Wilfred, that Fairfax was shot and killed while making his escape. Point then asks Elsie to marry him, but she instead accepts the proposal of Fairfax in his disguise of Leonard. Just at this moment, the real Leonard arrives with a reprieve for Fairfax. Elsie is overjoyed to discover that "Leonard" and Fairfax are one and the same, and all ends happily for everyone except Jack Point who sings: "Misery me, Lackadaydee! . . . All for the love of a lady!"

THE YEOMEN OF THE GUARD

Or, The Merryman and His Maid

Characters

SIR RICHARD CHOLMONDELEY, *Lieutenant of the Tower*
COLONEL FAIRFAX, *under sentence of death*
SERGEANT MERYLL, *of the Yeomen of the Guard*
LEONARD MERYLL, *his son*
JACK POINT, *a strolling jester*
WILFRED SHADBOLT, *head jailor*
ELSIE MAYNARD, *a strolling singer*
PHOEBE MERYLL, *Sergeant Meryll's daughter*
DAME CARRUTHERS, *housekeeper of the Tower*
YEOMEN OF THE GUARD
HEADSMAN
TWO ASSISTANTS TO HEADSMAN
CROWD, *men and women*
WOMEN

SCENE 1

TIME: *The sixteenth century.*

SETTING: *The Tower of London: Tower Green. Stone wall extends across back of stage and rises left to form an archway that leads to Cold Harbour Tower. In right upstage corner of wall is gateway to other parts of Green. Tree is right with bench and spinning wheel under it. Another bench is set against back wall. Behind wall, backdrop shows turrets and battlements of the White Tower at far side of Green. Exit down right, below tree, leads to outside the Tower. Another exit is down left.*

AT RISE: PHOEBE MERYLL *is alone on stage, seated at spinning wheel.*

PHOEBE (*Singing as she spins*):

> When maiden loves, she sits and sighs,
> She wanders to and fro;
> Unbidden teardrops fill her eyes,
> And to all questions she replies
> With a sad "heigho!"
> 'Tis but a little word—"heigho!"
> So soft, 'tis scarcely heard—"heigho!"
> An idle breath—yet life and death
> May hang upon a maid's "heigho!"

(WILFRED *enters from Tower*.)

WILFRED: Ah, Mistress Meryll, you have brought your spinning out here on the Tower Green.

PHOEBE (*Looking up*): It's much more pleasant than spinning in the house. Now go away, Wilfred.

WILFRED: Haven't you anything to say to me?

PHOEBE (*Coldly*): Yes, I have! Are all the locks, chains and bolts in good order? The racks and thumbscrews ready for work?

WILFRED: I didn't become head jailor because I like the job. (*Sarcastically*) We can't *all* be sorcerers, you know.

PHOEBE (*Rising; indignantly*): Colonel Fairfax is *not* a sorcerer! He's an alchemist and a man of science.

WILFRED: Whatever he is, it won't be for long. He's going to be beheaded today for dealings with the devil.

PHOEBE: You're a cruel monster to speak so unfeelingly of the death of a young and handsome soldier.

WILFRED (*Under his breath*): Curse him!

PHOEBE: Why, I believe you're jealous of him—jealous of a man I've never spoken to. What a fool you are! (*Moves spinning*

wheel to behind tree. WILFRED *exits angrily into Tower.* YEO-
MEN OF THE GUARD, *carrying halberds, march in through
gateway to form a diagonal line at left.*)

YEOMEN (*Singing as they march in*):
       Tower Warders, under orders,
       Gallant pikemen, valiant sworders!
       Brave in bearing, foemen scaring,
       In their bygone days of daring!
       Ne'er a stranger, they, to danger—
       Each was o'er the world a ranger;
       To the story of their glory
       Each a bold contributory!
(DAME CARRUTHERS *enters through gateway.*)

DAME: Good day to you!

YEOMEN (*Together*): Good day, Dame Carruthers!

1ST YEOMAN: Are you busy today?

DAME: Aye! Last-minute preparations for the execution of Colonel Fairfax have kept me busy enough.

PHOEBE (*Fervently*): It's a barbarous thing that so gallant a hero
should lose his head. Colonel Fairfax is the bravest and best
young gentleman in England. Twice he saved my father's
life. Oh, this wicked Tower!

DAME: Silence, you silly girl. I love this Tower! There's not a
stone in these old walls that is not as dear to me as my own
right hand. (*Sings*)
       When our gallant Norman foes
       Made our merry land their own,
       And the Saxons from the Conqueror were flying,
       At his bidding it arose,
       In its panoply of stone,
       A sentinel unliving and undying.
       Insensible, I trow,

As a sentinel should be,
Though a queen to save her head should come a-suing,
There's a legend on its brow
That is eloquent to me,
And it tells of duty done and duty doing.
"The screw may twist and the rack may turn,
And men may bleed and men may burn,
O'er London Town and its golden hoard
I keep my silent watch and ward!"

YEOMEN (*Singing as they exit into Tower, followed by* DAME CARRUTHERS):
"The screw may twist and the rack may turn,
And men may bleed and men may burn,
O'er London Town and its golden hoard
I keep my silent watch and ward!"
(SERGEANT MERYLL *enters through gateway.*)

PHOEBE (*Running to him*): Father! Has a reprieve arrived for Colonel Fairfax?

MERYLL: No, my lass, but there's one hope yet. Your brother Leonard has been appointed a Yeoman of the Guard. He comes from Windsor this morning, and he may bring a royal reprieve with him. (LEONARD *enters down right.*) Leonard, my boy, I'm right glad to see you! (*They shake hands warmly.*)

PHOEBE: Oh, Leonard, have you brought Colonel Fairfax's reprieve?

LEONARD: Alas, no. I wish I could have brought one. Father, is there no way to save him?

MERYLL: There *is* a way, Leonard, if you are willing to lend him your name and identity, and disappear for a while. Will you do that?

LEONARD: Gladly! Did he not save your life? And is he not my foster brother?

MERYLL: Listen, then. You have come to join the Yeomen of the Guard. Has anyone seen you but ourselves?

LEONARD: Only a sentry who took little notice of me.

MERYLL: Good! You must get away at once. (*Giving* LEONARD *purse*) Here is money, and I'll send you more. Hide for a while. I'll get a Yeoman's uniform to the Colonel—he can shave off his beard and no one will know him. I'll introduce him as my son, the brave Leonard Meryll, and he'll be welcomed by my brother Yeomen. Now, how to get into his cell? Phoebe, your sour-faced admirer, Wilfred, keeps the key—

PHOEBE: I think I can get anything I want from Wilfred.

MERYLL: Then get away, son—and bless you for this sacrifice.

PHOEBE (*Embracing* LEONARD): Take my blessing, too, dear brother. (LEONARD *exits quickly down right.*)

MERYLL: Be of good cheer, Phoebe! We may save Colonel Fairfax yet.

PHOEBE (*Pointing down left*): Look, Father! They are bringing Colonel Fairfax now. Surely it is not time already, is it?

MERYLL: No, no—they are taking him to Cold Harbour Tower to await his end in solitude. But here comes Sir Richard Cholmondeley [*Pronounced "Chumley"*], the Lieutenant of the Tower [*Pronounced "Left-tenant"*]. Don't let him see you crying. (*Seats her on bench under tree.* SIR RICHARD *enters left from Tower and waits, center, as the bearded* FAIRFAX *and two* YEOMEN *enter down left.*)

SIR RICHARD: Halt! (*As* YEOMEN *stop*) Colonel Fairfax, my friend, we meet sadly.

FAIRFAX: Sir, I greet you with all good will.

SIR RICHARD: You face this bravely, as a brave man should.

FAIRFAX: Believe me, sir, my lot could be worse.

PHOEBE (*Aside to* MERYLL, *sobbing*): Oh, Father, I cannot bear it!

FAIRFAX (*Walking to bench*): Pretty one, why do you weep? Such a life as mine is not worth weeping for. (*Sees* MERYLL) Sergeant Meryll! My old comrade-in-arms! (*Shakes his hand*) We are soldiers, you and I, and we know how to die. (*To* PHOEBE) Come, come, pretty one, you mustn't grieve for me. Take my word for it, it is easier to die well than to live well. I know, for I have tried both. (*Sings*)

> Is life a boon?
> If so, it must befall
> That Death, whene'er he call,
> Must call too soon.
> Though fourscore years he give,
> Yet one would pray to live
> Another moon!
> What kind of plaint have I,
> Who perish in July?
> I might have had to die,
> Perchance, in June!

(*At the end,* PHOEBE, *still weeping, is led off by* MERYLL *down right.* FAIRFAX *draws* SIR RICHARD *aside and speaks confidentially*) Sir Richard, I have a favor to ask. My cousin has falsely accused me of sorcery. He desires my death because he is my heir, and he will inherit my estate if I die unmarried.

SIR RICHARD: As you will most surely do.

FAIRFAX: As I will most surely *not* do! I intend to marry immediately, if you will help me.

SIR RICHARD: But how? To whom?

FAIRFAX: I don't care—I have only an hour to live—fetch me the first woman who comes. She will have my dishonored name and a hundred crowns besides. (FAIRFAX *takes purse from his doublet and gives it to* SIR RICHARD.)

SIR RICHARD: It's a strange request, but I'll see what can be done.

FAIRFAX: A thousand thanks, Sir Richard. (*Turns to* YEOMEN)
I am ready, good fellows. (*Exits with* YEOMEN *into Tower*)

SIR RICHARD: A man of great courage—it's a pity he should die.
Now, how to find him a bride on such short notice. (*Weighing
purse in his hand*) Well, the task should be easy. (*Exits
down right.* JACK POINT, *dressed in jester's costume and cap
and carrying folly stick, races in through gateway with*
ELSIE MAYNARD, *carrying tambourine. They are pursued by
an eager* CROWD *of men and women.* CROWD *surrounds couple and tries to trap them.* POINT *and* ELSIE *elude several attempts to seize them. Finally* 1ST MAN *playfully catches*
ELSIE. POINT *taps him on the head with folly stick and he
lets go of her.* CROWD *laughs.*)

CROWD (*Chanting loudly in unison*):
        Here's a man of jollity,
        Jibe, joke, jollify!
        Give us of your quality,
        Come, fool, follify!
        If you vapor vapidly,
        River runneth rapidly,
        Into it we throw
        Cock who doesn't crow!
        Banish your timidity,
        And with all rapidity
        Give us quip and quiddity—
        Willy-nilly, O!

POINT: My masters, I pray you be patient, and we will satisfy
you, for we are merry folk who would make all as merry as
ourselves. We can rhyme you couplet, triolet, quatrain, son-
net, rondolet, ballads, what you will. Or we can dance you
saraband, gondolet, carole, pimpernel, or Jumping Joan.
(POINT *claps his hands after he mentions each dance as a
command to* ELSIE *to give a little suggestion of each, which
she does, shaking tambourine.*)

ELSIE: Let's give them the song of the Merryman and his Maid.

CROWD (*Ad lib*): Aye, the Merryman and his Maid! A good song!
(*Etc.* CROWD *groups itself about stage. In the following duet,
the singing member of the couple stands aside while the non-
singing member pantomimes and dances the action of the
song.*)

POINT (*Singing*):
　　I have a song to sing, O!

ELSIE (*Singing*):
　　Sing me your song, O!

POINT (*Singing*):
　　　　　It is sung to the moon
　　　　　By a love-lorn loon,
　　　　　Who fled from the mocking throng, O!
　　　　　It's the song of a merryman, moping mum,
　　　　　Whose soul was sad, and whose glance was glum,
　　　　　Who sipped no sup, and who craved no crumb,
　　　　　As he sighed for the love of a ladye.
　　　　　Heighdy! Heighdy! Misery me, lackadaydee!
　　　　　He sipped no sup, and he craved no crumb,
　　　　　As he sighed for the love of a ladye.

ELSIE (*Singing*):
　　I have a song to sing, O!

POINT (*Singing*):
　　What is your song, O?

ELSIE (*Singing*):
　　　　　It is sung with the ring
　　　　　Of the songs maids sing
　　　　　Who love with a love life-long, O!
　　　　　It's the song of a merrymaid, peerly proud,
　　　　　Who loved a lord, and who laughed aloud
　　　　　At the moan of the merryman, moping mum,

Whose soul was sad, and whose glance was glum,
Who sipped no sup, and who craved no crumb,
As he sighed for the love of a ladye.
Heighdy! Heighdy! Misery me, lackadaydee!
He sipped no sup, and he craved no crumb,
As he sighed for the love of a ladye.

POINT (*Singing*):
    I have a song to sing, O!

ELSIE (*Singing*):
    Sing me your song, O!

POINT (*Singing*):
        It is sung to the knell
        Of a churchyard bell,
        And a doleful dirge, ding dong, O!
        It's a song of a popinjay, bravely born,
        Who turned up his noble nose with scorn
        At the humble merrymaid, peerly proud,
        Who loved a lord, and who laughed aloud
        At the moan of the merryman, moping mum,
        Whose soul was sad, and whose glance was glum,
        Who sipped no sup, and who craved no crumb,
        As he sighed for the love of a ladye.
        Heighdy! Heighdy! Misery me, lackadaydee!
        He sipped no sup, and he craved no crumb,
        As he sighed for the love of a ladye.

ELSIE (*Singing*):
    I have a song to sing, O!

POINT (*Singing*):
    Sing me your song, O!

ELSIE (*Singing*):
        It is sung with a sigh
        And a tear in the eye,
        For it tells of a righted wrong, O!

It's a song of the merrymaid, once so gay,
Who turned on her heel and tripped away
From the peacock popinjay, bravely born,
Who turned up his noble nose with scorn
At the humble heart that he did not prize:
So she begged on her knees, with downcast eyes,
For the love of the merryman, moping mum,
Whose soul was sad and whose glance was glum,
Who sipped no sup, and who craved no crumb,
As he sighed for the love of a ladye.

ELSIE *and* POINT (*Dancing together as they sing*):
Heighdy! Heighdy! Misery me, lackadaydee!
His pains were o'er, and he sighed no more,
For he lived in the love of a ladye.
(*Repeating*)
Heighdy! Heighdy! Misery me, lackadaydee!
His pains were o'er, and he sighed no more,
For he lived in the love of a ladye.

CROWD (*Applauding, ad lib*): Well sung! Well danced! (*Etc.*)

1ST MAN (*Seizing* ELSIE): A kiss for that, pretty maid!

MEN: Aye, a kiss all round!

POINT (*Defending* ELSIE): Back, sirs, back! This is going too far!

ELSIE (*Fighting off* 1ST MAN): Help! Help! (SIR RICHARD *enters down right with* YEOMEN. CROWD *falls back.*)

SIR RICHARD: What's the trouble here?

ELSIE: Sir, we sang to these folk, and they would repay us with insults and discourtesy.

SIR RICHARD (*To* YEOMEN): Clear the rabble! Away with them! (YEOMEN *drive* CROWD *off and go off with them.* SIR RICHARD *turns to* ELSIE.) Now, my girl, who are you and what are you doing here?

ELSIE: May it please you, sir, we are two strolling players, Jack Point and I (*Bobbing curtsy*)—Elsie Maynard, at your worship's service. We go from fair to fair, singing and dancing, and so we make a poor living.

SIR RICHARD: Are you man and wife?

POINT: No, sir. Her mother travels with us, but now she's ill, and we have come here to earn some money to buy medicine for her.

SIR RICHARD: Well, my girl, how would you like to earn a hundred crowns?

ELSIE: A hundred crowns! That would save Mother's life!

SIR RICHARD: Then listen! A worthy gentleman is to be beheaded in an hour on this very spot. (*Indicating place where* POINT *is standing;* POINT *leaps aside in terror*) For certain reasons, he wants to marry before he dies, and he has asked me to find him a wife. Will you be his wife?

POINT: Sir, I am concerned in this. Elsie is promised to me. Have we your word that this gentleman will die today?

SIR RICHARD: Nothing is more certain, I'm sorry to say.

POINT: Then I consent. It is for Elsie to speak.

ELSIE: Alas, I am very poor, and I badly need the money—I, too, consent. (*She accepts purse from* SIR RICHARD *and puts it into pocket of skirt.* WILFRED *enters from Tower wearing a cape.* SIR RICHARD *whispers to him, and* WILFRED *removes cape, draping it over* ELSIE'S *head so she is covered to her knees.*)

SIR RICHARD (*Explaining to* ELSIE): A necessary precaution, my girl. You must not see the gentleman and the gentleman must not see you. (WILFRED *leads* ELSIE *into Tower.* SIR RICHARD *turns to* POINT.) So, my good fellow, you are a jester.

POINT (*Making a tragic face*): Aye, sir, and out of a job.

SIR RICHARD: Perhaps I can find you one. What are your qualifications?

POINT: Marry, sir, I have a pretty wit. (POINT *punctuates the following speeches by leaps about the stage and gestures appropriate to each of the qualities and jests he mentions.*) I can convulse you with quip and conundrum. I can be merry—wise—quaint—grim—and scornful. I know all the jests—ancient and modern—past, present, and to come. I can riddle you from dawn of day to set of sun. Oh, sir, a pretty wit, I warrant you!

SIR RICHARD: Can you give me an example? Say that I sat down hurriedly on something sharp.

POINT: Sir, I should say that you had sat down on the spur of the moment.

SIR RICHARD (*Not amused*): Humph! Is that the best you can do?

POINT: It has always been much admired, sir, but we will try again.

SIR RICHARD: Let's suppose that I caught you kissing the kitchen wench under my very nose.

POINT: Under *her* very nose, good sir—not under yours! *That* is where *I* would kiss her. Well, sir, do I get the job?

SIR RICHARD: Follow me, Jack, and we will discuss this matter further. (SIR RICHARD *exits through gateway and* POINT *dances off after him.* WILFRED *enters from Tower, leading* ELSIE. *He removes cape and steps inside Tower to dispose of it.*)

ELSIE (*Aside*): It's done! I am the bride of a bridegroom I have never seen. And in an hour, I shall be a widow. Poor man! (*Exits down right.* WILFRED *re-enters and looks off after* ELSIE.)

WILFRED: I wonder what business Colonel Fairfax and his chaplain could have had with that strange girl. I tried to spy on them, but they stopped up the keyhole. (*Sits on bench under tree*) Now what could he have wanted with her? (PHOEBE *and* MERYLL *enter through gateway, unobserved by* WILFRED.)

MERYLL (*Aside to* PHOEBE): There's Wilfred. Get the keys from him and give them to me. (MERYLL *hides behind tree.*)

PHOEBE: Wilfred—has no reprieve arrived?

WILFRED: None. Your adored Fairfax is to die.

PHOEBE (*Sitting beside him, on his right, so that he is turned away from Tower*): Now, Wilfred, you know I have only pity for the poor man.

WILFRED (*Pouting*): I know that he is more to you than I am.

PHOEBE: Why, that's not true, dear Wilfred. (*Putting arms around* WILFRED'S *waist, she slyly takes bunch of keys from his belt.*) I think you are a delightful companion. You're roguish, and lighthearted, and ever so clever! (*Hands keys to* MERYLL, *who enters Tower, unnoticed by* WILFRED)

WILFRED (*Responding to flattery boisterously*): I'm a mad wag! I believe I'm the merriest dog that barks! Oh, Phoebe, you and I could be so happy together. Just suppose we were married—

PHOEBE (*Eluding his embrace, crossing to center*): It's a charming picture—but I don't know—and yet—*were* I your bride—

WILFRED (*Eagerly, going to her*): Yes? Yes?

PHOEBE (*Singing, carries on a flirtation with* WILFRED):
Were I thy bride,
Then all the world beside

Were not too wide
To hold my wealth of love—
Were I thy bride!
Upon thy breast
My loving head would rest,
As on her nest
The turtle dove—
Were I thy bride!

(MERYLL *re-enters from Tower, gives keys to* PHOEBE, *still unnoticed, then hides behind tree.* PHOEBE *replaces keys on* WILFRED's *belt, as she continues to sing.*)

This heart of mine
Would be one heart with thine,
And in that shrine
Our happiness would dwell—
Were I thy bride!

(*Breaks off singing and speaks mischievously*) But then, of course, you see (*Tweaking* WILFRED's *nose*), I'm *not* your bride! (PHOEBE *laughs and runs off through gateway.*)

WILFRED: No, you're not—not yet! But, lord, how she wooed me! (*Runs off after* PHOEBE)

MERYLL (*Coming out of hiding*): What a helpless ninny is a love-sick man! (FAIRFAX *enters from Tower, without beard and moustache, and dressed in Yeoman's uniform.*) Ah, Colonel Fairfax!

FAIRFAX: My kind friend, what a risk you are taking!

MERYLL: No risk at all, sir. No one will recognize you. Here come the Yeomen to greet you. Remember, you are now my brave son, Leonard Meryll.

YEOMEN (*Singing as they enter from Tower and move into formation back and left stage*):
Leonard Meryll! Leonard Meryll!
Dauntless he in time of peril!

Man of power, knighthood's flower,
Welcome to the grim old Tower!
(*Cheering*) Hurrah! Hurrah! Hurrah!

FAIRFAX: Thank you, comrades, but the tales you have heard of my prowess are greatly exaggerated. (PHOEBE *enters, followed by* WILFRED. *She rushes to* FAIRFAX *and throws her arms about him.*)

PHOEBE: Leonard!

FAIRFAX (*Startled*): I beg your pardon?

PHOEBE: Don't you know me? I'm Phoebe—your own little sister!

FAIRFAX (*Pretending to recognize her*): What! Little Phoebe? It can't be! Why, how you've grown! (*A church bell begins to toll.* CROWD *re-enters and assembles right stage. Execution block is brought from Tower and set in place upstage by* TWO ASSISTANTS. HEADSMAN *follows, carrying a huge axe, and takes his position behind block.* YEOMEN *form line.* SIR RICHARD *and* POINT *enter.* SIR RICHARD *directs* WILFRED, *the disguised* FAIRFAX *and two* YEOMEN *to bring the prisoner; they exit into Tower.*)

CROWD (*Chanting*):
The prisoner comes to meet his doom;
The block, the headsman, and the tomb.
The funeral bell begins to toll—
May heaven have mercy on his soul.
(FAIRFAX, WILFRED *and* YEOMEN *return in great excitement.*)

FAIRFAX (*To* SIR RICHARD, *as a Yeoman*): My lord, I scarcely know how to tell you—we went to the prisoner's cell—he is not there! (CROWD *reacts.*)

SIR RICHARD: What! The prisoner has escaped? (*To* WILFRED) Then your life must be forfeit! Arrest him! (ASSISTANTS *seize* WILFRED.)

WILFRED (*Shouting as he is taken into Tower*): I didn't set him free! I hate the man!

ELSIE (*Aside to* POINT): Oh, woe is me! I am his wife, and he is free!

POINT (*Bitterly*): Oh, woe is *you?* Oh, woe is *me,* I rather think! You are his bride—and I am left alone.

SIR RICHARD (*Announcing in a loud voice*): A thousand marks for the recapture of Colonel Fairfax, alive or dead! (*Everyone, except* FAIRFAX, ELSIE *and* HEADSMAN, *rushes offstage in different directions to hunt for the fugitive.* ELSIE *faints into the arms of* FAIRFAX, *and the* HEADSMAN *stands with axe behind execution block. Curtain closes.*)

*   *   *   *   *

SCENE 2

TIME: *Two days later.*

SETTING: *Same as Scene 1. Execution block has been removed.*

AT RISE: POINT *enters down right, in low spirits, reading from a large volume.*

POINT (*Reading*): "The Merrie Jests of Hugh Ambrose." (*Shuts book with a bang*) Bah! It's a sad state of affairs when poor, heartbroken, jilted Jack Point must turn to a joke book for his jests! (*Tosses book on bench under tree.* WILFRED *enters left from Tower, also in low spirits.* POINT *goes to him.*) Is there any news of the escaped prisoner?

WILFRED: No—they've searched all over the Tower, but there's no sign of him. I've been dismissed for negligence of duty.

POINT: Come, take heart, and be merry, as I am! (*Aside, dolefully*) As I am!

WILFRED: You know, I've often considered being a jester myself. It shouldn't be difficult, seeing as you are one.

POINT: Difficult? Nothing easier! I'll prove it to you.
  (*Sings or recites*)

> Oh, a private buffoon is a light-hearted loon,
> If you listen to popular rumor;
> From morning to night he's so joyous and bright,
> And he bubbles with wit and good humor!
> He's so quaint and so terse, both in prose and in verse;
> Yet though people forgive his transgression,
> There are one or two rules that all family fools
> Must observe, if they love their profession.
> If your master is surly, from getting up early
> (And tempers are short in the morning),
> An inopportune joke is enough to provoke
> Him to give you, at once, a month's warning.
> Then if you refrain, he is at you again,
> For he likes to get value for money;
> He'll ask then and there, with an insolent stare,
> If you know that you're paid to be funny!
> Though your head it may rack with a bilious attack,
> And your senses with toothache you're losing,
> Don't be mopey and flat—they don't fine you for that,
> If you're properly quaint and amusing!
> Though your wife ran away with a soldier that day,
> And took with her your trifle of money;
> Bless your heart, they don't mind—they're exceed-
>   ingly kind—
> They don't blame you—so long as you're funny!

(*Speaks to* WILFRED) So, master jailor, you want to be a jester, do you?

WILFRED (*Enthusiastically*): Aye, that I do!

POINT: Then listen! My sweetheart, Elsie Maynard, was secretly married to Fairfax half an hour before he escaped. While he lives, she is dead to me and I to her, so my jokes notwithstanding, I am the saddest dog in England. If you will swear that you shot this Fairfax while he was trying to swim the river, and that he sank and was seen no more, I'll make you the very archbishop of jesters. (*Picking up book, shows it to* WILFRED) What do you say?

WILFRED: It's a bargain! (*They shake hands.* POINT *puts his jester's cap on* WILFRED'*s head, gives him his folly stick, then they link arms and skip off down right.* FAIRFAX *enters from Tower, still disguised.*)

FAIRFAX: I am free! Free—but for the bonds of matrimony. I wonder who the woman was that I married. I couldn't tell if she was young or old—her face and figure were concealed from me. (MERYLL *enters through gateway.*) Ah, Sergeant Meryll! How is your pretty charge, Elsie Maynard? I hope she has fully recovered from her fainting spell.

MERYLL: She is quite well again and leaves us today.

FAIRFAX: Thanks to Dame Carruthers' kind nursing, I suppose?

MERYLL: Aye, deuce take the old witch! I've been trying to avoid marriage with Dame Carruthers for years. (DAME CARRUTHERS *enters through gateway.*) Good lord, here she is! I'll be going—(*Starts to leave*)

DAME: Don't go, Sergeant Meryll—nor you, Master Leonard. I've something to tell you about Elsie Maynard. She has a liking for you, Master Leonard.

FAIRFAX: And I for her, Dame Carruthers.

DAME: Then be warned in time, and give not your heart to her. She's a married woman!

MERYLL: A married woman! Tush, old lady—she's promised to Jack Point, the jester.

DAME: Tush to you, old man! I overheard her talking in her sleep. She spoke of marrying someone she'd never seen who was to die within the hour. I believe it was that Fairfax whom she married.

MERYLL (*Aside to* FAIRFAX) : Is this true, sir?

FAIRFAX (*Aside to* MERYLL): Is it true? (*Trying to deceive* MERYLL) Why, the girl was raving in her sleep! (*Aloud to* DAME CARRUTHERS) Why should Elsie marry a man who had only an hour to live?

DAME: There be those who would marry only for a minute, rather than die old maids. (*Looks reproachfully at* MERYLL)

MERYLL: Aye—and I know one of them! (*Exits hastily into Tower, pursued by* DAME CARRUTHERS.)

FAIRFAX: So my mysterious bride is Elsie Maynard. (*Pleased*) I might have fared worse with my eyes open! (*Glancing off through gateway*) Here she comes! I shall test her to see how faithful a wife she is. (ELSIE *enters*.) Good morning, Mistress Elsie. I'm glad to see that you are feeling better.

ELSIE: Dame Carruthers is a good nurse.

FAIRFAX: Elsie, I recall that you fainted in my arms the other day. Were you faint with joy because Colonel Fairfax had escaped?

ELSIE: It may be so.

FAIRFAX: Then I am jealous of him. (*Passionately*) Elsie, I love you! (ELSIE *is surprised and alarmed*.) I have loved you these two days, and I ask you to be my wife.

ELSIE: But Master Leonard, I am not free—I *am* a wife!

FAIRFAX: Whose wife? Tell me his name, and his hours are numbered!

ELSIE: Oh, sir, I beg you, keep my secret. My husband is none other than Colonel Fairfax!

FAIRFAX (*Pretending indignation*): The most *ill*-mannered, *ill*-natured, *ill*-tempered dog in Christendom!

ELSIE: He is nothing to me, for I never saw him—I was blindfolded. He was to have died within the hour, but he escaped.

FAIRFAX (*Seizing her hand*): Be mine! He will never know. Fly with me, Elsie—we will be married tomorrow.

ELSIE (*Firmly, withdrawing her hand*): I *am* married, and I have a duty. Shame on you, Master Leonard! (*A gunshot is heard from offstage.* MERYLL *hurries in from Tower left, followed by* DAME CARRUTHERS. SIR RICHARD *and* PHOEBE *enter through gateway.*)

SIR RICHARD: What was that?

FAIRFAX: A gun—fired from the wharf, I think.

ALL (*Ad lib*): What can it mean? A gun fired in broad daylight! Are we being attacked? (*Etc.* WILFRED *and* POINT *run in down right, out of breath.*)

SIR RICHARD: Who fired that shot?

WILFRED: I did, m'lord!

POINT: He did, m'lord!

WILFRED: I found Colonel Fairfax hiding on the wharf.

POINT: In a fishmonger's stall. Phew! (*Pinches nostrils*)

WILFRED: We fought—Fairfax dove into the river—and I shot him. His body sank like a stone.

POINT: A lump of lead! (*Sinks to ground with a grunt*)

WILFRED (*Exasperated by* POINT's *interruptions*): Whether stone or lump of lead—anyhow, the man is dead!

SIR RICHARD (*Clapping* WILFRED *on shoulder*): Bravely done! Come, jailor, show me where it happened. (WILFRED, SIR RICHARD, MERYLL *and* DAME CARRUTHERS *exit down right. Others remain onstage.*)

FAIRFAX (*Speaking to* POINT): Are you sure it was Colonel Fairfax?

POINT: I saw him with both eyes at once (*Pointing to each eye*)— this one and that one. And now, Elsie, you are free to choose again, so behold me! (*Strikes a pose*) I am young—I have a pretty wit—

FAIRFAX: Tush, man, you don't know how to court a woman. Listen to me. (*Goes down on one knee*) Mistress Elsie, there is one here who loves you well.

POINT (*Hand on heart*): That he does—right well!

FAIRFAX: He is only a man of poor estate, but he will be a true and trusty husband to you. Tell me, will you be this poor good fellow's wife?

ELSIE: Yes, I will be his true and loving wife. (*They embrace.*)

PHOEBE (*Greatly agitated*): Why, what's all this? Brother—it is not proper!

POINT: Enough, Master Leonard! You go too far!

FAIRFAX: That is for Elsie to say. (*Puts arm around* ELSIE *and leads her through gateway.*)

POINT (*Facing front with woebegone expression and singing*):
When a jester is outwitted,
Feelings fester, heart is lead!
Food for fishes only fitted,
Jester wishes he was dead!

Oh, the doing and undoing,
Oh, the sighing and the suing,
When a jester goes a-wooing,
And he wishes he was dead!
(POINT *exits down right, drooping dejectedly.*)

PHOEBE (*Bursting into tears*): Was it for this I helped to save Fairfax's life? (*Sinks on upstage bench*)

WILFRED (*Entering down right*): Phoebe, my girl! Why are you crying?

PHOEBE: I cry for jealousy.

WILFRED (*Sitting beside her*): But I have never given you cause for jealousy.

PHOEBE: You? Huh! I am jealous because of a better man than you. And he's going to marry Elsie Maynard!

WILFRED (*Staring at* PHOEBE, *bewildered*): The man you love is to marry Elsie Maynard? Why, your brother, Leonard Meryll, wants to marry her—or so Point tells me. Surely you do not mean your own brother!

PHOEBE (*Jumping to her feet*): Oh, mercy, what have I said?

WILFRED (*Rising in a fury*): You liar! Who is this man you called brother? Is it—Fairfax? (PHOEBE *starts.*) It *is!* It's Fairfax—

PHOEBE (*Retorting sharply*): Whom you have just shot, remember, and who lies at the bottom of the river! (*Pleadingly*) Wilfred, don't give away the secret—if you don't, I will marry you.

WILFRED: Is that a promise? (PHOEBE *nods reluctantly.* LEONARD MERYLL *enters down right.*)

LEONARD: Phoebe! Good news! Colonel Fairfax's reprieve was signed two days ago. His scheming cousin tried to conceal it, but now it is in the hands of Sir Richard.

PHOEBE: Then Fairfax is free? Oh, my darling! I'm beside myself with joy! (*Hugs* LEONARD)

WILFRED (*Dancing with rage*): Come away from him, you hussy! As for you, sir, I'll skin you for this! Phoebe, who is this man?

PHOEBE: Peace, fool! He is my brother.

WILFRED: Another brother! Are there any more of them?

PHOEBE: This is the *real* Leonard, you dolt! Come, Wilfred, don't be angry. I am your Phoebe (*Wryly*)—and we will be married in a year—or two—or three. (MERYLL *enters through gateway, followed stealthily by* DAME CARRUTHERS, *who listens, unobserved, behind tree.*)

MERYLL: Phoebe, have you heard the good news?

PHOEBE: Yes, Father—but Wilfred has learned our secret about Fairfax, and the price of his silence is—

WILFRED: Phoebe's heart!

PHOEBE (*Correcting him*): No—Phoebe's *hand!* (*Offers hand to* WILFRED, *who takes it*)

WILFRED: It's the same thing.

PHOEBE: *Is* it? (*Boxes* WILFRED's *ear.* DAME CARRUTHERS *comes out from behind tree.*)

DAME: So! A plot! One word from me, and three heads will roll!

MERYLL: Not at all. Colonel Fairfax has been reprieved. (*Aside*) Yet I would fare badly if my part in the plot were known.

Plague take the old meddler! (*Aloud*) Dame Carruthers, what is the price of your silence?

DAME: Meryll's heart!

MERYLL: No—Meryll's *hand!*

DAME: It's the same thing.

MERYLL: *Is* it? (DAME *nods vigorously.* MERYLL *throws up his hands in resignation, and joins* LEONARD *down left. Procession of* WOMEN *enters through gateway, singing and strewing flowers.* ELSIE *follows, wearing bridal veil and carrying bridal bouquet.* YEOMEN *enter from Tower and take positions left stage. Principals are grouped front of stage.*)

WOMEN (*Singing as they enter*):
Comes the pretty young bride.
Brightly thy summer is shining,
Fair as the dawn of the day;
Take him, be true to him—
Tender his due to him—
Honor him, love and obey.
(*Trumpet sounds.* SIR RICHARD *enters through gateway and comes downstage to* ELSIE.)

SIR RICHARD: Mistress Maynard, I bring you news! Colonel Fairfax, your husband, is alive. He is free and comes to claim his bride.

ELSIE (*Distracted*): Oh, no! It cannot be! (*Falls, weeping, into* DAME CARRUTHERS' *arms. Trumpet sounds again.* FAIRFAX *enters through gateway, handsomely dressed.*)

FAIRFAX (*Sternly, to* ELSIE, *who is still weeping in* DAME'S *arms*): All thought of Meryll put aside—I claim you as my bride!

ELSIE (*Turning slowly to* FAIRFAX; *sadly*): Sir, I obey. (*Looks up and recognizes* FAIRFAX) Leonard!

FAIRFAX: My own! (*They embrace. General rejoicing, which subsides as* POINT *enters down right, a tragic figure, strumming a guitar.*)

POINT (*Speaking to audience*): Good people, attend to me, and shed a tear or two (*Singing*)—
> For I have a song to sing, O!

ALL (*Singing*):
> Sing me your song, O!

POINT (*Singing*):
> It is sung to the moon
> By a love-lorn loon,
> Who fled from the mocking throng, O!
> It's the song of a merryman, moping mum,
> Whose soul was sad and whose glance was glum,
> Who sipped no sup and who craved no crumb,
> As he sighed for the love of a ladye.

ALL (*Singing*):
> Heighdy! Heighdy! Misery me, lackadaydee!
> He sipped no sup and he craved no crumb,
> As he sighed for the love of a ladye.

ELSIE (*Singing*):
> I have a song to sing, O!

ALL (*Singing*):
> What is your song, O!

ELSIE (*Nestling head on* FAIRFAX's *shoulder; singing*):
> It is sung with the ring
> Of the songs maids sing
> Who love with a love life-long, O!
> It's the song of a merrymaid, nestling near,
> Who loved her lord—but who dropped a tear
> At the moan of the merryman, moping mum,
(ELSIE *turns sympathetically to* POINT.)

Whose soul was sad and whose glance was glum,
Who sipped no sup and who craved no crumb,
As he sighed for the love of a ladye.

(ELSIE *turns to* FAIRFAX; POINT *exits.* YEOMEN *form arch with crossed halberds, and* ELSIE *and* FAIRFAX *pass under it.*)

ALL (*Singing*):

Heighdy! Heighdy! Misery me, lackadaydee!
He supped no sup and he craved no crumb,
As he sighed for the love of a ladye.

(*Curtain*)

THE END

THE YEOMEN OF THE GUARD

Characters: 7 male; 3 female; as many male and female as desired for Yeomen, Crowd, Women; 2 male or female for Assistants.

Playing Time: 30 minutes.

Costumes: Sixteenth-century dress. Elsie wears brightly colored skirt and bodice. In Scene 2, she wears a bridal veil. Dame Carruthers and Phoebe wear more elaborate dresses. Fairfax, as prisoner, wears costume of gentleman of the period, beard and moustache. He changes into yeoman's uniform and is clean-shaven. Leonard is dressed as Elizabethan gentleman. Jack Point wears jester's costume and cap. Meryll, Sir Richard and Yeomen wear costumes similar to those worn by modern-day Beefeaters at the Tower of London. Wilfred wears dark brown; he has a cape briefly in Scene 1. Headsman is dressed in black, with head covered by black mask. Crowd and women wear typical dress of villagers of the period.

Properties: Spinning wheel, halberds, two purses, jester's folly stick, tambourine, bunch of keys on ring, execution block, axe, large book, guitar.

Setting: Tower Green of the Tower of London. A stone wall extends across back of stage. At left it rises to form an archway. In right upstage corner of wall is a gateway leading to other parts of the Green. Under a tree at right are a bench and spinning wheel. Another bench is set against back wall. Backdrop shows turrets and battlements of the White Tower. An exit down right leads to outside the Tower grounds. Another exit is down left.

Lighting: No special effects.

Sound: Church bell, gunshot, trumpet, as indicated in text.

Music for songs on following pages.

WHEN MAIDEN LOVES

Phoebe

When maiden loves she sits and sighs, She

wanders to and fro; Un - bidden teardrops fill her eyes

And

to all questions she replies with a sad "Heigh - ho!"

'Tis but a little word-- "Heigh-ho!" So soft 'tis scarcely heard

"Heigh-ho!" An i-dle breath -- Yet life and__

death May hang up - on a maid's "Heigh - ho!"

TOWER WARDERS, UNDER ORDERS

Yeomen

Tower warders, under orders, gallant pikemen, valiant sworders! Brave in bearing, Foemen scaring, In their bygone days of daring! N'er a stranger There to danger-- Each was o'er the world a ranger: To the story of our glory, Each a bold, a bold con-trib-u - to-ry!

WHEN OUR GALLANT NORMAN FOES

Dame Carruthers

When our gallant Norman foes Made our merry land their own, And the Saxons from the Conqueror were flying, At his bidding it arose, In its panoply of stone, A sentinel un-living and un - dy-ing. In - sensible, I trow, As a sen-ti-nel should be, Tho' a queen to save her head should come a-suing; There's a legend on its brow That is el-o-quent to me, And it tells of du - ty___ done___ and duty do -

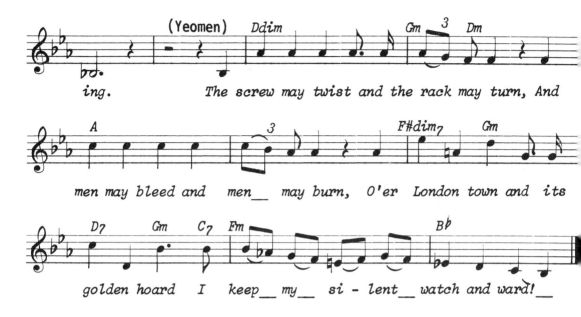

(Yeomen) *Ddim* *Gm* *3* *Dm*

ing.   The screw may twist and the rack may turn, And

A *3* *F#dim₇* *Gm*

men may bleed and men__ may burn, O'er London town and its

D₇ *Gm* *C₇* *Fm* *B♭*

golden hoard I keep__ my__ si - lent__ watch and ward!__

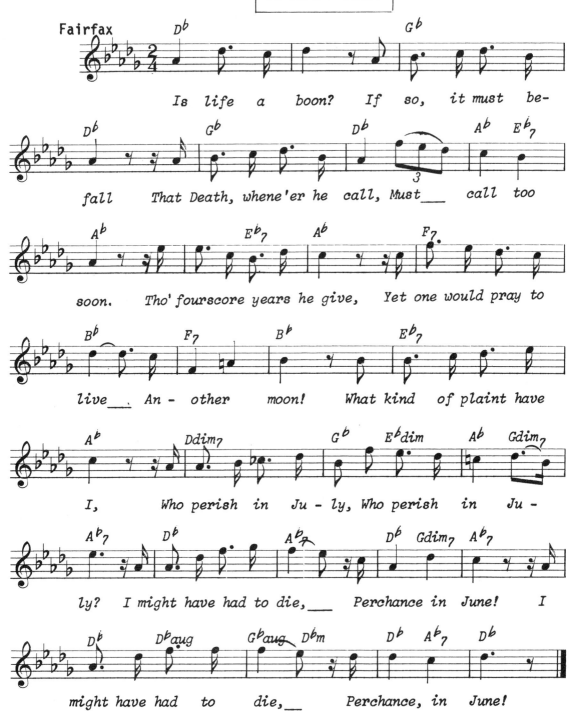

IS LIFE A BOON?

Fairfax

Is life a boon? If so, it must be-
fall That Death, whene'er he call, Must___ call too
soon. Tho' fourscore years he give, Yet one would pray to
live___. An - other moon! What kind of plaint have
I, Who perish in Ju - ly, Who perish in Ju -
ly? I might have had to die,___ Perchance in June! I
might have had to die,___ Perchance, in June!

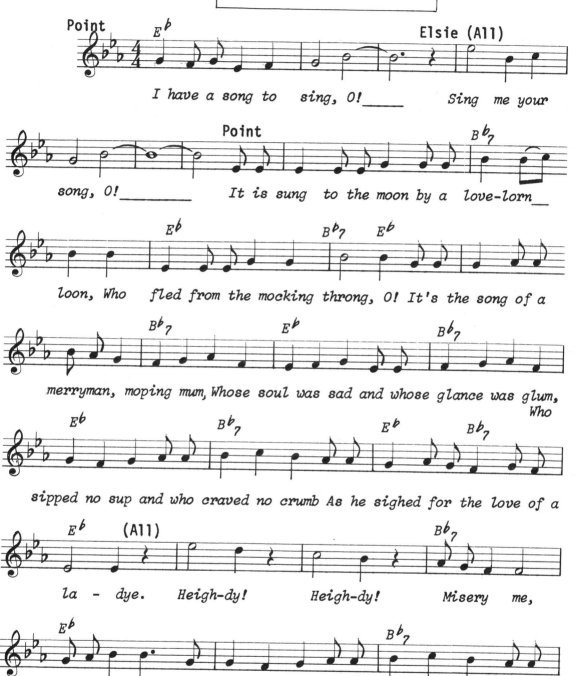

I HAVE A SONG TO SING, O!

I have a song to sing, O!_____ Sing me your

song, O!_____ It is sung to the moon by a love-lorn__

loon, Who fled from the mocking throng, O! It's the song of a

merryman, moping mum, Whose soul was sad and whose glance was glum, Who

sipped no sup and who craved no crumb As he sighed for the love of a

la - dye. Heigh-dy! Heigh-dy! Misery me,

lackaday - dee! He sipped no sup and he craved no crumb, As he

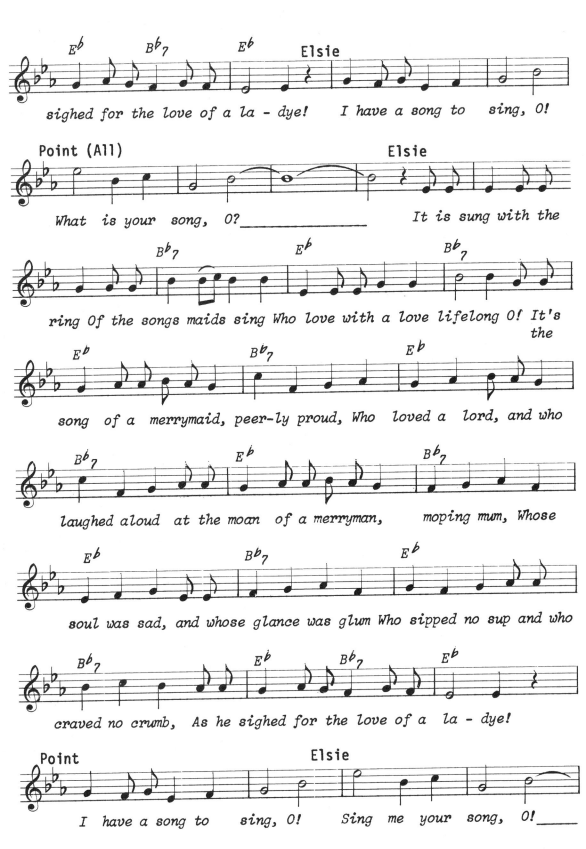

Point

B♭7

It is sung to the knell Of a churchyard bell And a

E♭   B♭7   E♭

doleful dirge, ding dong, O! It's a song of a pop-in-jay,

B♭7   E♭   B♭7

bravely born, Who turned up his noble nose with scorn At the

E♭   B♭7   E♭

humble merrymaid, peerly proud, Who loved a lord, and who

B♭7   E♭   B♭7

laughed aloud At the moan of a merryman, moping mum, Whose

E♭   B♭7   E♭

soul was sad, and whose glance was glum Who sipped no sup and who

B♭7   E♭   B♭7   E♭

craved no crumb As he sighed for the love of a ladye! Heighdy!

B♭7   E♭

Heighdy! Misery me, lackaday-dee! He sipped no sup and he

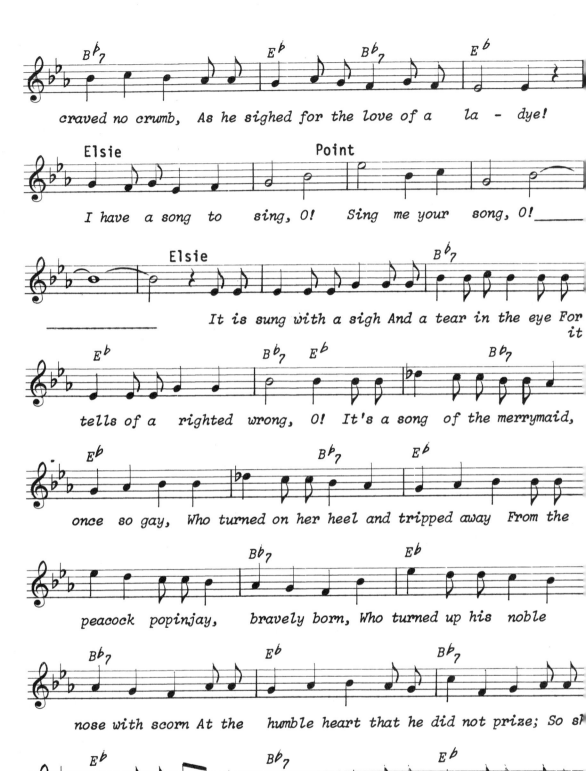

craved no crumb, As he sighed for the love of a la - dye!

Elsie **Point**

I have a song to sing, O! Sing me your song, O!____

Elsie

____ It is sung with a sigh And a tear in the eye For it

tells of a righted wrong, O! It's a song of the merrymaid,

once so gay, Who turned on her heel and tripped away From the

peacock popinjay, bravely born, Who turned up his noble

nose with scorn At the humble heart that he did not prize; So sh

begged on her knees with downcast eyes, For the love of the merryman

moping mum, Whose soul was sad and whose glance was glum, Who

sipped no sup, and who craved no crumb, As he sighed for the love of a

la - dye! Heighdy! Heighdy! Misery me, lackaday-

dee! His pains were o'er, and he sighed no more, For he

lived in the love of a la - dye! Heighdy! Heighdy!

Misery me, lackaday-dee! His pains were o'er, and he

sighed no more, For he lived in the love of a la-dye!____

WERE I THY BRIDE

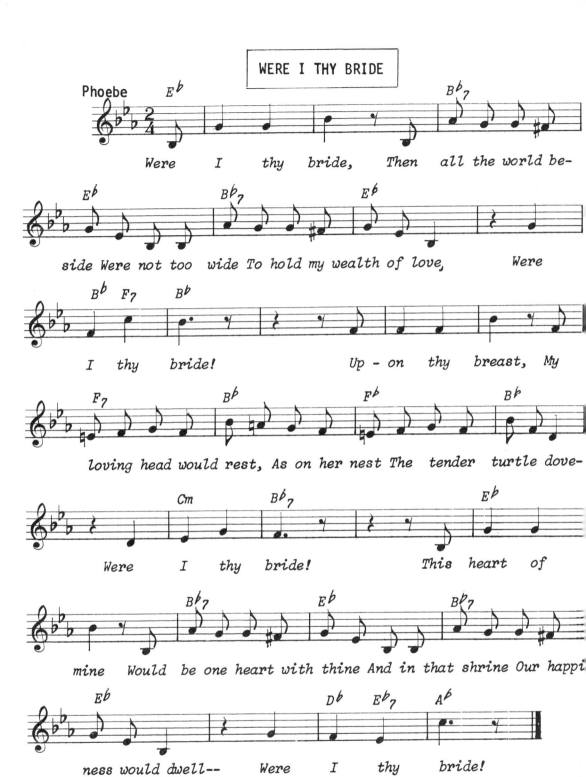

Were I thy bride, Then all the world be-side Were not too wide To hold my wealth of love, Were I thy bride! Up - on thy breast, My loving head would rest, As on her nest The tender turtle dove- Were I thy bride! This heart of mine Would be one heart with thine And in that shrine Our happi ness would dwell-- Were I thy bride!

OH! A PRIVATE BUFFOON IS A LIGHTHEARTED LOON

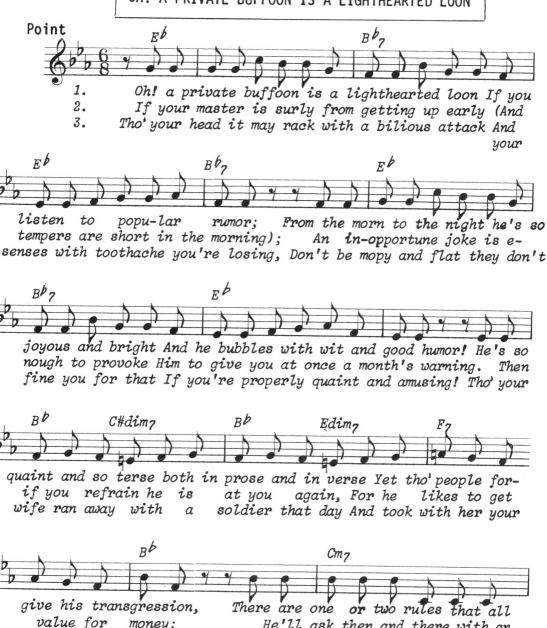

Point

1. Oh! a private buffoon is a lighthearted loon If you
2. If your master is surly from getting up early (And
3. Tho' your head it may rack with a bilious attack And

your

listen to popu-lar rumor; From the morn to the night he's so
tempers are short in the morning); An in-opportune joke is e-
senses with toothache you're losing, Don't be mopy and flat they don't

joyous and bright And he bubbles with wit and good humor! He's so
nough to provoke Him to give you at once a month's warning. Then
fine you for that If you're properly quaint and amusing! Tho' your

quaint and so terse both in prose and in verse Yet tho' people for-
if you refrain he is at you again, For he likes to get
wife ran away with a soldier that day And took with her your

give his transgression, There are one or two rules that all
value for money; He'll ask then and there with an
trifle of money. Bless your heart they don't mind, they're

ex-

fami - ly fools Must observe if they love their profession.
insolent stare "If you know that you're paid to be funny?"
ceedingly kind, They don't blame you as long as you're funny!

WHEN A JESTER IS OUTWITTED

Point

When a jester is out-wit-ted, Feelings fester, heart is lead! Food for fishes on-ly fitted, Jester wishes he was dead! Oh, the doing and undo-ing, Oh, the sighing and the suing, When a jester goes a-wooing, And he wishes he____ was dead!

COMES THE PRETTY YOUNG BRIDE

Women

Comes the pretty young bride, Brightly thy summer is shinin Fair as the dawn, as the dawn of the day; Take him, be true to him, Tender__ his due to him, Honor him__ love and obey.__

282

IOLANTHE

The story of

IOLANTHE

Years ago, Iolanthe, a fairy, married a mortal, contrary to fairy law, and she was sentenced to death. But the Fairy Queen, who loved her, banished her instead, and for twenty-five years, Iolanthe has been serving her sentence at the bottom of a river. As the operetta opens, the fairies—Iolanthe's sisters—plead with the Queen to restore Iolanthe. The Queen consents, but she forbids Iolanthe to see her husband.

Iolanthe's son, Strephon, is a handsome young shepherd who is engaged to Phyllis, a shepherdess and a Ward in Chancery. Phyllis is being wooed by a number of noble peers, but she loves only Strephon. However, Phyllis's guardian, the Lord Chancellor, refuses to consent to the marriage—in fact, he wants to marry Phyllis himself.

Strephon asks his mother's aid to solve his romantic problems. Phyllis sees him kissing Iolanthe, and refuses to believe that this woman, who looks seventeen, can be his mother. Indignant at Strephon's apparent faithlessness, Phyllis announces that she will marry one of the peers. Strephon appeals for help to the Fairy Queen, who declares that she will punish the Chancellor and the peers by sending Strephon to Parliament, where he will pass all sorts of alarming reforms; the peers will not be able to oppose them because of her fairy magic.

A few weeks later, outside the Houses of Parliament, with Private Willis on guard, the fairies and the peers sing of Strephon's reforms as a member of Parliament. The Chancellor staggers in, having been kept awake night after night by his unrequited love for Phyllis. Iolanthe pleads with the Chancellor to let Strephon and Phyllis marry, and in desperation she reveals that the Chancellor is the man she married years before, and Strephon is their son. The other fairies announce that they have married peers. This is a breach of fairy law, and the Queen declares that they all must die. The Chancellor comes to the rescue by inserting a single word in the law to make it read: "Every fairy shall die who *doesn't* marry a mortal." This settles everything. Fairy wings sprout from the peers' shoulders, Phyllis and Strephon are reunited, and all fly off happily to Fairyland.

IOLANTHE

Or, The Peer and the Peri*

Characters

IOLANTHE, *a fairy*
STREPHON, *her son, an Arcadian shepherd*
QUEEN OF THE FAIRIES
CELIA }
LEILA } *fairies*
FLETA }
LORD CHANCELLOR
PHYLLIS, *his ward*
EARL OF MOUNTARARAT } *peers*
EARL TOLLOLLER }
PRIVATE WILLIS, *of the Grenadier Guards*
FAIRIES
PEERS

SCENE 1

SETTING: *An Arcadian fairy grove. A backdrop shows a river running through a meadow. River bank is at right, and beside it, a large bush. At back of stage is a rustic bridge with steps descending to stage level. Trees and bushes are at right and a tree stump is down left.*

AT RISE: IOLANTHE *is concealed behind large bush at right river bank.* FAIRIES, *led by* LEILA, CELIA *and* FLETA, *enter across bridge, and form circle at center.* FAIRY QUEEN *enters last and remains on bridge to watch* FAIRIES *sing and dance.*

---

* A beautiful fairy-like being from Persian mythology.

FAIRIES (*Singing as they dance*) :

> We are dainty little fairies,
> Ever singing, ever dancing;
> We indulge in our vagaries
> In a fashion most entrancing.
> If you ask the special function
> Of our never-ceasing motion,
> We reply, without compunction,
> That we haven't any notion!
> Tripping hither, tripping thither,
> Nobody knows why or whither;
> We must dance and we must sing
> Round about our fairy ring.

(FAIRIES *stop dancing and sigh wearily.*)

CELIA: It's all very well to sing and dance, but since the Fairy Queen banished our sister, Iolanthe, twenty-five years ago, our revels haven't been the same.

LEILA: Iolanthe was the life and soul of Fairyland.

FLETA: What did she do to deserve so terrible a punishment?

LEILA: She married a mortal. By our laws, a fairy who marries a mortal, dies!

CELIA: But Iolanthe didn't die.

FAIRY QUEEN (*Coming downstage from bridge*) : No—because I, your Queen, loved her so much, I changed her sentence from death to mere banishment—on the condition that she leave her husband and never communicate with him again. (*Exclaiming in distress*) But I never thought that she would go and live at the bottom of that stream! (*Points to river bank, right*)

LEILA: Think of the damp!

QUEEN (*Shuddering*) : And the frogs! Ugh! I'll never understand why Iolanthe went to live among the frogs.

FLETA: Why don't you summon her and ask her?

QUEEN (*Shaking her head*): If I set eyes on her, I shall forgive her.

CELIA: Then why not forgive her? Twenty-five years—it's a long time.

FLETA: Oh, give her back to us, Your Majesty! Do it for your sake as well as ours. (FAIRIES *kneel in supplication.*)

QUEEN (*Hesitating*): Oh, I *should* be strong—but I am weak. Well, well! It shall be as you wish. (FAIRIES *rise.* QUEEN *goes to river bank, takes a pinch of earth, breathes on it and flings it into river; then she makes a magical sign with her wand and calls out.*) Iolanthe! I invoke thee! From thy exile thou art summoned! Iolanthe, come! (IOLANTHE *slowly rises from behind bush at river's edge, wearing a mantle of waterweeds over her costume. Pinned to her hair is a long veil. She kneels before* QUEEN *with head bowed and arms crossed.* QUEEN *lightly touches* IOLANTHE's *shoulder with wand.*) Rise—thou art pardoned!

IOLANTHE (*Casting off waterweeds as she rises*): Pardoned!

FAIRIES: Pardoned! (CELIA *brings tiara to* QUEEN *who places it on* IOLANTHE's *head, and embraces her.* IOLANTHE *dances among* FAIRIES.)

FAIRIES (*Singing*):
>Welcome to our hearts again,
>Iolanthe! Iolanthe!
>We have shared thy bitter pain,
>Iolanthe! Iolanthe!
>Every heart and every hand
>In our loving little band
>Welcomes thee to Fairyland,
>Iolanthe!

(*All gather around* IOLANTHE *and* QUEEN *at center.*)

QUEEN: And now, tell me, Iolanthe, with all the world to choose from, why on earth did you decide to live at the bottom of a river?

IOLANTHE: To be near my son, Strephon. He comes here often.

QUEEN: I didn't know you had a son!

IOLANTHE: He was born soon after I left my husband—but he doesn't even know of his father's existence.

FLETA: How old is he?

IOLANTHE: Twenty-four.

LEILA: No one, to look at you, would believe you had a son of twenty-four. But, of course, that's one advantage of being immortal—we never grow old.

CELIA: Is your son handsome?

IOLANTHE: Very handsome. He's an Arcadian shepherd—and he loves a girl called Phyllis, whose guardian is the Lord Chancellor himself.

CELIA (*Disappointed*): The son of Iolanthe—a mere shepherd! Why, he is half supernatural.

IOLANTHE: Yes—he's one of us down to the waist—but his legs are mortal.

QUEEN: Dear me! I should like to see him. (*Offstage, flute is heard playing pastoral air.*)

IOLANTHE: Nothing could be easier, Your Majesty. (*Gesturing toward bridge*) Here he comes. (QUEEN *and* FAIRIES *quickly hide behind trees and bushes, peeking out at* STREPHON *as he enters across bridge. He is playing a shepherd's pipe.*)

STREPHON (*Singing*):
>   Good morrow, good mother!
>   Good mother, good morrow!
(*Goes to* IOLANTHE)
>   By some means or other,
>   Pray banish your sorrow!
>   With joy beyond telling
>   My bosom is swelling,
(*Waltzing with* IOLANTHE *around stage*)
>   So join in a measure
>   Expressive of pleasure,
>   For I'm to be married today, today—
>   Yes, I'm to be married today!
(*They stop dancing.*)

IOLANTHE: So, you are to be married to Phyllis! Wonderful! Has the Lord Chancellor given his consent, at last?

STREPHON: Not he! All he says is (*Pompously*)—"A shepherd lad is not a fit husband." (FAIRIES *and* QUEEN *come out of hiding.*) Nevertheless, I shall marry Phyllis today! (*Sees* FAIRIES) Mother, who are these ladies?

IOLANTHE: Rejoice with me, Strephon—my queen has pardoned me. (QUEEN *nods to* STREPHON. IOLANTHE *indicates* FAIRIES.) And these are my sisters.

STREPHON: Your sisters? Then they are my aunts! (FAIRIES *gather around him.*)

QUEEN: A pleasant piece of news for your bride on her wedding day.

STREPHON: Hush! My bride doesn't know that my mother is a fairy. I don't dare tell her that I'm not wholly mortal. What's the use of being half a fairy?

QUEEN: I think I can solve your dilemma. You have a brain like ours, and it can be put to use. How would you like to go into

Parliament? You won't feel out of place there, for many of the members are only half human.

IOLANTHE: That would be delightful! As a Member of Parliament, Strephon, you would be a proper husband for Phyllis, and the Lord Chancellor would have to give his consent to your marriage.

QUEEN (*To* STREPHON): Agreed?

STREPHON: Agreed, Your Majesty! (*Kneels and kisses her hand*)

QUEEN: Farewell for the present. If ever you are in doubt or danger, call us and we will come. (*Motioning to* FAIRIES) Now we must be taking wing for another fairy ring! (FAIRIES *and* QUEEN *exit left.* IOLANTHE *bids* STREPHON *an affectionate farewell, and follows.* STREPHON *plays a trill on his pipe. From offstage right,* PHYLLIS *sings an answering trill. He repeats trill, and again* PHYLLIS *answers. Then* PHYLLIS *enters across bridge.*)

PHYLLIS (*Singing*):
Good morrow, my lover,
My lover, good morrow!
I prithee discover,
Steal, purchase, or borrow
Some means of concealing
The care you are feeling—
(PHYLLIS *and* STREPHON *dance from center toward opposite sides of stage, then back together again as* PHYLLIS *continues to sing*)
And join in a measure
Expressive of pleasure,
For we're to be married today, today!

STREPHON *and* PHYLLIS: Yes, we're to be married today! (*They embrace.*)

STREPHON: My Phyllis! Today we are to be made happy forever.

PHYLLIS: Oh, Strephon, I tremble at the step I am taking by going against my guardian. I shall be of age in two years. Don't you think you could wait two years?

STREPHON: Who knows what will happen in two years? Why, you might fall in love with the Lord Chancellor himself! As it is, half the House of Lords is sighing at your feet. No—delays are dangerous, and if we are to marry, the sooner the better. (*Sound of trumpets and drums is heard off right.* STREPHON *and* PHYLLIS *hurry off left. Procession of* PEERS, *led by* LORD TOLLOLLER *and* LORD MOUNTARARAT, *enters, marching in single file across bridge. They sing as they march diagonally to down left corner of stage, across apron to down right corner, then upstage where they divide, each group lining up on opposite sides of stage to form an inverted "V".*)

PEERS (*Singing*):
>   Loudly let the trumpet bray—
> (*Raise hand to mouth as if holding trumpet*)
>   Tantantara!
>   Proudly bang the sounding brasses—
> (*Strike palms together in imitation of cymbals*)
>   Tzing! Boom!
>   As upon its lordly way
>   This unique procession passes!
>   Tantantara! Tzing! Boom!
> (*They repeat actions.*)
>   Bow, bow, ye lower middle classes!
>   Bow, bow, ye tradesmen, bow, ye masses!
>   Blow the trumpets, bang the brasses!
>   Tantantara! Tzing! Boom!
> (*Repeat actions*)
>   We are peers of highest station,
>   Paragons of legislation,
>   Pillars of the British nation!
>   Tantantara! Tzing! Boom!

(LORD CHANCELLOR *enters, trotting across bridge and downstage between lines of* PEERS. *He does a little dance step as he passes from one* PEER *to the next, squinting through his pince-nez in an effort to recognize each one.*)

CHANCELLOR (*Singing*):
        The Law is the true embodiment
        Of everything that's excellent.
        It has no kind of fault or flaw,
        And I, my lords, embody the Law.
        The constitutional guardian I
        Of pretty young wards in Chancer-*y*.
        [*Rhymes with "I"*]
        All are agreeable girls, and none
        Are over the age of twenty-one.
        A pleasant occupation for
        A rather susceptible Chancellor!

PEERS (*Singing*):
        A pleasant occupation for
        A rather susceptible Chancellor!

CHANCELLOR (*Singing*):
        And every one who'd marry a ward
        Must come to me for my accord;
        And in my court I sit all day
        Giving agreeable girls away.
    (*Pointing to one* PEER *after another*)
        With one for him—and one for he—
        And one for you—and one for ye—
        And one for thou—and one for thee—
        But never, oh, never a one for me!
        Which is exasperating (*Stamps hard, hurts foot, hops
            about*)—for
        A highly susceptible Chancellor!

PEERS (*Singing*):
        Which is exasperating for
        A highly susceptible Chancellor!

TOLLOLLER (*Stepping forward*): And now, my lords, to the business of the day.

CHANCELLOR: By all means. Your lordships have appealed to me to give my ward, Phyllis, to whichever of you she may select as a husband. If I could reconcile it with my duty, I would award her to myself. I know of no man who is so well fitted to make her exceptionally happy.

PEERS: Hear, hear!

CHANCELLOR: But I must waive my claim. I have summoned Phyllis to present herself before you and make her choice. (CHANCELLOR *claps his hands three times and beckons off left.* PHYLLIS *enters coyly, with downcast eyes, and curtsies to* CHANCELLOR.)

PEERS (*Ad lib, sighing*): Oh, rapture! How beautiful! How gentle! How dutiful! (*Etc.*)

TOLLOLLER (*Singing*):
> Of all the young ladies I know,
> This pretty young lady's the fairest;
> Her lips have the rosiest show,
> Her eyes are the richest and rarest.
> Her origin's lowly, it's true,
> But of birth and position I've plenty;
> I've grammar and spelling for two,
> And blood and behavior for twenty!

MOUNTARARAT (*Singing*):
> Though the views of the House have diverged
> On every conceivable motion,
> All questions of party are merged
> In a frenzy of love and devotion.
> If you ask us distinctly to say
> What party we claim to belong to,
> We reply, without doubt or delay,
> The party I'm singing this song to!

PHYLLIS (*Demurely*): My lords, you waste your time on me. My heart is already given. (PEERS *and* CHANCELLOR *are shocked.*)

CHANCELLOR: Given? To whom? Who has dared to do this? Who has defied my command? (STREPHON *steps out from behind bushes, left, and faces* CHANCELLOR *boldly.*)

STREPHON: It is I—a shepherd of Arcady! (*Taking* PHYLLIS's *hand*) Against the world I claim my darling's hand!

PEERS (*Speaking with hands on hearts*):
      Though our hearts she's badly bruising,
      (*Shaking fists at* STREPHON)
      In another suitor choosing,
      Let's pretend it's most amusing.
      Ha! Ha! Ha! Tan-ta-ra!
(PEERS *march, two by two, around stage, led by* TOLLOLLER *and* MOUNTARARAT, *and exit across bridge.* STREPHON *and* PHYLLIS *bring up the rear, mocking* PEERS *with exaggerated imitation of their march. As they reach the bridge, they are confronted by* CHANCELLOR, *who orders* PHYLLIS *to follow* PEERS *and restrains* STREPHON. PHYLLIS *exits across bridge.*)

CHANCELLOR (*Leading* STREPHON *downstage*): Now, young man, what excuse have you to offer for disobeying my orders?

STREPHON: I know no orders but those of nature. The bees—the breeze—the seas—the rooks—the brooks—the gales—the vales, all cry that Phyllis should be mine. You, sir, may be England's Lord High Chancellor, but are you Chancellor of birds and trees, winds and thunderclouds?

CHANCELLOR (*Giving question some thought*): Well—er—no, I'm not—but I can not accept as evidence what nature has *told* you. That's hearsay—it isn't legal. I must have first-hand, signed information. Now, if you can get an affidavit from the breeze you just mentioned, or a sworn statement from a heavy shower, I'll give them the attention they deserve. But until that evidence is produced, I positively forbid you to marry Phyllis. Good day, young man! (CHANCELLOR *exits majestically across bridge.* STREPHON *sits on tree stump down left in despair.*)

STREPHON: Oh, Phyllis! Phyllis! You have been taken from me just as I was about to make you my own. (IOLANTHE *enters up left and hastens to* STREPHON's *side.*)

IOLANTHE: What's this? My son in tears—and on his wedding day?

STREPHON: Oh, Mother, there's to be no wedding day for Phyllis and me. The Lord Chancellor has parted us forever!

IOLANTHE: The Lord Chancellor! (*Aside*) If Strephon only knew about the Chancellor! (*To* STREPHON) Take heart, Strephon. Our Queen has promised you her special protection. I will put your case before her.

STREPHON (*Rising*): My dearest Mother, how can I ever repay you? (*Embraces her*)

IOLANTHE: My dearest son, you repay me every hour—with your love. (*Lays her head on his shoulder.* PEERS *enter on bridge, walking stealthily on tiptoe with fingers to lips.* MOUNTARARAT *and* TOLLOLLER *are in front, leading* PHYLLIS *between them. She watches in horror as* STREPHON *and* IOLANTHE *speak affectionately together.*)

STREPHON: When the day is dark, I'll call on thee to chase the gloom away.

PHYLLIS (*Whispering to* MOUNTARARAT): What did he say?

MOUNTARARAT (*Whispering back*): He said he'd call on her some rainy day to while the time away. (PHYLLIS *is much agitated at* STREPHON's *supposed faithlessness.*)

IOLANTHE (*To* STREPHON): When tempests wreck thy bark, if thou shouldst need an ark, I'll give thee one.

PHYLLIS (*To* TOLLOLLER): What did she say?

TOLLOLLER (*Whispering*): She said she'd meet him in the park after dark, and give him one.

PHYLLIS (*Raising her voice angrily*): I'll give him one! (*Confronts* STREPHON) False Strephon! I worshiped you, but you worship another!

STREPHON (*Taken aback*): But, Phyllis, this lady is my mother.

PHYLLIS: Your *what?*

PEERS (*In derision*): He says she's his mother! (PEERS *laugh mockingly.* CHANCELLOR *enters, and* IOLANTHE *turns away, quickly covering her face with veil.*)

CHANCELLOR (*Elbowing his way through* PEERS): What are you laughing about? What's so funny?

MOUNTARARAT: This shepherd here—who must be all of twenty-four— is asking us to believe that a girl of seventeen (*Indicating* IOLANTHE) is his *mother!*

STREPHON (*Shouting*): I tell you, she *is* my mother—and has been ever since I was born!

PEERS (*Jeeringly*): Taradiddle, taradiddle, tol-lol-lay! (IOLANTHE *quietly exits unnoticed.* PHYLLIS *pulls ring from finger, throws it at* STREPHON's *feet.*)

PHYLLIS: Here—take your ring and go! I never want to see you again!

STREPHON (*Pleadingly*): Phyllis, listen to me—

PHYLLIS (*Turning her back on him*): Not a word! You have deceived me! (*To* PEERS) I will marry one of you—and I don't care which! (PEERS *crowd around, vying for her attention.* STREPHON *picks up ring, looks at it sadly and sighs, then puts it on little finger. Suddenly he brightens.*)

STREPHON (*Aside*): I'll call the Fairy Queen—she will set things straight. (*Plays a bird-call on his pipe*) Mighty protectress, come to my aid! (*Sound of harp is heard.* QUEEN *and* FAIRIES *enter left.*)

QUEEN: You have summoned us, Strephon. What is your pleasure?

STREPHON: I told my love and these gentlemen (*Indicating* PHYLLIS *and* PEERS) that the lady they found me talking to was my mother—and no one believed me. Please tell them that I spoke the truth.

QUEEN (*Sternly, to* PHYLLIS *and* PEERS): You have done this young man an injustice. The lady *is* his mother.

MOUNTARARAT: Taradiddle! If she's seventeen and he's twenty-four, her age at his birth must have been (*Reckoning on fingers*)—*minus* eight!

TOLLOLLER: To have a mother younger than her son is a very curious thing!

PEERS: Hear, hear!

CHANCELLOR (*To* QUEEN, *haughtily*): You have no right, madam, to interfere in this matter, madam. I order you to leave, madam—and take your brood with you.

QUEEN (*Outraged*): Brood indeed! Madam indeed! I'll teach you a lesson, you puffed-up, presumptuous mortal! (QUEEN *and* FAIRIES *level wands threateningly at* CHANCELLOR *and* PEERS, *who back away nervously.* QUEEN *recites*)
> Oh, Chancellor, unwary,
> Your manner arbitrary
> Is out of place
> When face to face
> With an influential fairy!

CHANCELLOR: Good heavens! She's a fairy! And I took her for the headmistress of a ladies' seminary.

QUEEN: I've had enough of your doubt and your driveling. The
    time has come for action—and for punishment.

>Mark well our sentence as we speak it—
>And *he* (*Pointing to* STREPHON) shall wreak it!
>Henceforth, Strephon, cast away
>Crook and pipe and ribbons so gay—
>Flocks and herds that bleat and low—
>Into Parliament you shall go!

CHANCELLOR: What! A shepherd in Parliament! It's never been
    done!

QUEEN (*Grimly*): It will be done this time. What is more, he shall
    be your leader.

>Every bill and every measure
>That may gratify his pleasure,
>Though your fury it arouses,
>Shall be passed by both your Houses!

PEERS: Oh!

QUEEN:

>You shall sit, if he sees reason,
>All year, in and out of season!

PEERS: No!

QUEEN:

>And hideous vengeance will pursue
>All noblemen who venture to
>Oppose his views
>Or boldly choose
>To question him—that's *treason!*
>
>(QUEEN *waves wand: thunder and lightning.*)

PEERS (*Cowering*): Mercy! Spare us! (*They rush offstage.* CHAN-
    CELLOR *leads away* PHYLLIS, *who looks back at* STREPHON, *as
    if pleading for forgiveness.* STREPHON *turns his back to her.
    Curtain closes.*)

*　　*　　*　　*　　*

SCENE 2

TIME: *A few weeks later.*

SETTING: *Palace yard, Westminster, in the moonlight. A backdrop shows the Houses of Parliament and the clock tower—Big Ben—in the distance. The face of Big Ben is illuminated. A high wrought-iron fence runs across back of stage with a gateway center. Right of gateway is a sentry box; left of gateway, a park bench. Entrances to yard are gateway and arches, right and left.*

AT RISE: PRIVATE WILLIS, *rifle on shoulder, goes through elaborate series of marching steps. He stops and stands at attention.*

PRIVATE WILLIS (*Singing*):

> When all night long a chap remains
> On sentry-go, to chase monotony
> He exercises of his brains;
> That is, assuming that he's got any.
> Though never nurtured in the lap
> Of luxury, yet I admonish you,
> I am an intellectual chap,
> And think of things that would astonish you.
> I often think it's comi*cal*—Fal, lal, la!
> How Nature always does contrive—Fal, lal, la!
> That every boy and every gal
> That's born into the world alive
> Is either a little Liber*al*
> Or else a little Conserva*tive!*
> [*Rhymes with "alive"*]

Fal, lal, la! (*Retires to sentry box and stands at attention.* FAIRIES, *led by* CELIA, LEILA *and* FLETA, *enter right, laughing and chattering.*)

CELIA: Strephon's a Member of Parliament!

LEILA: Carries every bill he chooses!

FLETA: Lords and Commons are both in the blues!

CELIA, LEILA *and* FLETA: Strephon makes them shake in their shoes! (*Exaggerated imitation of "shaking in shoes."*)

FAIRIES: Shake in their shoes! Shake in their shoes! Strephon makes them shake in their shoes! (PEERS *enter left, shouting angrily,* MOUNTARARAT *and* TOLLOLLER *in the lead.*)

PEERS: Strephon's a Member of Parliament!

MOUNTARARAT: Running amuck of all abuses!

TOLLOLLER: Carrying every bill he may wish!

MOUNTARARAT *and* TOLLOLLER: Here's a pretty kettle of *fish!* (*They stamp on word "fish"*)

PEERS (*Stamping*): Kettle of *fish!* Kettle of *fish!* Here's a pretty kettle of *fish!*

CELIA (*To* PEERS): Gentlemen, you seem annoyed.

TOLLOLLER: Annoyed! I should say we are! Any bill that Strephon favors is automatically passed. No one disputes him.

CELIA: Of course not. We use our magic to influence the members, and they vote just as Strephon wants them to.

MOUNTARARAT: This is what comes of women's interfering in politics. If there's one institution which can't be improved at all, it is the House of Peers! (*He sings the following song with great dignity, giving the effect of a national anthem.*)
> When Britain really ruled the waves—
> (In good Queen Bess's time)
> The House of Peers made no pretence
> To intellectual eminence,
> Or scholarship sublime;
> Yet Britain won her proudest bays
> In good Queen Bess's glorious days!

When Wellington thrashed Bonaparte,
As every child can tell,
The House of Peers, throughout the war,
Did nothing in particular,
And did it very well;
Yet Britain set the world ablaze
In good King George's glorious days!
(FAIRIES *watch* PEERS *with interest during song.*)

CELIA (*Aside to* LEILA) : Attractive persons, aren't they?

LEILA: *Most* attractive!

TOLLOLLER (*To* CELIA) : Won't you *please* stop Strephon before it's too late?

CELIA: But we *can't* stop him. You shouldn't have insulted our Queen.

LEILA (*Regretfully*) : Oh, why did you defy us, you great geese? (PEERS *exit left, ruefully shaking their heads.* FAIRIES *gaze wistfully after them.*)

FLETA: They're really very charming.

CELIA: I'm growing quite fond of them.

FAIRIES (*Ad lib*) : So am I ... And I ... And I. (*Etc.* QUEEN *enters right in time to overhear* FAIRIES' *remarks.*)

QUEEN (*Angrily*) : For shame! Is this the way you obey the fairy laws? You know that it's death to marry a mortal.

LEILA: But it's not death to *wish* to marry a mortal.

FLETA: If it were, you'd have to execute every one of us.

QUEEN (*Reproachfully*) : This is weakness!

CELIA: We're not all as tough as you are, Your Majesty.

QUEEN: Tough! Do you suppose *I* am insensible to the effects of manly beauty? (*Pointing to* PRIVATE WILLIS) Look at that man—a perfect picture! Who are you, sir?

WILLIS (*Snapping to attention*): Private Willis, B Company, First Grenadier Guards.

QUEEN: You're a very fine fellow, sir.

WILLIS: I am generally admired.

QUEEN: I can quite understand that. (*To* FAIRIES) Now here is a man who has a most extraordinary effect upon me. I could love him—but I must be strong and maintain our fairy law. And so must all of you. (*Waving them off right*) Now be off —and let's hear no more about this weakness. (FAIRIES *exit.* QUEEN *pauses to look back longingly at* WILLIS *before she exits.* WILLIS *salutes, shoulders rifle, does an about-face, then marches out gateway and off up left.* PHYLLIS *enters down left, walks dejectedly to bench and sits.*)

PHYLLIS: I can't think why I'm not in better spirits. I'm engaged to two noblemen at once—both Mountararat and Tolloller. That ought to be enough to make any girl happy—but I'm miserable! Don't suppose it's because I care for Strephon. I hate him! No girl *could* care for a man who goes about with another girl—a pretty one, too—and then says she's his *mother!* (MOUNTARARAT *and* TOLLOLLER *enter left. They rush to* PHYLLIS *with open arms.*)

MOUNTARARAT: Phyllis! My darling!

TOLLOLLER: Phyllis! My own!

PHYLLIS (*Rising*): Well, my lords, have you settled which one it's to be?

TOLLOLLER: We would rather leave the decision to you.

PHYLLIS: But it doesn't concern me. You are both earls, both rich, and both plain. There's really nothing to choose between you. One of you must give way.

TOLLOLLER (*To* MOUNTARARAT): The awkward part is that if you rob me of the lady I love, we must fight a duel, and one of us must die. It's a family tradition. But George (*Clasping* MOUNTARARAT'*s hand*)—I have a very strong regard for you.

MOUNTARARAT (*Much affected*): My dear Thomas, if one of us is to destroy the other, let it be me. I couldn't bear to see you embittered for life because you had killed me.

PHYLLIS: My lords, I hope you are not going to quarrel with each other over me—it's not really worthwhile.

TOLLOLLER (*Looking at her closely*): No, I don't believe it is.

MOUNTARARAT (*Agreeing*): The sacred ties of friendship are much more important.

PHYLLIS: Then free me, please—and go your ways in friendship's name. (*They bow to her, then to each other, and exit left, arm in arm.* PHYLLIS *exits right.* CHANCELLOR *enters through gateway, looking haggard and depressed.*)

CHANCELLOR: My hopeless love for Phyllis has robbed me of sleep —it lies on my chest like a mad nightmare. (*Singing or reciting with appropriate gestures*)

> When you're lying awake with a dismal headache, and repose is taboo'd by anxiety,
> I conceive you may use any language you choose to indulge in, without impropriety;
> For your brain is on fire—the bedclothes conspire of usual slumber to plunder you:
> First your counterpane goes, and uncovers your toes, and your sheet slips demurely from under you.

Then the blanketing tickles—you feel like mixed pickles, so terribly sharp is the pricking,

And you're hot, and you're cross, and you tumble and
toss till there's nothing 'twixt you and the tick-
ing.

Then the bedclothes all creep to the ground in a heap,
and you pick 'em all up in a tangle;

Next your pillow resigns and politely declines to remain at its usual angle!

Well, you get some repose in the form of a doze, with
hot eyeballs and head ever aching.

But your slumbering teems with such horrible dreams
that you'd very much better be waking;

For you dream you are crossing the Channel, and
tossing about in a steamer from Harwich—[*Pronounced "Harrich"*]

Which is something between a large bathing machine
and a very small second-class carriage—

And you're giving a treat (penny ice and cold meat)
to a party of friends and relations—

They're a ravenous horde—and they all came on board
at Sloane Square and South Kensington Stations.

And bound on that journey you find your attorney
(who started that morning from Devon);

He's a bit undersized, and you don't feel surprised
when he tells you he's only eleven.

Well, you're driving like mad with this singular lad
(by the by, the ship's now a four-wheeler),

And you're playing round games, and he calls you bad
names when you tell him that "ties pay the
dealer";

But this you can't stand, so you throw up your hand,
and you find you're as cold as an icicle,

In your shirt and your socks (the black silk with gold
clocks), crossing Salisbury Plain on a bicycle:

(*Speaking in a loud, agonized voice*)

And you wake with a shudder despairing!

(*Singing at a very fast clip*)

You're a regular wreck, with a crick in your neck,
And no wonder you snore, for your head's on the floor,
And you've needles and pins from your soles to your
    shins,
And your flesh is a-creep, for your left leg's asleep,
And you've cramp in your toes, and a fly on your nose,
And some fluff in your lung, and a feverish tongue,
And a thirst that's intense, and a general sense
That you haven't been sleeping in clover;

(CHANCELLOR *pauses, sighs in relief, then sings slowly*)

But the darkness has passed,
And it's daylight at last,
And the night has been long—
Ditto, ditto my song—

(*Speaks quickly*) And thank goodness they're both of them over! (*Collapses on bench. After a moment, he rouses himself and straightens his shoulders.*) I can't go on like this, night after night. (*Rises with determination*) I'll make one more effort to convince myself that I have a right to marry Phyllis. Faint heart never won fair lady! (*Exits through gateway.* PHYLLIS *enters right, goes to look off after* CHANCELLOR, *then hears someone coming down left and hides in sentry box.* STREPHON *enters in very low spirits.*)

STREPHON: I suppose I ought to enjoy myself in Parliament, but I'm miserable—poor, brokenhearted fool that I am. (*Sinks on bench and buries face in hands*) Oh, Phyllis! Phyllis!

PHYLLIS (*Stepping forward*): Yes?

STREPHON (*Startled, leaping to feet*): Phyllis! Or should I say, "My lady"?

PHYLLIS (*Aloofly*): I haven't decided. You see, *I* have no *mother* to advise *me*—especially a *young* one!

STREPHON: She's not very young—a couple of centuries or so.

PHYLLIS (*Sarcastically*) : Oh? She wears well.

STREPHON: She does indeed. I've no longer any reason to conceal the fact—she's a fairy.

PHYLLIS: A fairy! (*Thoughtful pause*) Hm-m. That would account for a good many things. Then—you must be one of them too.

STREPHON: Yes, I am—at least, down to my waist.

PHYLLIS: Why didn't you tell me this before?

STREPHON: I thought you wouldn't want half a mortal.

PHYLLIS: Oh, Strephon, my dear, I'd rather have half a mortal I do love than half a dozen I don't! (*They embrace.* STREPHON *removes ring from his finger and puts it on* PHYLLIS's *finger.*) Does your mother know of our engagement?

IOLANTHE (*Entering right, smiling*): She does—and she welcomes it. (*Kisses* PHYLLIS) What about the Lord Chancellor? Will he consent?

STREPHON: Mother, no one can resist your fairy eloquence. Go to him and plead for us.

IOLANTHE (*Quickly*) : No, no—impossible!

STREPHON: But our very lives depend on his consent.

PHYLLIS (*Beseechingly*) : Surely you will not refuse to do this for us?

IOLANTHE: You don't know what you ask. (*Pauses*) The Lord Chancellor is my husband—and Strephon's father!

STREPHON *and* PHYLLIS: What!

IOLANTHE: But he must never know! He believes I died childless, and, dearly as I love him, I am bound, under penalty of death, never to reveal myself to him. (*Suddenly*) Oh—he's coming! Quickly, leave! (STREPHON *and* PHYLLIS *hurry off right*.) My veil! He must not see me. (IOLANTHE *drops veil over face and withdraws to sentry box.* CHANCELLOR *enters through gateway, rubbing his hands together gleefully.*)

CHANCELLOR: Victory! Victory! Success has crowned my efforts, and I may consider myself engaged to the darling of my heart. (IOLANTHE *goes to* CHANCELLOR *and kneels*.)

IOLANTHE: My lord, I beg you, listen to a mother's fond appeal! I plead for my son, Strephon. Give him your consent to marry Phyllis.

CHANCELLOR: Madam, I can't do that. Phyllis is my promised bride.

IOLANTHE: Your bride! Oh, no, it can not be! (*Lifting veil*) Behold! I am your wife!

CHANCELLOR (*Thunderstruck, raising* IOLANTHE *to her feet*): Iolanthe! You're not dead—you're alive!

IOLANTHE (*Sadly*): I live—and now I must die. I have broken my vow. My doom is speeding toward me. Hark! (*Sound of rushing wind is heard—sweeping chords on harp.* QUEEN, FAIRIES, STREPHON *and* PHYLLIS *enter right.*)

QUEEN (*As* IOLANTHE *kneels before her*): Iolanthe, once more you have broken your vows. You know the penalty—death! (*Raises her wand. Clap of thunder is heard.* PEERS *and* PRIVATE WILLIS *enter left.*)

LEILA (*Grasping* QUEEN'S *arm*): Stop, Your Majesty! If Iolanthe must die, so must we all (*Gesturing to* FAIRIES)—for we have all married Peers—and we are all fairy duchesses and countesses!

TOLLOLLER (*Sheepishly*): It's our fault, Your Majesty. They couldn't help themselves.

QUEEN (*Smiling grimly*): It seems they *have* helped themselves, and liberally, too! (*All laugh as* FAIRIES *and* PEERS *mingle together.*) You have all incurred the death penalty, but I can't slaughter the whole company. And yet, the law is clearly written here (*Reading a line engraved on her wand*)— "Every fairy must die who marries a mortal."

CHANCELLOR (*His arm around* IOLANTHE): Your Majesty, allow me to suggest the addition of a single word. Let the law read that every fairy must die who *doesn't* marry a mortal.

QUEEN: Very well. I shall alter the law and put it into effect immediately. (*Calls*) Private Willis!

WILLIS (*Coming forward*): Yes, ma'am! (*Salutes*)

QUEEN: To save my life, it is necessary that I marry at once. How would you like to be my royal guardsman?

WILLIS: Well, ma'am, I wouldn't think much of a British soldier who didn't save a female in distress.

QUEEN: Brave fellow! (*Touches him lightly with wand and a pair of wings springs from his shoulders. See Production Notes*) You are now one of us. (*Turns to* PEERS) And you, my lords, will you join our ranks?

PEERS: Hurrah! We will! We will! (QUEEN *waves wand and wings spring from shoulders of* PEERS, CHANCELLOR, PHYLLIS *and* STREPHON.)

QUEEN: Away we go to Fairyland!

ALL (*Singing*):
>Soon as we may,
>Off and away!

We'll commence our journey airy—
Happy are we—
As you can see,
Everyone is now a fairy!

CHANCELLOR *and* PEERS (*Singing*):
Up in the sky,
Ever so high,
Pleasures come in endless series;
We will arrange
Happy exchange—
House of Peers for House of Peris!
(*All are dancing as curtain closes.*)

THE END

Production Notes

IOLANTHE

Characters: 5 male; 6 female; as many male and female as desired for Peers and Fairies.

Playing Time: 35 minutes.

Costumes: Fairies and Iolanthe wear ballet-style gowns in pastel colors with wings attached. Iolanthe first appears wearing mantle of waterweeds over costume; pinned to her hair is a long veil. Queen's costume is a white Victorian-style gown with crinoline. Fairies wear tiaras, Queen has a crown. All carry wands. In Scene 1, Strephon and Phyllis should look like Dresden china shepherd and shepherdess. Scene 2, Phyllis wears evening gown and Strephon formal evening clothes. Chancellor is dressed in black, with black robe with border of gold braid, jacket, vest, knee-breeches, shoes with buckles. He has white British barrister's wig, and pair of pince-nez. Private Willis wears uniform of the Grenadier guards; he carries a rifle. In Scene 1, Peers, Mountararat and Tolloller wear coronets and ceremonial robes over formal evening dress. Coronets and robes are removed for Scene 2. Mountararat and Tolloller wear monocles. Note on fairy wings: If a method for having wings "spring" from shoulders cannot be devised, it is suggested that on Fairies' last entrance in Scene 2, each Fairy carry inconspicuously a pair of wings which she attaches to a Peer's shoulders at the specified time. Iolanthe puts wings on Chancellor, Queen on Private Willis. Strephon and Phyllis wear wings in Scene 2, but they are concealed until finale.

Properties: Shepherd's pipe for Strephon; tiara for Iolanthe; ring for Phyllis.

Setting: Scene 1: An Arcadian fairy grove. Backdrop shows a river running through a meadow. River bank is at right, and beside it, a large bush. At back of stage is a rustic bridge used for entrances and exits. Steps descend from bridge to stage level. Trees and bushes are at right and a tree stump is down left. Space at center is clear. Scene 2: Palace yard, Westminster. A backdrop shows Houses of Parliament and Big Ben. A high wrought-iron fence runs across back of stage with a gateway at center. To right of

310

gate is a sentry box; left, a bench. Entrances are gateway and
  arches right and left.
Lighting: Scene 2: Moonlight; lightning.
Sound: Recorded flute and harp music, trumpets and drums, thunder
  and wind.
Music for songs on following pages.

WE ARE DAINTY LITTLE FAIRIES

We are dain-ty lit-tle fair-ies,

Ev-er sing-ing, ev - er danc - ing; We in-

dulge in our va - ga-ries In a fash-ion most en-

trancing. If you ask the special function Of our

never-ceas-ing mo - tion, We re - ply, without com-

punction, That we haven't an - y no - tion! Tripping

hither, tripping thither, Nobody know why or whither, We must

dance and we must sing Round a - bout our fair-y ring.

WELCOME TO OUR HEARTS AGAIN

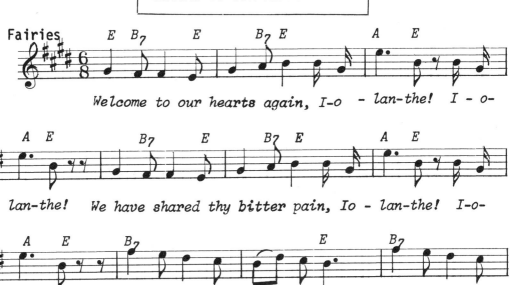

Fairies

Welcome to our hearts again, I-o - lan-the! I - o-

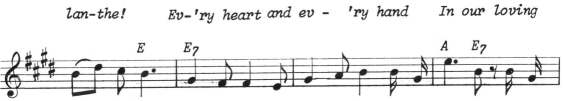

lan-the! We have shared thy bitter pain, Io - lan-the! I-o-

lan-the! Ev-'ry heart and ev - 'ry hand In our loving

lit - tle band Welcomes thee to Fairyland, Io - lan-the! I-o-

lan - the! I - o - lan - - - - - - the!

GOOD MORROW, GOOD MOTHER
(Good Morrow, My Lover)

Strephon (1)
Phyllis (2)

1. Good morrow, good mother,__ Good mother, good
2. Good morrow, my lover,_____ My lover, good

morrow!____ By some means or other Pray
morrow!____ I prithee discover Steal,

banish your sorrow! With joy beyond telling My
purchase or borrow Some means of concealing The

bosom is swelling, So join in a measure Ex - pressive of
care you are feeling, And join in a measure Ex - pressive of

pleasure, For I'm to be married to - day, to - day! Yes,
pleasure, For we're to be married to - day, to - day! Yes,

I'm to be married to - day!_____
We're to be married to - day!_____

LOUDLY LET THE TRUMPET BRAY

Loud-ly let the trum - pet bray, Tan-tan-ta - ra,

tan-tan-ta-ra! Proud-ly bang the sound-ing__ brasses, __

__ As upon its lord - ly__ way This u-

nique pro - ces - sion__ pass-es. Tan-tan - ta-ra,

tan-tan-ta-ra! Bow, bow, ye lower middle classes! Bow,

bow, ye tradesmen, bow, ye masses, Blow_ the__ trumpets,

bang the brasses, Tan-tan-ta-ra, Tzing, boom!

We are__ Peers of__ high-est__ station,

Par - a - gons of__ leg - is - la - tion,

Pil - lars__ of the__ Brit - ish__ Na - tion.

Tan-tan-ta - ra, Tan-ta-ra, Tzing, boom, tzing, boom, tan-ta-

ra, Tzing, boom!

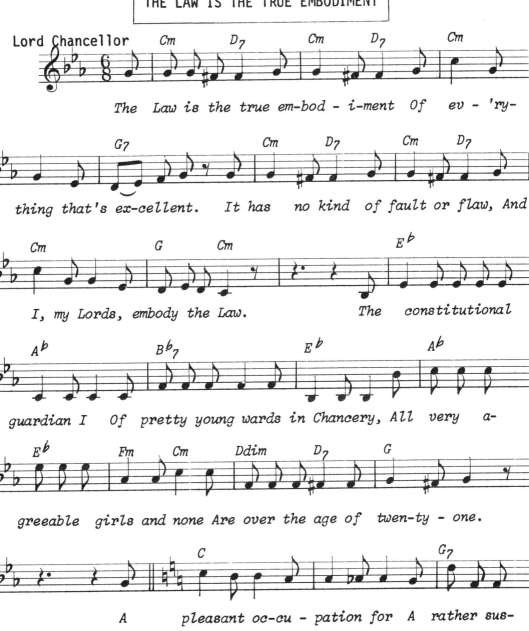

Lord Chancellor

The Law is the true em-bod-i-ment Of ev-'ry-thing that's ex-cellent. It has no kind of fault or flaw, And I, my Lords, embody the Law. The constitutional guardian I Of pretty young wards in Chancery, All very a-greeable girls and none Are over the age of twen-ty-one. A pleasant oc-cu-pation for A rather sus-ceptible Chancellor! And ev-'ryone who'd

marry a ward Must come to me for my__ accord, And in my

court I sit all day, Giving a-greeable girls away,

With one for him and one for he And one for you and

one for ye, And one for thou and one for thee But never, oh never a

one for me! Which is ex-as-per-at-ing

for A highly susceptible Chancellor!

Tolloller

Of all the young ladies I know____This

pretty young lady's the fairest; Her lips have the rosiest show,__

____ Her eyes are the richest and rarest. Her origin's lowly, it's

true,___ But of birth and po-si-tion I've plenty; I've

grammar and spelling for two, And blood and be-ha - vior__ for

Mountararat

twen-ty! Though the views of the House have di-

verged__ On ev-'ry conceivable motion, All questions of

party are merged__ In a frenzy of love and devotion! If you

ask us distinctly to say_____ What party we claim to be-

long to, We re-ply without doubt of de-lay_____ The

party I'm singing this song to!__ If you ask__ us dis-

tinctly to say, We re - ply____without doubt or delay, The

party we claim to be-long to Is the party we're singing
                                                      this

song to! The party we claim to be - long to's the party
                                                      we're

singing this song to!

WHEN ALL NIGHT LONG

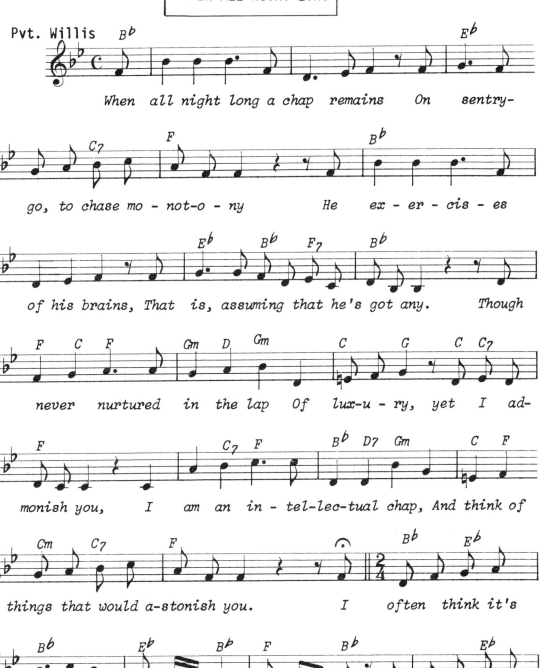

Pvt. Willis

When all night long a chap remains On sentry-
go, to chase mo - not-o - ny He ex - er - cis - es
of his brains, That is, assuming that he's got any. Though
never nurtured in the lap Of lux-u - ry, yet I ad-
monish you, I am an in - tel-lec-tual chap, And think of
things that would a-stonish you. I often think it's
comical-- Fal, lal, la! Fal, lal, la! How nature always

does contrive, Fal, lal, la, la! That__ ev-'ry boy and__
ev'ry gal That's born into the world alive Is either a little
Liberal Or else a little Con-serv-a-tive. Fal, lal, la,

Fal, lal, la!

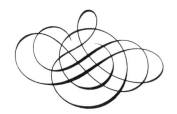

WHEN BRITAIN REALLY RULED THE WAVES

Mountararat

1. When Britain really ruled the waves (In good Queen Bess's
2. When Wellington thrashed Bonaparte As ev'ry child can

time) The House   of Peers made no pretence To   in-tel-lect-ual
tell, The House   of Peers thru-out the war, Did   nothing in par-

eminence, Or   scholarship sublime;   Yet   Brit-ain won her
ticular, And   did it ver-y well: Yet   Brit-ain set the

proudest bays   In   good   Queen Bess's   glo - rious days!
world ablaze   In   good   King George's   glo - rious days!

323

WHEN YOU'RE LYING AWAKE WITH A DISMAL HEADACHE

Lord Chancellor

When you're lying awake with a dismal headache and re-

pose is taboo'd by anx - i -e - ty, I conceive you may use any

language you choose to indulge in without impro-prie-ty; For your

brain is on fire_ and the bedclothes conspire of usual slumber to

plunder you; First your counterpane goes and uncovers your toes and
your

sheet slips demurely from under you; Then the blanketing tickles, you

feel like mixed pickles so terribly sharp is the pricking, Then the

bedclothes all creep to the ground in a heap and you pick 'em all up in a

tangle;   Next your pillow resigns and politely declines to re-

main at its us-u-al   angle.   Now you dream you are crossing the

Channel and tossing about in a steamer from Harwich,   Which is

something between a large bathing machine and a very small second class

carriage.   And you are giving a treat (Penny ice and cold meat) to

a party of friends and relations--   A   ravenous horde and they

all came aboard at Sloane Square and South Kensington Stations; But

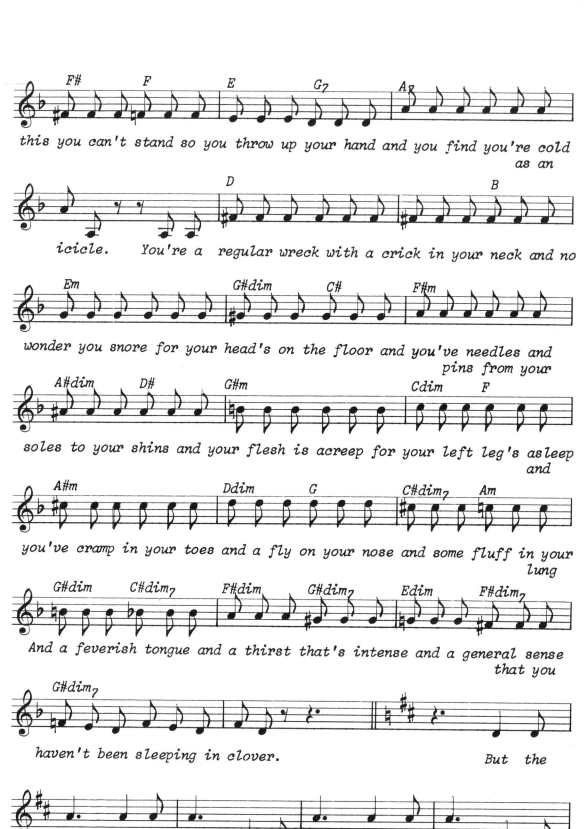

this you can't stand so you throw up your hand and you find you're cold as an

icicle.   You're a   regular wreck with a crick in your neck and no

wonder you snore for your head's on the floor and you've needles and pins from your

soles to your shins and your flesh is acreep for your left leg's asleep and

you've cramp in your toes and a fly on your nose and some fluff in your lung

And a feverish tongue and a thirst that's intense and a general sense that you

haven't been sleeping in clover.   But   the

dark - ness has passed And it's day - light at last   and the

night has been long-- ditto, ditto my song--

And thank goodness they're both of them o - ver!

SOON AS WE MAY

All (1)
Chan. & Peers (2)

1. Soon as we may, Off and a - way!
2. Up in the sky, Ev-er so high,

We'll com - mence our jour-ney air - y-- Hap-py are
Plea-sures come in end-less se - ries: We will ar-

we, As you can see, Ev - 'ry one is
range Hap-py ex - change-- House of Peers for

now a fair - y!
House of Pe - ris!

Index of Songs

After Much Debate Internal (Patience)   239

Behold the Lord High Executioner (Mikado)   73

Carefully on Tiptoe Stealing (Pinafore)   37
Comes the Broken Flower (Trial by Jury)   141
Comes the Pretty Young Bride (Yeomen)   282
Commonplace Young Man, A (Patience)   238

Flowers That Bloom in the Spring, The (Mikado)   84
For He's Going to Marry Yum-Yum (Mikado)   79
For He's Gone and Married Yum-Yum (Mikado)   87
For the Merriest Fellows Are We (Gondoliers)   177
From Every Kind of Man (Mikado)   82
From the Sunny Spanish Shore (Gondoliers)   179

Gaily Tripping (Pinafore)   32
Good Morrow, Good Mother (Iolanthe)   314
Good Morrow, My Lover (Iolanthe)   314

Hail, O King of a Golden Land (Gondoliers)   190
He Is an Englishman (Pinafore)   38
Here's a How-de-do (Mikado)   80

I Am the Captain of the *Pinafore* (Pinafore)   30
I Am the Monarch of the Sea (Pinafore)   33
I Am the Very Model of a Modern Major-General (Pirates)   117
I Cannot Tell (Patience)   220
I Have a Song to Sing, O! (Yeomen)   275
I Stole the Prince (Gondoliers)   181
If That Is So (Mikado)   86
If You Want to Know Who We Are (Mikado)   70
If You Want a Receipt (Patience)   222
If You're Anxious for to Shine (Patience)   226
I'm Called Little Buttercup (Pinafore)   28
In Enterprise of Martial King (Gondoliers)   180
Is Life a Boon? (Yeoman)   274
I've Got a Little List (Mikado)   75

Law Is the True Embodiment, The (Iolanthe)   317
List and Learn (Gondoliers)   176
Loudly Let the Trumpet Bray (Iolanthe)   315

Magnet and the Churn, The (Patience)   233
Many Years Ago, A (Pinafore)   39
My Object All Sublime (Mikado)   83

Never Mind the Why and Wherefore (Pinafore)   36
Now, Jurymen, Hear My Advice (Trial by Jury)   137

O'er the Season Vernal (Trial by Jury)   142
Of All the Young Ladies I Know (Iolanthe)   319
Oh, Better Far to Live and Die (Pirates)   115

Oh, Gentlemen, Listen I Pray ("You Cannot Eat Breakfast
    All Day") (Trial by Jury)   145
On a Tree by a River ("Titwillow") (Mikado)   85
One of Us Will Be a Queen (Gondoliers)   183

Policeman's Lot Is Not a Happy One, A ("When a Felon's Not
    Engaged in His Employment") (Pirates)   119
Poor Wandering One (Pirates)   116
Pour, O Pour the Pirate Sherry (Pirates)   113
Prithee, Pretty Maiden (Patience)   228
Private Buffoon Is a Lighthearted Loon, A (Yeoman)   287

Rising Early in the Morning (Gondoliers)   185
Rollicking Band of Pirates We, A (Pirates)   120
Royal Prince, The (Gondoliers)   189

Schoolgirls We (Mikado)   76
Silvered Is the Raven Hair (Patience)   231
So Go to Him (Patience)   236
Soon As We May (Iolanthe)   327

Then Away We Go (Gondoliers)   184
There Lived a King (Gondoliers)   187
Things Are Seldom What They Seem (Pinafore)   35
Three Little Maids from School Are We (Mikado)   77
Titwillow ("On a Tree by a River") (Mikado)   85
Tower Warders, Under Orders (Yeomen)   271
Turn, Oh Turn (Patience)   232
Twenty Love-Sick Maidens We (Patience)   219

Wandering Minstrel I, A (Mikado) 72   72
We Are Dainty Little Fairies (Iolanthe)   312
We Sail the Ocean Blue (Pinafore)   27
Welcome to Our Hearts Again (Iolanthe)   313
We're Called Gondolieri (Gondoliers)   178
Were I Thy Bride (Yeomen)   280
When All Night Long (Iolanthe)   321
When Britain Really Ruled the Waves (Iolanthe)   323
When a Felon's Not Engaged in His Employment ("A Policeman's
    Lot Is Not a Happy One") (Pirates)   119
When First My Old, Old Love I Knew (Trial by Jury)   138
When the Foeman Bares His Steel (Pirates)   118
When Frederic Was a Little Lad (Pirates)   114
When I, Good Friends, Was Called to the Bar (Trial by Jury) 139
When I First Put This Uniform On (Patience)   224
When I Was a Lad (Pinafore)   34
When a Jester Is Outwitted (Yeomen)   282
When Maiden Loves (Yeomen)   270
When a Merry Maiden Marries (Gondoliers)   182
When Our Gallant Norman Foes (Yeomen)   280
When You're Lying Awake with a Dismal Headache (Iolanthe)   324
With a Sense of Deep Emotion (Trial by Jury)   143

You Cannot Eat Breakfast All Day ("Oh, Gentlemen, Listen
    I Pray") (Trial by Jury)   145